MW01713289

Rosie O'Dell

"*Rosie O'Dell* is one of those books with such brilliant writing as to lull you into forgetting you're actually reading."
CAROLYN R. PARSONS, THE PILOT

"Yes, it's Bill Rowe—back this time with his third novel, which I think is by far his best. Probably one of the better novels to come out in the past few years—depending on your own tastes, of course."
THE NORTHEAST AVALON TIMES

"[A] deeply emotional page-turner by one of the country's finest writers."
MEGAN MURPHY, INDIGO

"This is a terrific story that hinges on a woman who is like quicksilver, running through all the cracks."
THE GLOBE AND MAIL

"It's well-written (Rowe is an experienced and accomplished writer), the characters are excellently drawn and much of the writing is just plain funny."
THE PEI GUARDIAN

"There is not a false note in this book. All the characters are drawn with skillful insight, the descriptions are so vibrant you can almost hear the water and feel the mist of St. John's, Newfoundland. Although it has elements of a thriller, this is no gothic soap opera, but rather a brilliantly crafted look into the hearts and souls of ordinary people who are thrown into extraordinary circumstances."
ATLANTIC BOOKS TODAY

"This novel is a real page-turner, with lots of tension and mystery."
THE TELEGRAM

Praise for

Danny Williams, Please Come Back

"I started to really appreciate Rowe's ability to narrow down a topic and come up with something pithy and witty to say about it, week after week."
THE TELEGRAM

"Like any columnist worth his salt Rowe is provocative and a number of the columns deal with topics whose lessons are still relevant."
THE NEWFOUNDLAND QUARTERLY

"Rowe's columns on Williams's persona, bellicose manner and political antics truly shine. What Danny Should Do in the Crab War? (May 7, 2005) puts a delightful Shakespearian twist on Williams's strategic positioning; Is Danny a Dictator? (June 25, 2005) will stand as a classic."
THE CHRONICLE HERALD

"A brisk read and a fine book to have in your personal library."
THE COMPASS

"[Rowe] does it all, of course, with his usual blend of droll good humour and common sense."
THE GLOBE AND MAIL

"With a mind—and a pen—as sharp as a paper cut, the elegant, affable Rowe remains Newfoundland's literary agent provocateur, provoking, teasing, sometimes coddling his subjects, but all the time digging towards truths that cause discomfort for the province's Who's Who and everyman alike."
THE BUSINESS POST

Praise for

Danny Williams: The War with Ottawa

"Interesting book about a successful Canadian politician . . ."
THE GLOBE AND MAIL

"Bill Rowe's *Danny Williams: The War with Ottawa* is an enjoyable read."
TIM POWERS

"[*Danny Williams: The War with Ottawa*] is captivating. [Bill Rowe] spares no punches."
THE COMPASS

"The most interesting political book to be released in Canada in some time . . ."
THE BUSINESS POST

"Rowe's Ottawa chronicle [is] absorbing, humorous."
THE TELEGRAM

"I quickly realized that this was not going to be a dry political memoir. To the contrary, not only is the book interesting and revealing of this contentious time, it is very funny in places."
THE CHRONICLE HERALD

"An exciting read."
THE NEWFOUNDLAND QUARTERLY

"[One of] three of this year's most controversial and talked about political books."
THE HOUSE, CBC RADIO

"Rowe has a more humanistic side to politics. It is as if a citizen managed to be a fly on the wall while Danny Williams fought."
CURRENT MAGAZINE

More praise for

Danny Williams: The War with Ottawa

"An eye-opening, often hilariously funny, account of life among Ottawa power brokers and civil servants."
CANADIAN LAWYER MAGAZINE

"Bill Rowe has a lot to say. There are dozens of interesting stories told, and comments passed on . . ."
THE NORTHEAST AVALON TIMES

"A fascinating and frequently funny read."
DOWNHOME

"Written with the knowledge and insight that only an insider could possess, this book (sub-titled 'The Inside Story of a Hired Gun') is a timely reminder of the duplicity of far too many of our elected leaders—no matter what their political stripe." **ATLANTIC BOOKS TODAY**

"The writer's good English style—rare today—his knowledge of all kinds of personalities in the political world and his misadventures in getting a basic office set up (which took six of the eight months he was there) all make for amusing and exciting reading." **THE PEI GUARDIAN**

The Premiers Joey and Frank

Also by Bill Rowe

ROSIE O'DELL

DANNY WILLIAMS, PLEASE COME BACK

DANNY WILLIAMS: THE WAR WITH OTTAWA

IS THAT YOU, BILL?

THE TEMPTATION OF VICTOR GALANTI

CLAPP'S ROCK

The Premiers Joey and Frank

Greed, Power, and Lust

BILL ROWE

FLANKER PRESS LIMITED
ST. JOHN'S

Library and Archives Canada Cataloguing in Publication

Rowe, William N. (William Neil), 1942-, author
The premiers Joey and Frank : greed, power, and lust / Bill Rowe.

Includes index.
Issued in print and electronic formats.
ISBN 978-1-77117-266-0 (pbk.).--ISBN 978-1-77117-267-7 (epub).--
ISBN 978-1-77117-268-4 (kindle)

1. Rowe, William N. (William Neil), 1942-. 2. Smallwood, Joseph R., 1900-1991. 3. Moores, Frank D. (Frank Duff), 1933-2005. 4. Newfoundland and Labrador--Politics and government--20th century. I. Title.

FC2175.1.R68A3 2013 971.8'04 C2013-905122-8
C2013-905123-6

PRINTED IN CANADA

MIX
Paper from responsible sources
FSC www.fsc.org FSC® C103567

This paper has been certified to meet the environmental and social standards of the Forest Stewardship Council® (FSC®) and comes from responsibly managed forests, and verified recycled sources.

Cover Design: Graham Blair Edited by Paul Butler

Cover photos: Joseph Roberts Smallwood courtesy of the Centre for Newfoundland Studies Archives (J.R. Smallwood Collection 075, 5.05.061), Memorial University of Newfoundland Library, St. John's, Newfoundland; Frank Moores courtesy of The Rooms Provincial Archives, A 86-68

FLANKER PRESS LTD. PO BOX 2522, STATION C ST. JOHN'S, NL CANADA
TELEPHONE: (709) 739-4477 FAX: (709) 739-4420 TOLL-FREE: 1-866-739-4420
WWW.FLANKERPRESS.COM

9 8 7 6 5 4 3

Canada Canada Council for the Arts Conseil des Arts du Canada Newfoundland Labrador

We acknowledge the financial support of the Government of Canada through the Book Publishing Industry Development Program (BPIDP) for our publishing activities; the Canada Council for the Arts, which last year invested $157 million to bring the arts to Canadians throughout the country; the Government of Newfoundland and Labrador, Department of Tourism, Culture and Recreation.

In memory of my mother and father,
Edith Butt of Woody Point and Fred Rowe of Lewisporte

Contents

Author's Note

For years I had close political involvement, as colleague or adversary, with Joey Smallwood and Frank Moores. This book is my memoir of those first two premiers of Newfoundland and Labrador and the cast of characters around them.

The book is not a work of historical research. It consists almost entirely of my own memories and reminiscences, some of which have been sparked by conversations with acquaintances and by clippings, notes, and documents in my personal files.

I have tried to present remembered facts as accurately and objectively as possible. My opinions are my own subjective musings. With both facts and opinions, I have endeavoured not to pull any punches or soften hard truths. And wherever I could, I have sought to convey the humour of the bizarre situations encountered.

Some readers may deem my memories of events and persons factually wrong or misremembered. Others may consider my assessments of actions and motives harsh or ill-considered. I would urge them to offer and argue their suggested corrections for the public record, perhaps even by writing memoirs of their own.

My hope is to put out another book of candid memoirs later, covering other premiers I have known and observed through my participation in politics and media.

Bill Rowe

St. John's
Newfoundland and Labrador
August 2013

CHAPTER ONE

A Sunny Day Tomorrow

THE VOICE BOOMED out of the sky like God announcing doomsday. The year was 1948, and I was six years old. My schoolmate Rickie and I were playing with a ball in the backyard, but we dropped it to gawk up at the small aircraft swooping low over the St. John's houses. We listened transfixed to the words blaring out of its loudspeaker: ". . . a rainy day tomorrow." But then the words became ". . . a sunny day tomorrow." The man up there sounded very sure of himself, but he wasn't making much sense. I ran into our house to ask my mother. Inside, I heard my younger brother crying. He was in bed with a fever today, and he'd been rudely awakened from his nap by the bellowing from on high. My mother was already heading toward his room without seeing me, and I heard her muttering to herself as she went: "Bloody moron."

"Mr. Smallwood," she said later, smiling when I asked her what she'd meant by moron. "Or it might have been Peter Cashin. It was definitely one or the other." And what were they talking about—rainy day tomorrow, sunny day tomorrow? Well, if it was Mr. Smallwood, she replied, he was saying that Confederation with Canada would mean a sunny day tomorrow, and Responsible Government would mean a rainy day tomorrow. But if it was Mr. Cashin, he was saying the exact opposite.

I was perplexed. "But which one is right, Mom?"

"More than likely they're both right," she said. I'd be a few years older before I fully grasped her point.

Meanwhile, my father, Fred Rowe, shared none of Edith's—his wife's—skepticism or sense of irony over the issue. He was an enthusiastic supporter of Confederation—so much so that Joseph R. Smallwood made him one of his fifty Confederate vice-presidents. Becoming one of Joey Smallwood's army of vice-presidents was a "greatness" that was thrust upon men, often without their knowledge. Aiden Maloney told me he'd heard for the first time that he'd become a Confederate vice-president by way of a telegram from an appalled anti-Confederate family member. Aiden was managing a fish plant on the southwest coast of Newfoundland at the time, and Smallwood must have assumed, because the owner of the fish plant was a Confederation backer (the promise of a senate seat being involved), that anyone working for him was ipso facto a Confederate as well. It was the kind of quantum leap in logic, or rosy thinking, that associates of Joey Smallwood would contemplate with head-scratching befuddlement over the next quarter century.

My father openly supported Confederation despite the fact that, as principal of Curtis Academy, a big new school in St. John's, he was expected by the many anti-Confederate mercantile and professional members on the school board to shut his damned mouth about the boons of joining Canada. Smallwood moved Ramsay, Bill, and Clara—his children—from their other schools in the city to Curtis, off Pleasant Street. Dad would tell me later that Smallwood's kids had been coming under verbal, and even physical, abuse at school over the Confederation issue, and Joey knew they would be safe at Curtis. In years to come, I recall older students at Curtis Academy reminiscing about Clara arriving in the mornings on a pony which she'd tether outside the school. She had ridden the animal all the way from their house out on Kenmount Road, where Smallwood had a farm.

My father, like so many of his generation who'd been dumped into the Great Depression just as they were graduating from high school, struggled for years to complete his university education. Thus it happened by coincidence, just before the second referendum resolved the issue in favour of Confederation, that he was able, finally, in his mid-thirties, to make financial arrangements to complete his doctorate at the University of Toronto.

Joey had other plans for him and didn't want him to go. But Dad knew that if he didn't realize his lifelong dream now, he never would. He resigned as principal of Curtis and he and Edith took their four sons—Fred, Bud, George, and me—to Toronto for the 1948-1949 academic year. On top of his studies there, Dad gave weekly talks on CBC Radio designed to familiarize Canadian listeners with Newfoundland and our curious ways.

I went into grade two at a school in Toronto where I soon became acquainted with some curious Upper Canadian ways. Feeling extremely shy in this strange, foreign land, I would respond to my teacher's questions with a mute nod or shake of my head. She would thereupon tell me to stop answering "like a little Eskimo," which would make the class titter, and she'd urge me to use spoken words like a civilized child now that I was a Canadian. The charming woman also seated the children in rows ranging, according to her likes and dislikes, from smart to stupid, and she divided the children's singing voices into categories running from "canaries" for the sweetest sounds, to "robins" for the tolerable, to "crows" for the most grating and raucous. A little girl I liked for her quiet humour and her sharp mind found herself seated in the stupidest row and singing with the crows. Even with my child's eyes and ears, as yet unschooled in prejudice, I couldn't help drawing a link between her place in the class and her poor manner of dress and different accent.

Good luck to that little human being in clawing her way out of the Toronto welfare cycle.

As my father finished his studies at U of T, he faced a choice. He could accept one of the offers he'd received to lecture at a university in the United States or Canada, or he could accept brand-new premier Smallwood's offer to become the first deputy minister of Welfare, revamp—essentially help create—that department, and then run for the House of Assembly at the first opportunity.

Dad told me that if Confederation had not taken place, he would not have returned to Newfoundland but would instead have made a life for himself and family elsewhere in North America. In the event, though, he accepted Joey's offer and came back. Decades later and retired from provincial politics, he would ask me if he'd made the right decision way back then. I'd reply that, yes, he had: look at the interesting, eventful life he'd lived. And he'd slowly shake his head in humour and disbelief at the travails he'd undergone during his twenty years as Premier Smallwood's point man.

Back from Toronto to St. John's again in 1950, I was happy to enter grade three under Miss Drodge, our caring and cheerful classroom teacher. To say my year in that Toronto school coloured my view of Ontario for life would be an exaggeration. But I did retain this lifelong healthy attitude: some waspy Upper Canadians with mean-spirited bigotry were all too ready to jump to judgment and put other peoples and provinces in their preordained lesser place. When I would hear Mr. Smallwood, our "only living father of Confederation," extolling the multitudinous "blessings" of our union with Canada on the radio, I never had trouble restraining myself from dancing about the room in joy.

IN THE EARLY 1950s, Joey recruited Dad to run as the Liberal candidate in the district of Labrador. Harold Horwood had resigned from the seat because, according to Joey, he could not abide being passed over for a position in the cabinet after all he'd done for Joey's

Confederate cause. Joey's more slanderous explanation to me in the late 1960s for slighting his old Confederate comrade-at-arms was that in those days the electorate was not as easygoing as they were now about a fellow who was too fond of the company of pretty young men. Whatever the truth of the matter, Horwood's newspaper columns for years afterwards showed vicious spite against Joey and his own replacement, Fred Rowe, as well as some others in the Smallwood entourage.

Dad got elected to the House of Assembly and became minister of Mines and Resources. In this role, I remember, his greatest pride and joy, backed by Smallwood's enthusiasm, was planning the string of provincial parks throughout the province, designed to hold these beautiful spots in perpetuity for the benefit of the people. (The two of them would have been heartbroken decades later to see the government of Clyde Wells begin the cost-cutting process of dismantling or selling off many of these provincial parks.)

Throughout his years as member for Labrador, Dad would make long summer visits by vessel to every community in the straits, on the coast, and in Lake Melville. "Pay close attention to your district," he told me Smallwood always urged. "Any fool can get elected once—the real challenge for a politician is to get re-elected next time." Often, Dad would take family members with him on his tours, and when my turn came in the mid-1950s, we headed north from Notre Dame Bay in the motor vessel *Bonnie Nell.* All went well until we reached the Strait of Belle Isle. There the captain had to make a crucial decision: according to the forecast, a storm was brewing, and if we didn't cross over to Labrador right away we could be stuck on the Newfoundland side for several days. He and Dad decided between them to proceed. After all, the narrow waterway was only ten or twelve miles across.

Dad was not a religious man. But he looked like he was praying to the Almighty for salvation that day. Halfway across the straits, at the point of no return, the wind had turned savage. Waves towered far above the vessel and, in the opinion of everyone on board, it was only the skill of the skipper—a Captain Lewis from Twillingate, I believe—that kept her from swamping with all hands. My father told me later that he had resigned himself to causing the death of his wife and two young sons on board.

After hours of his vessel being buffeted about, the captain managed to put in, finally, at a snug little haven called Occasional Harbour. There, cut off from radio connection, we had to stay for three days while the storm blew over. When communications were re-established, we learned that officials in St. John's feared we'd been lost, and Premier Smallwood had ordered, when weather permitted, a rescue or recovery operation. After we got home again, my pals treated me with the awe reserved for the resurrected hero in a Saturday afternoon movie serial.

DURING MY BOYHOOD, as Dad became minister of different government departments under Smallwood, I sensed a certain amount of work-related tension in our home. Dad himself had long discovered the vast difference between the coddling you received from a political leader who was trying to recruit you and the conduct of a leader who now has you exactly where he wants you. My mother was a reserved but plain-spoken woman who wouldn't play-act if her life depended on it. She had an uncanny ability to zero in on the essential character of a person, and it was not in her nature to be taken in by anyone's bullshit.

Over the years to come, I'd hear her from time to time change her earlier muttered "bloody moron" to "bloody crook." That generally happened whenever Smallwood would, on a spontaneous whim, prevail upon Dad to do something immediately or go somewhere right away, interfering unreasonably with a long-planned family event. By the word "crook" she told me she did not necessarily mean she thought Joey was a criminal; she used the word, she said, in its other Newfoundland sense—"crooked," meaning someone who was contrary, wilfully disagreeable, and generally obnoxious.

There was no doubt in my mind what she meant, though, when, earlier than most, she applied the term "crook" to Joey's economic development saviour, the Latvian Alfred Valdmanis. She could never believe what she saw at social events whenever Valdmanis was around Joey: Valdmanis would click his heels and bow low before Joey and address him as "Mine Premier," which was only a small step away, in my suspicious mother's disgusted view, from "Mein Führer." She had a beloved younger brother, a war hero, who'd been badly wounded and nearly killed in the Second World War.

Dad told me that, earlier in his career, Joey had owned a dog named Wolf. When Valdmanis informed him that the name was the same as one of Hitler's last dogs, a pup of his famous Blondi, Joey responded that that was only a coincidence: "There have been millions of dogs called Wolf," he said. Dad told me he was struck by Valdmanis's smirk of satisfaction as he replied, "Of course, Mine Premier."

We had an irreverent neighbour nearby—a blunt, unrepentant Tory we all liked, despite our Liberal household, for his outrageously frank and funny views. One Saturday morning he dropped off some rabbits he'd snared for us. We always told him he only brought such welcome gifts so that he'd have an excuse to argue politics. He never denied it. This morning he made the suggestion that the next time Valdmanis was sitting in a chair, someone should sneak up behind him and whisper "Heil Hitler" in his ear and watch him jump to his feet and extend his arm by reflex in a Nazi salute before he caught himself.

Dad, who had no love for the economic saviour, nevertheless managed to suppress his grin at the suggestion. Mom, on the other hand, nearly fell off her chair laughing at the brilliant idea. (My younger brother, George, who was present with us in the kitchen at the time, must have picked up on the notion. Years later at a party, he would in fact sneak up behind one of Joey's leftover German businessmen from Valdmanis's great industrialization days and whisper "Heil Hitler" in his ear, and the man did leap to his feet in a Nazi salute, before coming to his senses and claiming that he was only joking.)

There was no laughing around our house, though, when Valdmanis was arrested at Joey's behest and charged with taking bribes and kick-backs from Germans over his industrial development of Newfoundland. Joey himself escaped serious criticism by painting himself as the victim, betrayed by the greatest male love of his life, and describing the pain of having to turn in his golden boy to the police. Mom, I'm sure, always believed he'd wormed his way out of it somehow. "That Joey," she said to me, "Cute as a cut cat."

I think Mom's main problem with Smallwood was that she feared her husband might be caught up in something sinister. She had no doubt about Dad's honesty, but she considered him scholarly and academically inclined, and lost in thought a lot—too much so for the brutal realities of politics—and lacking the street smarts of Joey and some of his cronies, the likes of Al Vardy and Les Curtis and Greg Power. "Fred, you're always in a daze," she'd say to him with a laugh, not unkindly, which he'd concede with a nod and a smile. To her, it was telling that Dad often referred to his own father's "wasted" life.

His father, Eli, was the captain of a fishing vessel that went for years to the Labrador fishery. He was good at it, but he seemed to have despised every isolated second of it. He couldn't give it up because his family would starve if he didn't keep at it. When he finally saw his way clear to stay home with his family by opening up a store, it wasn't long before the Great Depression struck. Eli suffered a debilitating stroke caused, Dad believed, by the financial strain. All Dad's father ever wanted to do was read, discuss, write, and lecture. If he'd had his life to relive, he told Dad, he would have striven to become a history teacher.

I think Mom suspected that Dad was talking about himself. He should have accepted one of the university offers instead of falling for King Joey's blandishments and coming back to join the long line of courtiers hopping to it at his decree. Seeing how much responsibility Joey was piling on him, she feared that, in his essential guilelessness, he might be cajoled or sucked into doing something stupid at the boss's orders. Or hurt by Joey's callousness and one-way loyalty.

Despite the workload Dad carried in the government, Joey would tell me years later that he always considered him to be somewhat lazy and frivolous. Why? Because Dad liked to sit back occasionally and listen to music and read poetry and play a few hands of bridge with friends. To Joey, if you were awake and not performing politics or thinking politics or talking politics or reading a political history or biography, you were not a serious and engaged politician. You were shirking and slothful. Dad once told me that, on a trip to Paris with Joey and a couple of other ministers, Joey and his entourage "did" the Louvre, one of the biggest museums in the world, in twenty minutes. Then Joey forged on to speed walk through Notre Dame Cathedral in ten minutes. To think that when my future colleague, Ed Roberts, from his experience as Joey's executive assistant, described him to me years later as a philistine, I actually contradicted him.

DAD NEVER HOBNOBBED socially with his colleagues in the cabinet during off-hours, except for those crowded, endless, brutal Christmas cocktail parties every household seemed to throw once a year in the 1950s for everyone they knew. And I don't remember being in Joey's presence at all at home until my early teens. Then, one Friday night our whole family was gathered in our living room to watch a movie on our ancient film projector. Every couple of weeks Dad, as part of his shirking, slothful family participation, would bring home with him from a film library an acclaimed old movie for us to watch. This night it was the 1946 black and white film of Charles Dickens's *Great Expectations,* starring the young Jean Simmons. We were all watching it, enthralled, when the doorbell rang—the *front* doorbell. This was highly unusual since, normally, visitors came to the more accessible side door. I went out, prepared to get rid of whoever it was quickly and return to our engrossing movie.

Standing there on the veranda was a man whose big face and bulbous eyes I recognized from his pictures in the papers. It was one of

Joey's favourite henchmen, O. L. "Al" Vardy. All I really knew about Vardy, from Dad and Mom's talk around the house, was that he'd been earlier forced to bow out of running in a St. John's seat because the dirty Tories (i.e. Peter Cashin) had threatened to reveal that he had served prison time in the States for armed robbery. Joey had been infuriated by the threat: people today had no idea what it was like during the Depression, he'd raged, for men desperately trying to feed their starving families. But the Tories intended to reveal all, Dad had murmured to Mom, because Vardy had been going around during the campaign insinuating that someone close to Cashin was a homosexual.

In any event, the convicted felon now standing before me at the door was Smallwood's deputy minister of Economic Development and Director of Tourism. This latter position required Al Vardy to spend nearly every day in the summer out on Conception Bay aboard the government vessel the *Altuna*, catching and then being photographed beside a gigantic tuna fish hanging by its tail from the weigh scales. Some wag, probably our Tory neighbour, claimed they were hanging the wrong oily, fishy critter—it should have been the one standing next to the tuna.

Vardy had either achieved already or soon would achieve the record for the biggest tuna caught, nearly 900 pounds, and Joey would offer a reward for any tuna of a thousand or more pounds caught on rod and reel. Years into the future, when the tuna was considered to be verging on extinction, I would say to Vardy that it must be gruesome now to contemplate his having to go out on the bay back then, day after day, waiting for hours on end for a bite and then pulling in yet another monster fish, all in aid of a tourist effort now dead. Vardy replied, "Gruesome? Are you off your goddamned head? I loved it."

All that and my more sinister encounters with the economic development deputy were yet to come. But now, at the front door to our house, the deep, ballsy voice that had given Vardy early prominence as a radio announcer, where he had become friendly with Joey, inquired, "Is your father home?" When I said, yes, he was, Vardy turned and called down to the sidewalk, "He's here." I looked down. Four or five men, not together in a bunch but strung out along the sidewalk from a big black Chrysler Imperial, slowly and self-importantly moved toward us in unison. Then another man got out of the car and advanced as well.

He was diminutive and dressed in a long black overcoat, with a black homburg down over his ears: Joey Smallwood himself. It was the kind of hat that would also be later known as a godfather hat from the way it so suited the image of movie gangster Al Pacino. I'd already seen my own father in that outfit and figured that it was his own peculiar, personal taste and idea of the dignity of his office. Now I realized, from seeing Joey and his other cabinet ministers advancing toward me, that it was the premier's idea of a uniform for himself and his colleagues. Not only did it lend a look of dignified gravity where perhaps none naturally existed, he would say to me years later, but it also made it easier, combined with ostentatiously low licence plate numbers (Joey's was 1001), for the police to recognize and acknowledge cabinet ministers.

Tonight, without any request to come in, or even so much as a "by your leave," Joey and his cohorts came up the steps and walked into the house. He took it for granted that, if Dad was home, he would want to have him in, that, indeed, Dad would welcome him with open arms no matter what else the family might be doing.

For the next couple of hours, only two sounds were heard in our living room. One was the clink of ice being rattled in glasses as Joey's disciples signalled to Dad, their captive host, that their glasses needed refilling pronto with rum and Coke or rye and ginger. The other sound was Joey's voice. This was a phenomenon I'd never witnessed before: one man in private company talking continuously for hours without interruption and without anyone else in the room even trying to comment or contribute. It was as if Joey owned the airspace and the sound waves, which everyone else was willing to concede to him without demur or protest. To interrupt or butt in would have seemed like a sacrilegious trespass.

I have no idea now what he talked about, but I do remember that I was fascinated. It was not in the least boring regardless of what the content might have been. The mere form of his speech was interesting in itself: not a word out of place or groped for, and each sentence containing its impact at the end so as to hold your attention to its finish. It was similar to his public speeches that I was fairly familiar with, but different in that tonight there was no repetition. Every now and then, without breaking stride in his words, Joey would thrust his empty sherry glass at one of his cronies, who would then hustle over to refill it from the bottle of Bristol Cream Dad had miraculously caused to materialize from the liquor cabinet. He told me later that he kept it in the cupboard just in case something like tonight might happen.

I noticed that Dad was trying not to nod off. Evidently, he'd heard all of this from Joey before, as had the others, whose eyes varied from swivelling randomly in their heads to glazing over as if they possessed the translucent eyelids of a reptile. I couldn't understand at the time their lack of interest, but, then again, this was my first time. I understood it better years hence on the second, third, and fiftieth intrusion of a topic on my eardrums. Joey didn't mind or pay any heed to them tonight. As long as he could talk to what gave the appearance of being the semblance of an audience, all was well.

Mom brought out a sumptuous array of cookies and cake, which the hangers-on glommed into without let or hindrance until there was literally not a crumb left. One had pressed his forefinger down on the plate to salvage that last crumb. But Joey waved away every offer of the plate, and finally placed his order: "One or two crackers and a little cheddar cheese and a cup of tea, Mrs. Rowe, thank you." I never heard him then or later call any woman except his two Claras, wife and daughter, by anything but Mrs. or Miss and her surname.

After Joey and his gang were gone, and we were cleaning up the place, I heard Mom say to Dad that it was a wonder Smallwood hadn't issued this order to her: "Mrs. Rowe, give us the room." She had been utterly flabbergasted months before when she'd accompanied Dad to Joey's house one weekend afternoon and heard, as the men gathered around the premier in the living room to talk strategy, his peremptory command to his wife: "Clara, give us the room." This had sent her resentfully out with the two or three other women. Mom had decreed to Dad after that occasion, "That bloody ignoramus—don't ever ask me to go there again."

I DID SEE Mom genuinely moved by sympathy for Joey once during my youth. That happened in May of 1957, after ambulances and police cars, sirens shrieking, had raced past our house on Cornwall Avenue travelling from west to east, and all of us stood rooted at the window wondering what catastrophe had befallen some poor unfortunates out there. As we turned on the radio news, the telephone call came through for Dad to let him know that a helicopter carrying Joey's son Ramsay and Ramsay's wife had hit high-voltage wires out at his farm on Roaches Line and crashed. The pilot and Joey's daughter-in-law, to whom Joey had yielded the seat intended for himself so that she could enjoy a ride with her husband, were killed, and Ramsay was gravely burned. Years later, Joey would tell me and others that he wished every day of his life thereafter that he had selfishly refused to relinquish his seat to Ramsay's wife.

His long-time colleague Les Curtis intoned, "You were spared for the sake of Newfoundland, Joe."

Joey didn't agree with him aloud. But he didn't disagree either.

CHAPTER TWO

Students for Joey

I WAS IN my first year at Memorial University when one of the most dramatic events of Smallwood's reign took place. That was the strike of loggers employed by the old Anglo-Newfoundland Development Company (AND), whose paper mill was in Grand Falls. The strike started on December 31, 1958, in support of the demand by the loggers' new union, the International Woodworkers of America (IWA), for increases in wages and better living conditions in their woods camps. The low wages and the atrocious camps, which appeared to be unfit for human habitation, the IWA was saying, had persisted under the loggers' largely useless previous union, the Newfoundland Loggers' Association (NLA). But even before Joey entered the fray, many members of the public and the media, and some members of the labour movement itself, were supporting the NLA in fighting the IWA's raid on their members.

The IWA organizers—particularly H. Landon Ladd, their charismatic chief—were depicted by some as violent anarchists, aggressive radicals, and out-and-out communists. I remember chatting with an executive member of the Newfoundland and Labrador Federation of Labour a decade or so later. He was from central Newfoundland and he told me that one of the IWA organizers during the strike had shown him the Communist Party card he carried and told him they were going to organize everything and everyone in the province, from domestic workers to government workers, and that they were going to bring Joey Smallwood's government crashing down.

The man said there was nothing wrong with what the IWA wanted to get for the loggers but that their way of thinking and their actions were not very appealing to his fellow workers in the mill or to Newfoundlanders generally. Nobody wanted anything to do with a strike involving violence, kicking men out of their camps, or trashing company property and pitching it out. He told me the IWA organizers even threw coins into garbage cans so that kids would go after them, and then they'd take pictures and claim that the youngsters were so poor and hungry they had to eat garbage. He said that the IWA wouldn't even talk to other union or labour leaders. If they had done that instead of saying to hell with everyone, and if they'd organized peacefully, he believed, the IWA would be rolling in union dues today. I would frankly wonder during his narration how much of the man's description was an after-the-fact rationalization for what Joey did to the IWA back in 1959 with the zealous support and encouragement of a lot of Newfoundlanders, including that man.

For, although most loggers had voted to have the IWA as their union, I certainly recall Newfoundland public opinion—in the media, on the street, at the university—gradually building against the union during the winter weeks that the bitter strike went on. And I remember the feeling in my own household, no doubt created partly by my father's words, that the general public's opposition to the IWA had reached such a height that the government would be derelict in its duty if it didn't intervene. Accordingly, everyone in the province saw or heard Premier Smallwood appear on television and radio one evening around Valentine's Day in 1959 to denounce utterly, to castigate and flay, the IWA and its commandant Landon Ladd. In a speech that had to be one of the most effective pieces of negative propaganda in our province's history, Joey's words seared into people's brains. I had to look it up to see if it still seemed as effective now as I had remembered it. Here's just a sample:

> "How dare these outsiders come into this decent Christian province and by such desperate, such terrible methods try to seize control of our province's main industry. How dare they come in here and spread their black poison of class hatred and bitter and bigoted prejudice. How dare they come among decent God-fearing people and let loose the dirt and filth and poison of the last four weeks. The very presence of the IWA in Newfoundland tonight is an insult to every decent Newfoundlander. Every decent Newfoundlander should feel that he had been made dirty by the presence of this wicked and mischievous body of reckless and irresponsible wreckers."

The next day our irreverent Tory neighbour whispered to me, "How come Smallwood went so easy on them? He never even called them 'rotten fucking pricks.'"

Soon after his speech Joey had the House of Assembly pass legislation decertifying the IWA, stripping it of its right to bargain in this province, and "sending it packing." He proposed to replace the IWA and Landon Ladd—its top gun—with a union called the Newfoundland Brotherhood of Wood Workers, to be organized by Max Lane, one of his own government colleagues. National and international labour organizations and much of the mainland media denounced Joey for destroying the freedom of trade unionism. But public support in Newfoundland for Joey's actions seemed strong, and when a confrontation in March between police and loggers in Badger became a riot in which a Newfoundland Constabulary member, William Moss, was fatally injured, the support grew phenomenally.

Meanwhile, at Memorial University, our student body was so sympathetic to Joey's position, as surprising as this may seem in retrospect, that senior student leaders tried to organize a march in support of him and Max Lane's union and against Landon Ladd and the IWA. One chant, heard all over the campus, and proposed for the march, went like this: "Pick up your axe and follow Max and lop off Landon's lad."

Before the march could take place, however, Vice-President Mose Morgan banned it. He wasn't against the anti-IWA sentiment we wanted to express, but he feared our demonstration in the streets would be too fraught with danger and could easily lead to violence. I remember great disappointment among students and many faculty members that we were prevented from going out. (It was interesting, not to say hilarious, to recall this 1959 pro-Joey and anti-IWA attitude of much of the university, when, years later, Landon Ladd came back to give a speech at Memorial. He received a tumultuous standing ovation, as if the university had always been solidly behind him.)

I didn't know Landon Ladd and never saw him speaking on a platform, but Steve Neary would tell me, after I got to know him well years into the future, that Ladd was one of the most persuasive orators he'd ever seen in action. He was the equal, Steve thought, of Joey himself. Steve figured Smallwood was genuinely afraid of Ladd—not just affronted that Ladd had dared to come into Joey's own provincial turf and create such a fuss, but actually frightened that Ladd's speaking and organizational abilities and ruthlessness might cause serious political inroads in Joey's bailiwick.

I had my doubts about that on general principles, but Steve believed it, and in the election Joey called in 1959, Steve ran for the Newfoundland Democratic Party to show his labour colours then. And I can certainly testify that, even years later, when I ran in the overwhelmingly Liberal district of White Bay South, there were loggers and their families in communities like Westport and Hampden who would not vote for Smallwood or his party to save their own lives. Such was their deep bitterness that still festered so badly against the premier who drove their beloved union and its revered leader out of Newfoundland. The fact that Joey's new loggers' union ended the strike in 1959 by signing a collective agreement with the AND Company containing benefits that were mostly a carbon copy of those proposed by the IWA added insult to injury. (In 1962, Max Lane would be defeated in St. Barbe South, which some claimed was a direct consequence of 1959, but several livyers there told me that it had more to do with issues concerning the hospital in Norris Point, Bonne Bay.)

The IWA war in 1959 having been settled with Joey's complete victory, it would have been difficult to hold the election he wanted on that issue alone without appearing altogether too opportunistic. Luckily for the premier, however, Prime Minister John Diefenbaker was asinine enough to provide him with just the right excuse.

A Royal Commission set up under Term 29 of the Terms of Union between Newfoundland and Canada had recommended the payment by the federal government to the provincial government of an annual $8 million into the indefinite future. Diefenbaker, in revenge for Joey's vicious attack on him for preventing RCMP reinforcements from coming to the province during the IWA strike, now announced that the $8 million under Term 29 would terminate in 1962. To say that Smallwood stirred up a shitstorm over Diefenbaker's betrayal of Newfoundland would have been a gross understatement. Right off, I recall, he declared three days of mourning and caused all flags to be flown at half-mast. Some of the provincial PC Opposition members even sided with Joey against their federal Tory counterparts over Diefenbaker's stab in this province's back. The PC Party here was set back in its development for many years by splits and defections during that Term 29 debacle.

At the university our postponed march and bottled-up support for Joey's action against the IWA now took place. We marched, not on the IWA matter, but on Diefenbaker's treachery on Term 29. From the old Parade Street campus to the House of Assembly, then located in the Colonial Building, we trudged in our hundreds behind a coffin draped in black, waving placards, shouting that Newfoundland should separate from Canada, and chanting, "Diefenbaker, thief and faker."

Joey came out of the Colonial Building where he was lurking in wait for us and made a speech, thanking us for our support. In the middle of it, a student—I believe it was George Ivany—bawled out, "What about the new university?" Instantly, Joey responded with a promise to get cracking on its construction, not two years from now, not next year, but now, this year, right away. He proclaimed that the new campus would open within three years. (Less than three years later, in the fall of 1961, at the start of my own final undergraduate year, we would move into the brand new university buildings on the modern Elizabeth Avenue campus in St. John's.)

Meanwhile, back in 1959, after bringing the simmering resentments to an explosive boil, Joey called a provincial election for August. Diefenbaker's Term 29 betrayal, his intervention to stop RCMP reinforcements during the IWA violence, and his prolonged failure to name a chief justice to replace Sir Albert Walsh (which Joey lambasted as criminally negligent and unspeakably arrogant) all gave Joey his heaven-sent election ammunition. Indeed, a few months earlier, around the tenth anniversary of Confederation, Smallwood had dramatized the situation by offering to resign immediately if Diefenbaker's reason for treating Newfoundland so atrociously was because of the PM's personal grudge against him. If only the prime minister, Joey said, would give our poor struggling province a fair deal, he would resign the very next day. He had desperately hoped, he added with a straight face, that by this tenth anniversary of Confederation, the province would have been well off enough financially to allow him to drop out of politics altogether. Diefenbaker had cruelly disappointed him in his longed-for retirement plans.

Right before the election, two Tory MHAs—Jim Higgins, known to everyone locally as a prominent criminal lawyer, and Gus Duffy, a likeable gentleman who lived up the road from our house—bolted from the PC Party, formed something called the United Newfoundland Party, and supported Joey's position on Term 29. Duffy was elected along with another UNP candidate, John R. O'Dea, but Jim Higgins was defeated. For his pains, at Joey's behest when the Liberals under Pearson got back in government federally a few years later, Higgins was appointed to the Supreme Court of Newfoundland where, in my experience, he was a drunk and a bully high up there on his bench, and a racist everywhere else.

I remember one morning, not long after I became a lawyer, standing in the registry of the Supreme Court with a lawyer who was of East Indian origins, when Mr. Justice Jim Higgins came in. His breath stinking of stale booze, he looked at my exotic companion and turned to me to say loudly, "Every goddamned Turk wants his day in court."

Back to that 1959 election: Joey's Liberals returned with thirty-one seats out of thirty-six, to just three for the PCs under leader Malcolm Hollett. The Newfoundland Democratic Party had been quickly founded by the Federation of Labour to run as a protest against Joey's decertification of the IWA during the loggers' strike. They ran eighteen candidates under the leadership of a former Corner Brook *Western Star* editor, Ed Finn, Jr., but none got elected. A couple of years later the party became the New Democratic Party in Newfoundland.

In addition to winning a provincial election, with a demonized federal Tory prime minister, John Diefenbaker, as his overwhelming issue, Joey next embarked on an extensive speaking tour across Canada against Dief the thief. I recall hearing from Dad that the high point of the crusade was Smallwood's speech to the Canada Club in Ottawa which brought about an unheard-of standing ovation. It was a unique reaction from that particular audience, Joey openly proclaimed, for a Liberal premier.

Despite the rancorous animosity, Joey invited Diefenbaker to the opening of the new university campus in 1961. Initially the PM refused, naturally fearing that the local political madman would use the occasion to attack him. And why wouldn't he fear that? Joey had made it very public that this prime minister of Canada was petty and small-minded enough to exact personal revenge against him for their political battles: Diefenbaker had discovered that Joey's residence and office, called Canada House, on Circular Road, was owned by the Government of Canada, and issued orders to sell the house, preceded by an eviction notice sent to the Newfoundland premier.

When Smallwood assured him, however, that he would not make a fool of him at the university opening but honour and extol him as the prime minister, Diefenbaker did come, in great uneasiness and trepidation. But, like Eleanor Roosevelt (representing President Kennedy), the Duke of Devonshire (representing the British government), the new MUN chancellor, Lord Thomson of Fleet, scores of university presidents flown in from all over the world, and the Jamaican steel drum band, Diefenbaker received a tremendous welcome from Smallwood and the more than 10,000 school kids bused in from all over the province to march in a gigantic parade bearing banners.

AS AN ASIDE, I recall that the appointment of His Lordship Roy Thomson as chancellor of Memorial University was true to form for Joey's habit of acting now and then finding out afterwards if it made any sense. He would tell me later that, in the early 1950s, he had wanted to appoint as chancellor a man loaded with money who could make a prodigious donation to the university. Someone had told him soon after Confederation that a filthy-rich man by the name of Killam of Nova Scotia would like to be chancellor of a university, and MUN would suit him fine.

Joey's consideration of the suggestion consisted of pronouncing the man's name. Killam. Kill 'im? He didn't think that would go over very well here, he said. He was already facing the challenge of putting another funny name—Pickersgill—across to the electorate when he'd recruit him to run here in the 1953 federal election. So he turned the Killam idea down and appointed Lord Rothermere as chancellor of MUN instead. Killam died a couple of years later with no children and an estate of tens of millions, most of which, judging from his widow's philanthropy, would certainly have come to Memorial, as against less than a measly million from Rothermere. Joey wasn't going to make that mistake again, and so this time he appointed another self-made Canadian, maggoty with money, Lord Thomson of Fleet. Only afterwards did he have Thomson's history of philanthropy researched. He discovered, he told me, that no one could find even one solitary example of His Lordship ever having made a substantial donation to anything anywhere at any time. He turned out to be the stingiest, most miserly rich man, Joey figured, in the entire history of the world: as tight, one of his ministers proclaimed, as a hen's ass.

I myself would visit Lord Thompson at his office in London when I was studying in England in 1964-1965. I think Smallwood's office had lined up the encounter to broaden my horizons as a young Newfoundlander abroad. Ushered into the Lord's office and shown to a chair in front of his big desk, I looked at him as he peered at me through eyes that swam eerily behind those Coke-bottle-bottom glasses he wore. After about thirty seconds of that terrifying silent inspection, he opened up to wonder frankly why I was there. I blurted out the fib that I had always wanted to meet him because I too was interested in making big money one of these days. I was glad to see that my feigned greed for lucre seemed to have broken the ice; he finally smiled faintly. Then his eyes swam over me for another thirty seconds as if he was looking for grubs in a slab of meat, and finally he pronounced, as if he'd found a few,

"You'll never make big money. You haven't got the fire in your gut." Thus ended that historic rendezvous.

BACK TO THE opening of the new university campus in the early 1960s: Joey's cordial welcome there of Prime Minister Diefenbaker amazed us all. Over the next year, though, he reverted true to form and played a leading role across Canada in reducing Diefenbaker's Tory Party, which had received a record-high number of seats in the last election, to minority status in the House of Commons, and to actual defeat in the 1963 election against Lester Pearson's Liberals.

During my four years at Memorial, I became a member of the Liberal Club. At the time of the club's "Nuke Bell Island" policy, I may even have been its president. The Bell Island ferry was in the news constantly then, as it always had been and, seemingly, always would be. Our club issued a statement that, owing to the obviously unsolvable nature of the ferry problem, Bell Island should be made useful by being turned into a nuclear testing ground.

This was intended by us to be a satirical proposition, not a strictly serious one. It was supposed to bring attention to the plight of resident travellers, along the lines of, "If the government is not going to provide an adequate ferry service, they might as well bomb the place out of its own misery." No one outside of the student body, however, seemed to see the satire, or any humour at all. Steve Neary, who was about to move to the Liberals and get elected as the member for Bell Island in the 1962 election, went off the head altogether. He took to the public airwaves to urge the Bell Island Commuters' Committee, Wabana municipal leaders, provincial politicians, and "all right-thinking Newfoundlanders" to greater and greater denunciation of us renegade Grits on campus. The Tory Official Opposition noted publicly that one of the ringleaders of this appalling proposal was none other than the son of the premier's senior minister, Fred Rowe. Smallwood issued a proclamation that the Liberal Club's position did not in fact represent his government's policy vis-à-vis Bell Island, and even students should realize that some issues were far too serious to be joked about.

When Dad got home, I came down to face the music. In choice language, he detailed how I had embarrassed him and the government. He seemed to be struggling to keep his face expressionless. I figured he must be trying not to either weep or explode over the stupidity of his son. Only later did I learn that he'd been trying to keep himself from bursting out laughing. Apparently, in the secrecy of the cabinet room, after the "Nuke Bell Island" story hit the media, Joey had characterized my suggestion as the brilliant vision of a modern young Winston Churchill. The cabinet meeting had been given over to mirth for many minutes on our zany notion, so refreshingly different from the normal litany of woe on the ferry.

Years later there'd be a small ironic twist: in the 1970s, as a practising lawyer, I would be retained by the Federation of Municipalities to intervene against an application to the Public Utilities Board (PUB) by the operators of the Bell Island ferry to increase the fares. Our intervention to stop the fare increase and to improve the service turned out successful, and I was hailed as a bit of a local hero. Needless to say, I had stated nothing in my submission to the PUB about solving the ferry problems by dropping an atomic bomb on the charming island.

DURING MY LAST year at Memorial on the new campus, the Liberal Club invited Premier Smallwood to speak to the students, and the New Democratic Party invited their new national leader, Tommy Douglas. Both of them spoke over separate lunch hours in the "Little Theatre." And both times the place overflowed with students who gave each leader a tumultuous reception. I introduced Premier Smallwood. A few weeks later, at some sort of a function where Joey was present, he mentioned to me that he'd heard about Douglas's visit to the university on the media, and he was wondering what kind of a welcome the NDP leader had received. I told him it was enthusiastic. Did Douglas get a standing ovation at the end as he had received? Yes, I said, he did. How did I think the students rated Douglas's speech and his own? About equal, I responded: students thought that both speeches were tremendous. At this point the premier lost interest in our conversation. I had the distinct impression that he didn't want to hear that anyone else's oration—national leader visiting the province or not—could have been equal to his own, or received as favourably.

Years later Smallwood would tell me that Tommy Douglas always got far too much credit. Joey himself had introduced a precursor to medicare in Newfoundland for everyone up to sixteen years old, and had thereby pointed the way for the rest of the country long before Douglas brought his plan into Saskatchewan.

AFTER GRADUATING FROM Memorial in 1962, I spent the summer break working on a survey crew in the Bay of Islands before going to law school that fall. Diefenbaker called a federal election for June, and a huge Liberal rally was organized in Corner Brook. Provincial premier Smallwood, and not the federal Liberal candidate, was billed as the chief speaker.

Before the rally that evening, I found myself in Smallwood's suite at the Glynmill Inn with party brass and some provincial ministers. He talked and sipped from a glass of transparent liquid which I was naive enough to take for water, especially since he was about to speak at a big public event.

Before leaving the hotel for the rally, Joey lay back for a nap in the sitting room of his suite. Everyone present, from ministers to flunkies, now sat still or crept about in absolute silence. Many grinned at each other, but nobody spoke. At first I couldn't believe the imposition he was inflicting on everyone in the room: his bedroom adjoined the sitting room and he could have been in there napping away to his heart's content while we sat out here enjoying a chat. But then I grasped that no one in the sitting room considered it an imposition. Everyone seemed to be honoured that "the Skipper" had deigned to have his snooze in their presence.

At the rally that night, I would witness again what I had remarked before, and would confirm many times in the future: Joey loved to—he lived to—personalize his politics by demonizing his enemies. While other politicians, when acting or speaking ruthlessly, might rationalize, "It's not personal; it's only politics," Joey was having none of that. His maxim seemed to be, "This is not only politics; it's damn well personal too." I saw it in the IWA strife when, among other personal attacks, Joey had somehow linked Landon Ladd to the then-notorious American Teamsters Union: I recall Joey looking up at the gallery of the House of Assembly one day when Larry Daley, the head of the Teamsters in Newfoundland, was sitting there. His very presence seemed to galvanize Joey to an outburst: the Teamsters were infamously led in the States by Jimmy Hoffa, who was suspected of Mafia connections—*ergo*, Landon Ladd of the IWA, who was Daley's buddy, was a gangster too. It was a line of baseless logic designed to add to the demonization and destruction of Ladd personally and had nothing to do with the local issues at stake in the strike.

I would see and hear the same in his private vilification of Peter Cashin years after their public political scraps, even after Joey had given Cashin a plum job as payback for Cashin having run as an Independent in a federal election to split the Opposition vote and push Joey's candidate to victory. Cashin's new job entailed blasting off a city-wide siren now and then as a sort of fire drill warning that St. John's was under nuclear attack. Joey would sometimes bring up Cashin's mental state during conversations, stating that Peter had a steel plate in his skull as a result of World War I wounds and was completely off his head and indeed a dangerous, raving lunatic. He instanced Cashin's physical assault on him on the floor of the National Convention as just one proof. His total inability to get along with anyone, whether father, mother, other family members, or strangers, was another. When I would suggest to

Joey the anomaly of his having appointed a man whom he characterized as a madman to the job of saving us from nuclear annihilation, he only grinned.

I would hear similar demeaning of others for years to come. What of his colleague, and later opponent, Alex Hickman? Well, he was a weak man motivated solely by an obsessive need to impress his own wife. And his leadership rival, John Crosbie? John was actuated entirely by greed and a pathological need to line his own pockets and those of the entire Crosbie tribe. His colleague and supporter Ed Roberts, after Ed had annoyed him about something? Oh, Ed was among the most brilliant men he'd ever encountered in politics, second only to Alfred B. Morine, but, as with Morine, there was a close affinity between near-genius and serious instability. What about former cabinet minister Val Earle, after he'd defected from Joey's Liberals to the PCs? The man was the utter personification of "stupidity, cupidity, and malignant self-esteem." Well, then, Frank Moores—wasn't he a clever man? Yes, clever, of course; by no means a stupid man—he possessed a very big brain indeed, but, regrettably, it hung between his legs.

And now, at the huge Liberal rally in Corner Brook during that 1962 federal election, it was William J. Browne's turn to get it. "Billy" Browne, as Joey called him, had long been involved in politics. He'd been a member of the House of Assembly and of the last cabinet before Commission of Government took over, and after Confederation he was in and out of the House of Assembly and the House of Commons as a Progressive Conservative, most crucially as a member of Diefenbaker's cabinet at the time of Term 29. Thus, Joey had all the legitimate ammunition he needed to launch against him any political attack he wanted. But, on top of that, he seemed to have a visceral need to demonize Browne with personal slander.

Much of Joey's speech that night in Corner Brook consisted of building up to and then leading the audience in a prolonged chant of abuse of Billy Browne. First, he brought up a matter to make Browne look like an enemy of the people. This involved a dangerous, narrow curve on the Conception Bay Highway in the Topsail area, hundreds of miles away from where Joey was then speaking. Many people in the St. John's area, following Smallwood's lead, already called this part of the road "Judge Browne's Corner"—a reference to Browne's time as a magistrate between political gigs. Joey always claimed that the land adjoining the road there was owned by Billy Browne, and that the government could not widen the road and make it safe for drivers because Browne was demanding too much money for his land. Therefore, the greedy and avaricious Billy Browne was putting the lives of innocent drivers and their families at serious risk of injury or death. (A few years later, when Joey brought the subject up in private conversation, I asked him why the government had not simply expropriated the land in the public interest under the law, widened the road, and had the question of compensation decided by arbitration. Joey looked at me in pity, as if I were a cute but intellectually challenged child struggling vainly to understand the basics of political life.)

Back to Joey's speech in Corner Brook: First he made a few more points about how devious Billy Browne was. There was the "well-known fact" that Billy had a crafty and cunning deal with organizers of parish garden parties in any district he represented. When the donation bucket was going around, Billy would drop in a twenty-dollar bill. Of course, word would circulate among the parishioners about how generous the Honourable W. J. Browne was as everyone gawked in amazement at yet another twenty the sainted man had contributed. Later, his cronies, the organizers, would give Billy back nineteen dollars in change on the rationale that Billy earlier hadn't had the right change to make his intended one-dollar donation. Joey's anecdote drew combined howls of laughter and execration.

In this federal election, Browne was running for the Tories in St. John's West, which was way over on the Avalon Peninsula. And here was Joey, making him the main focus of his ridicule and venom in a rally 700 kilometres away in the Humber-St. George's riding, as he now led the audience in a rousing chant of "Billy Browne is going down." Joey did an inspiring job of conducting the refrain. I can see clearly in my mind's eye the huge crowd of all sorts, including respectable businessmen and professionals and their oh-so-proper spouses, sitting there with flushed faces and fervent eyes, caterwauling out their frenzied malediction of someone they'd barely heard of, let alone knew, on the other side of the island: "Billy Browne is going down, Billy Browne is going down."

One lone dissenter in the audience, a drunken heckler, started shouting out his low opinion of Smallwood and his arguments. The premier told him to come closer to the stage so that he could hear him properly. Up swaggered the stalwart. Once there, Joey said to him, "That's important. Everyone should hear that." He reached down from the stage, grasped the man's hand, and pulled him up onto the stage, the political leader's 140 pounds lifting the heckler's beer-bellied 180. Then he led the man to the mic and urged him to speak to the crowd. The man looked out over the ocean of expectant, smirking faces and did a pretty good impression, albeit involuntary, of Jackie Gleason's TV chump, Ralph Kramden: "Homma, homma, homma, homma." Then Smallwood led the drunk man to his own seat and sat him down, where the paralyzed disrupter stayed soundless for the rest of Joey's speech.

And Billy Browne did go down. The up-and-coming Richard Cashin defeated him by a couple of dozen votes in that federal election way over in St. John's West.

But then Browne resurrected himself once more in the provincial election in the fall of that same year by getting himself voted into the House of Assembly. I was in law school at the time, but during a visit back home in the winter or spring of 1963, I went to the House of Assembly to view proceedings. There Smallwood was on his feet lambasting Browne to his face. His voice dripping with contempt and derision, he made several remarks to the effect that here the great man was, reduced to being "back in this House." I was a little perplexed that the premier would consider it a scornful insult of an opponent that he'd gotten himself re-elected to the legislature, where Joey himself had spent his entire political life.

Years later, in 1970, after Billy Browne's third wife had just died, Joey would tell me in conversation that the reason Browne had been married so many times was that he killed off his wives by giving them cervical cancer. Billy was a carrier of the "germ" responsible for the disease, claimed Smallwood, which he transmitted to his unsuspecting wives. One question had never been satisfactorily answered, he said: Where had such a pious, religious, proper man picked up the death-dealing microbe to begin with? Oh, Billy might give the impression that butter wouldn't melt in his mouth, he concluded, but the man was a walking death machine of sexually transmitted disease. He alleged all this to me some years before it was generally understood that infection by the human papilloma virus was medically implicated as a cause of cervical cancer.

Joey would also wonder aloud to me whether the reason for Browne's rather mediocre achievements in politics might be the fact that, by becoming a Rhodes Scholar and studying at Oxford, a person might ascend intellectually so far above the common herd that it was impossible for him ever to relate to ordinary people or to be a good politician thereafter. He never mentioned my own stint as a Rhodes Scholar, but his statement about Browne came at a time, as we shall see, when he was intimating that, along with Ed Roberts, I was seriously endangering my own political career by putting up roadblocks to his more madcap initiatives involving John Shaheen and John C. Doyle.

MEANWHILE, BACK IN the early 1960s, I was at law school on the mainland, where the raising of Premier Smallwood's name by anyone often evoked reactions of admiration and fascination. Not always, though. Sometimes a sneer or sarcastic word or outright laughter was the response. Once in labour law class, the professor, who was by no means a raving socialist, mentioned Smallwood's decertification of the IWA, called him a union buster, and opined that my premier had set back the evolution of labour law in Newfoundland by a hundred years. "I don't know what's wrong with those fellows down there," he concluded, and the whole class looked at me in general merriment.

At least twice more during my law school career, Joey's antics raised guffaws among my fellow students. The first was after the NHL playoffs in 1963 where our own great Alex Faulkner had stood out so prominently for Detroit, including two game-winning goals in the semifinals against Chicago and a game-winner in the finals against Toronto. That was all admirable enough. Nothing but accolades there. The guffaws came after Joey proclaimed "Alex Faulkner Day," and declared a school holiday in order to hold a celebratory parade and a ceremony hosted by the premier himself. The whole shebang received Canada-wide prominence as the Newfie joke kicker at the end of national news. Honest to God, my classmates chortled at me, you're all so darned adorable and quaint down there.

The second general guffaw occurred when a law student in a class ahead of me came into the common room for a smoke one day and reminisced to me about his boarding school in New Brunswick, where a fellow student was a young guy by the name of Valdmanis. Quite frequently, young Valdmanis received brown paper parcels, which he said came from his dad in Newfoundland. At first everyone thought they were the usual "care packages" sent from their homes to kids at the school. But this Valdmanis boy never followed the normal ritual of opening them to share the goodies with the other students. Instead, he hid the packages and quickly passed them unopened either to his mother or to a man who would soon thereafter make a visit. No one, said my law school colleague with a fake look of wonderment on his face, could ever figure out what was in those packages. Ha ha ha, went all my fellow Clarence Darrow fledglings. A few years after that conversation, I learned that Joey's Valdmanis had a brother living in New Brunswick. The male visitor would have been the young Valdmanis's uncle. No one ever figured out what happened to all the money that Valdmanis, Sr., stole as Joey's industrial tsar, which, according to some accounts, may have amounted to over a million dollars—probably over $8 million in today's dollars.

DURING MY STUDENT days, I travelled to some conventions of the Liberal Party of Canada in Ottawa. In my first year at Memorial, I had talked my father into taking me to the Liberal leadership convention in January of 1958 as an observer. Louis St. Laurent had resigned on the heels of his loss of the government, the year before, to Diefenbaker. Now Lester Pearson and Paul Martin were the main contenders for the leadership.

At one get-together of Newfoundlanders in his suite at the Château Laurier, Premier Smallwood was frank about the potential for the party's success in an election led by either of those two candidates. "What a choice we have been presented with!" he said. "Oh, they are two great men to be sure. Statesmen to the core. But is either of them the man who can return the Liberal Party to power? One man cross-eyed and the other man lipsy?" The "cross-eyed" one was Paul Martin, Sr., a cabinet minister of great distinction in several Liberal governments. The candidate with the lisp—the "lipsy" one, in Newfoundland parlance—was Lester Pearson, world-renowned Nobel Peace Prize winner. He went on to win the leadership at that convention and to lead the party into an election against Diefenbaker that same year, with the result that Diefenbaker's PCs elected the greatest number of MPs in history, and the Liberal Party fell to historically low levels. Joey had been dead-on.

At the next convention a year or two later, I was in Joey's suite again at the Château Laurier with his large retinue when his phone rang. Joey answered it himself and said loud for the rest of us, "Good afternoon, Mr. St. Laurent." He thanked the former prime minister of

Canada for returning his earlier call. They agreed to get together right away in Joey's suite. The premier cast his eye around the room at Don Jamieson, Les Curtis, my father, and several other ministers, and settled on me as the obvious gofer in the group. "I'll have one of our most promising young Liberals," he said into the phone, "go out and meet your elevator."

Down the corridor, at the elevators, I waited only a few minutes before a door opened and Louis St. Laurent stepped out by himself. He stood there looking around, erect and immaculately dressed in a double-breasted suit, exuding great natural dignity. He was now not far from eighty years old, Joey had said.

I introduced myself and, as I led him back to the suite, he became interested in where I was studying, my subjects, and my impressions of the convention so far. In there, he stood and talked with Smallwood and the others for half an hour, reminiscing about the Confederation battle a dozen years ago just before he'd become PM and was honoured to usher Newfoundland into Canada. It had been by far the greatest achievement of his time in office, he said.

Joey noted the irony of Don Jamieson's presence today, since he'd been one of the strongest, most persuasive voices against Confederation at the time. And now here he was contemplating running for the House of Commons as a candidate for his former enemy, the Liberal Party of Canada. Someone mentioned the further irony that it had probably been Jamieson who'd persuaded Ches Crosbie, Jamieson's boss, to boycott the signing of the Terms of Union in Ottawa and to go home in an attempt to scuttle the deal.

Don Jamieson replied that he doubted if, in those days, he'd had the moral suasion with Ches Crosbie to induce him to take such steps. Ches was happy enough to have him around as a mouthpiece, he said, but in most other things he didn't treat him very seriously—he would even call Don by the name "Donald Duck." Joey interrupted to say he thought Greg Power had invented that name because of Don's powerful, penetrating voice. No, said Jamieson, Ches Crosbie had come up with it, because, owing to Don's weight and fat arse, he waddled like a duck when he walked. That caused good-natured laughter in the room, and Joey replied, "You mean to say there was something nasty said that Greg Power didn't invent?"

The get-together ended on those amusing notes, and I couldn't help remarking on the ingratiating skill of Jamieson: in a couple of lines he had turned his attempted sabotage of Confederation a decade before into a joke about himself, and he had made everyone present here today appreciate him for his self-effacing humour. Well, perhaps not everyone. A few years later I would listen to Joey tell a bunch of us, "Don Jamieson is so great an egotist, so completely a narcissist, so utterly full of himself, that, rather than not talk about himself at all, he will say something extremely negative about himself."

Jamieson would get elected to the Commons in a by-election in 1966, and Smallwood would do everything in his power for two solid years to keep him from going into the cabinet as Newfoundland's minister. Some would speculate that Joey saw any strong advancement by Don as a possible threat to his own leadership of the provincial Liberal Party. Joey himself would insist, however, that he could not permit the intolerable insult to the younger but senior Richard Cashin, elected in 1962, that would result if Jamieson leapfrogged over him into the cabinet. As we shall see, these too-cute-by-half machinations of Joey's would cause a serious fracture in his leadership not long afterwards.

Back in Smallwood's suite in the Château Laurier that day, Mr. St. Laurent decided to return to his own room, and I was directed to lead him out to the elevator again. Walking along the corridor with him, I wondered to myself why a former PM of his age was going about alone and unaccompanied—not that he was doddering or needed guidance, but where was his retinue? Where was his security? Was it because, as Liberal leader, he had lost the federal election to Diefenbaker in 1957 that he was accorded so little ceremony and scant respect at this Liberal convention? And was that why Smallwood had not asked leave to visit the former prime minister who had been in power when we joined Canada, but instead forced the great man to come down and pay court to the provincial premier?

Chatting amiably as we walked, I decided that all those questions could be answered by reference to Louis St. Laurent's essential character. The statesman was simply modest, non-pretentious, and had no desire to stand on any ceremony whatsoever. He was very pleased, he told me, that Premier Smallwood had been considerate and thoughtful enough to make a special effort to get together with an old has-been warhorse like him, long past his prime and of no political use to anyone. This was, in fact, a characteristic of Joey—taking considerate notice of powerless has-beens—that I would notice in the future myself.

IN 1963, DURING law school, urged on by Professor E. R. Seary, under whom I'd majored in English at Memorial, I applied for the Rhodes Scholarship. My father thought it was a great idea—until I mentioned to him some of the selection committee members: big Tory Fabian O'Dea, appointed as Lieutenant-Governor by the Tory Diefenbaker government; big Tory Robert Furlong, appointed as Chief Justice of our Supreme Court by the Tory Diefenbaker government on the recommendation of big Tory and Joey's arch-enemy, Billy Browne; big Tory lawyer Herb Morgan, brother of the academic critic of Joey, Mose Morgan; and big Tory James Greene, leader of the provincial PC Party. "Hmm," said my father dubiously as I listed the names. And a few days later, he told me he had mentioned my application casually to Premier Smallwood, who had replied that it was good to apply for these things just for the practice if for nothing else, but I shouldn't get my hopes up on this one. For one thing the timing was awkward—hadn't Neil Murray, the son of another of Joey's cabinet ministers, Myles Murray, won the Rhodes last year?

With forlorn hope that fall, I went through the motions of being interviewed by committee members. I could have kicked myself for my answer when one of the Tory pillars asked if I intended to do anything in addition to practising law when I finished my studies. I replied that I was considering entering politics later on. Oh, brilliant! Just like me to be stupid enough to bring attention to my close ties to the Liberal Party. He grinned and said, "Oh, good! Another candidate for the PC Party next election." A little sarcasm there, I thought amidst the laughter—a harbinger, no doubt, of my doom. A few weeks later, I was notified at law school of my selection as Rhodes Scholar for 1964.

Years after that, I mentioned all this to Fabian O'Dea during a private conversation, and he said that, in his experience, the politics of a person's family had nothing whatsoever to do with the selection committee's decision. We both agreed, though, that there was already prejudice and unfairness enough in the Rhodes Trust by its exclusion of female applicants. I told him that, judging by the superior brains of some of the women I'd known at Memorial University, there was no chance I would have won the Rhodes if females had been permitted to apply. It would be 1977 before that appalling sexual chauvinism would be removed and women allowed by law to become Rhodes Scholars.

Home during one of the breaks from law school after the Rhodes announcement, a knock came at our door, and when I answered, a man I didn't know was standing there holding a book. He introduced himself as Nimshi Crewe. I recognized his name from my father's mention of him as one of Newfoundland's great minds and a close friend of Smallwood's, especially during the pre-Confederation debates at the Methodist College Literary Institute (MCLI). Mr. Crewe told me now that the book in his hand, *The Trefoil*, was one of his favourites, and he had read and reread it with great pleasure and profit, and he wanted me to have it as I started on my intellectual adventure. I was flabbergasted at the wonderful, thoughtful gesture by the good, remarkable man.

Years later, when Nimshi Crewe was in his last illness—I believe he died in 1971—I told Joey of that earlier visit, and he replied that that was exactly what Nimshi was like. He was the only man in Smallwood's life whom he considered his great mentor. Nimshi was responsible for much of the success of his career, Joey said. Joey had never missed a debate at the MCLI when he was in St. John's, and that was where he had first met his brilliant friend. He was the one man alive, Joey said, to whom he could listen all night in discussions without trying to destroy his arguments. He had spent long hours talking to him at his home over the years. The premier had tried to get him to run and join his cabinet simply because he was the most brilliant man in Newfoundland, but Nimshi wanted to stay far away from public life. Besides, if he were in his cabinet, he said, he might no longer feel free to tell Joey off whenever he felt like it.

Joey's eyes misted over at the memories of his old friend. Then he gave his quiet laugh. At debates, he recalled, Nimshi would sometimes close his eyes in concentration and get turned completely around in his enthusiasm, and would end up talking to the wall with his back to the audience, but still to greater effect than most other speakers. One time, when Nimshi was searching his mind for a commodity to illustrate the economic point he was making, he blurted out in debate, according to Joey, "Say, for instance, that you require a, a, a . . . a gross of French safes!"

DURING MY FIRST year at Oxford, I made plans with some Canadian and English friends to spend the summer vacation—the long vac—travelling in Europe. But then I got a letter from home saying that Premier Smallwood was planning a number of political events during that summer of 1965 and he thought it would be a good idea if I came home for a month and took part. I drastically curtailed my travel plans to oblige. Neil Murray and I and two other Canadian students did spend a couple of weeks beating around France at the beginning of the summer, and in September three British students and I occupied three weeks travelling around Italy and Greece, sleeping on beaches and hotel rooftops. But in between those beguiling wanderings, I flew home to Newfoundland.

There the word was that Smallwood was planning to have an election next year in the fall of 1966, right after the big Come Home Year celebrations planned for that summer. Meanwhile, he was spending this summer bombing about the province with an entourage of ministers, members, and would-be candidates, celebrating all the progress that was taking place under his political aegis. I didn't know then that, at twenty-three, I was being numbered among the possible candidates. Nor, apparently, did well-known media personality John Nolan, who was at a variety of events, along with others who would make an entry into politics. When I asked John if he was going to run in the next election, he was noncommittal, giving the impression, genuinely or disingenuously, that he didn't know. He didn't ask me—it would have been a ludicrous question at my age. Possibly the only one who did know all was Ed Roberts, who had graduated from law school the year before and was now much in evidence as the premier's executive assistant.

Among the other media events that summer, two stand out. One was Pearson's Peak. We all travelled to central Newfoundland in July for the unveiling of the monument to Prime Minister Pearson that commemorated the completion of the Trans-Canada Highway (TCH) across the island. The premier and the rest of us in his gang drove out from St. John's while Prime Minister Pearson drove from Port aux Basques (or at least that was the story) to meet at the halfway point of the paved TCH just outside of Grand Falls. Joey's mantra in the media and on billboards was, "We finished the drive in sixty-five, thanks to Mr. Pearson." The Pearson Liberal Government had increased the federal contribution up to ninety per cent to complete the TCH. The contributions of the previous Tory government of John Diefenbaker were given short shrift by Joey.

The rough-hewn, slender rock pillar nearly a hundred feet high was called a "shaft" on the plaque affixed to the monument, as in, "This shaft was unveiled by the Prime Minister . . . etc." and a number of witty observers remarked that the word was appropriate since that was exactly what Joey was giving his Tory opponents, provincial and federal—the shaft. I recall Mike Pearson unveiling the plaque on his shaft by yanking off the Union Jacks that covered it. I think that Joey and Jack Pickersgill, our minister in Ottawa and greatly responsible for the federal largesse, made speeches. Both of them were reputed to be among the most effective political speech-makers in the land, but what stands out in my mind from that day was the talk by Pearson.

Understated as a speaker, he was normally ridiculed across Canada for his funny way of talking and his uselessness at orating. But his decency and good humour at this event remain memorable to me today, nearly fifty years later. I could sense even then why he did not (and never would) form anything but minority governments, but I could also feel why he would come down in history, for his progressive social policies and his small-l liberal approach, as one our most esteemed prime ministers.

BETWEEN THE PUBLIC events, the premier got wind of the fact from my father that his brother-in-law, Art Scammell, the author of "The Squid Jiggin' Ground," among other delightful Newfoundland songs, was visiting us in St. John's from Montreal. Art was my uncle by marriage, having married my mother's sister, Rellie. Joey asked Dad to bring Uncle Art up to his office to meet with him, and I tagged along. Joey was effusive in his praise of Scammell and talked about the several remarkable native sons produced by Uncle Art's childhood home, Change Islands. Then, as he and Uncle Art were shaking hands goodbye, Joey exclaimed, "I would rather have written 'The Squid Jiggin' Ground' than be premier of Newfoundland." Uncle Art was charmed, if amused, at the compliment, naturally, but from what I could gather from later conversations, he remained a Tory.

*

AFTER THAT, PREMIER Smallwood was off to another great event with the rest of us in tow. The one that has stayed in my memory is the Bay d'Espoir hydro development. It must have been the official sod-turning or announcement of the start of the project that summer. Whatever it was, Joey spoke for an hour at the site, not only describing the development itself and reeling off its megawatts of power with its hydro lines criss-crossing the island and the cheap home-heating energy that would result to everyone, but also the super-city that would soon be in place at the Head of Bay d'Espoir with its maze of highways, cloverleafs, overpasses, and underpasses serving all the new industries attracted and the many hundreds of new employees and their families, and so forth and so on. Someone in our entourage commented to me there or on the way back, "The man is utterly mad."

I thought of that comment a few weeks later waking up from a night in a sleeping bag on a beach in Greece to the nearby staccato of early morning gunfire. Yes, Joey may have been utterly mad. But it seemed to be a pardonable madness compared to the civil strife then developing in the womb of democracy, which would lead to the *coup d'état* and tyranny of the Greek colonels a year and a half later in 1967. Give me the harmless "utter madness" of Joey Smallwood any day, I thought then.

OUT OF THE blue during my final term of law studies in 1966, I got a letter from Dad saying that Joey wanted to feel me out about running in White Bay South in the election expected that fall. What? I would only be twenty-four years old in June—not all that long out of short pants—and White Bay South was Dad's own district, into which he'd ploughed great effort, time, and projects. I knew all that because I had gone around the district with him as company on several visits.

While I took some time to ponder the notion, Myles Murray visited London, on his way home from leading a Newfoundland delegation to a First World War memorial ceremony, and invited me and his son, my good friend Neil Murray, down for a meal and some theatre. I don't remember what play we saw, but I do remember my gluttony and Neil's at the Guinea and the Piggy—all you could eat for a quid and a bob.

Myles told us, over our huge slabs of beef, about how he'd spoken before being spoken to by Smallwood at his very first cabinet meeting. Afterwards the premier told him he didn't realize that Myles disliked being in cabinet so much and wanted out so badly—otherwise why had he voiced his discontent so audibly? Myles took the hint and lasted many more years by opening his trap only when called upon to respond. We all laughed, and I asked myself if I really wanted to be part of that at this point in my life. Soon afterwards, Myles was appointed judge, and he would tell me later that he'd had no idea as one of Joey's genuflectors just how enjoyable the feeling of absolute independence and total security of tenure could be.

That spring of 1966, I wrote in reply to my father, balking at running that year and giving several excellent reasons. A few days later I was summoned out to the communal phone where I was living to take a long-distance telephone call from home. I was informed without equivocation that Joey was counting on me running, had me down as a candidate, and he wanted me to come home right after university and get cracking. Why? I asked. What was the big rush for me to run?

It began to emerge, as I read between the lines from the other end, that Dad was going to run in Grand Falls district, whether I ran in White Bay South or not, and I'd be nuts to pass up this opportunity and let someone else take the district. Why was Dad leaving his old district? Well, Joey had made it clear that this coming election would be his last hurrah. He was sixty-five now and would be retiring soon afterwards. But in his final triumph he wanted to win, not just a solid majority government, but as many seats as humanly possible, and increase his majority from last election.

Part of this master plan of Joey's was to get Dad to run in Grand Falls district, which had elected Tory Ambrose Peddle in the 1962 election, and try to win the district back from that popular member. He figured that someone with Dad's experience and reputation could win the seat, not to mention that he'd be positioning himself to take over the premiership from Joey himself in a year or so. Moreover, my running was part of Joey's great youth-oriented thrust. Opponents had been wondering aloud if someone receiving his old-age pension as Joey now was, after nearly twenty years as ruler, was not getting a bit too long in the tooth for leadership. Joey's answer was to show the world all the young men (women weren't even a consideration) that he could attract: John Crosbie, Clyde Wells, John Nolan, Bill Callahan, Ed Roberts, Alex Hickman, John Mahoney, and me.

CHAPTER THREE

Joey's Young Turks

WHEN I GOT home to St. John's in June of 1966, a no-frills command from Premier Smallwood's office was waiting for me by the phone: Come up see him without delay. Up I trundled to Confederation Building, where, after a longish wait in his outer office surrounded by stressed-out supplicants, I was pulled inside to be greeted by Joey in his bedroom slippers with the statement, not a question, that I was running in White Bay South. Whereupon he couldn't finish our conversation quick enough as he wrung my hand and steered me to the door and progressed to more substantial matters inside, this minor one being in the bag.

Now that I was evidently a candidate, I had to tell my new law firm. I had earlier signed up to do my nine-month articles with Alex Hickman, Q.C., of the legal partnership of Halley, Hickman, Hunt, and Steele. But Smallwood had just appointed Alex to his cabinet, so now Jim Halley, Doug Hunt, and Geoff Steele had to take me under their wings. I would have some great exchanges with Halley at the firm and outside for years afterwards. He'd been a zealous anti-Confederate, even coming up with the notion of economic union with the United States that nearly derailed Joey's Confederate drive. But I didn't get the idea that he was entirely delighted I would be goofing off from the law office for politics even before I was a real lawyer, especially when I now left town at once to travel about the distant reaches of White Bay South district for most of that summer.

I found there that a rumour was already percolating through the district that my running was a possibility, and I was pleasantly surprised at the number of friends and acquaintances I'd made from previous visits who encouraged me to do so. There were few, if any, real nomination meetings to select candidates for the Liberal Party in those good old days. Normally, if Joey said you were the candidate for the Liberal Party, then you were the candidate—any differences of opinion being mediated by him or his minions with carrot-and-stick offers that you couldn't refuse. Then each candidate was formally installed during a visit to the returning officer for the official nomination, accompanied by a cluster of supporters who were captured in a snapshot for the newspaper and the party propaganda. I described the process afterwards to a friend, perhaps inelegantly but, I fear, accurately: "Like the other Liberal candidates in that election, I got nominated and elected on Joey's shitty shirttails."

However, I think there was actually a provision for legitimate, contested nomination meetings in the party constitution, because I recall, after Dad announced his move to Grand Falls district, that Mayor Bill Eaton gave me and others the impression that he would be running for the Liberal nomination in White Bay South, and I thought I had a real contest on my hands. Bill was a well-known pilot and businessman and mayor in Baie Verte, the largest town in the district, and a member of the highly regarded Eaton family that included Doug and Cam. Ultimately Bill didn't run. I don't know if someone on behalf of Joey "encouraged" him out, but we remained friends, even after he decided to run as a Tory against me in two future elections.

*

BEFORE DISPATCHING US to our districts to campaign, Joey collected all the candidates together in a room in St. John's for a pep talk. Do not concern yourself with policies or issues, he told us, just leave all that to him. Thereupon, he unfurled an impressive-looking booklet called the Liberal Manifesto. Fellow candidate Aiden Maloney and I joked with each other that when we got a chance to read it after the election, we must see how much of it was a nostalgic throwback to the days when some British members of the Commission of Government had called Smallwood a Bolshevik. (We didn't find anything except the title.)

If anyone questioned you about policy, Joey instructed us, refer them to the Manifesto. It contained both historic Liberal achievements and future Liberal commitments. Indeed, it contained everything, he stressed—and that wasn't a word of a lie. I don't recall actually seeing a guaranteed passage to heaven or a superb sex life promised as part of our Newfoundland Liberal platform, but I'm sure they were in the Manifesto somewhere if I'd been valiant enough to look harder.

Now, as for your districts, Joey went on, that was your own full responsibility. As candidate, you had one job and one job only: knock on every door in the district and say hello to everyone in the district. Do not try to win arguments. You could win every argument in the district and still get defeated. So, don't, don't, don't get into any arguments or even discussions. Because, remember, if anyone tries to engage you in a discussion, you can mark that down as a sabotage attempt by the enemy to distract you as a Liberal candidate and fritter away your valuable time. You'll have four years after the election to sit down for a cup of tea with constituents and discuss whether the universe is expanding or contracting. But to arrive at that pleasure, you had to get elected first.

The first duty of a politician, he said, is to get elected; the second duty of a politician, he continued, is to get elected; the third duty of a politician is . . . most of the candidates got his drift. A super salesman is successful by never losing sight of this aim: Always Be Closing The Deal—ABCD. It's the same with a candidate: you close the deal by getting elected. Always be getting elected. You get elected by going door to door twelve hours a day every day. Worry about nothing else, and leave everything else to Joey.

Finally, he warned, do not give liquor to anyone and do not go into clubs licensed to sell liquor. This was especially true in areas with a large component of United Church, Salvation Army, and Pentecostal adherents. But it was also true in Roman Catholic places, because a bar visit there would only lead to a racket. Do not give anyone money except in payment for a legitimate service for which you will get a receipt, except for, perhaps, a small donation to laudable or charitable causes and to the good works of the clergy.

We were all sent downtown individually to Bill Petten's office in, I believe, the Board of Trade building, to pick up our campaign money. Bill Petten was the Liberal Party's "treasurer" or, more accurately, Joey's bagman. Like Ray, his father, who had performed an identical service for Joey, Bill would soon be appointed to the Senate of Canada, and Joey would joke that he had created the hereditary Petten senatorship.

When I first knew him, Bill Petten possessed an unusual physical affliction: his eyelids drooped constantly down over his eyes, giving him a sinister, hooded look, while the rest of his face remained extremely friendly. I always thought he should go into movies as a lovable-looking Mafia hit man. He was a great guy with a wonderful sense of humour. After Joey had him pitchforked into the Senate, he would have his eyelids surgically fixed—tucked up, so that his gaze became ordinary. When I ran into him in an airport sometime afterwards and commented on the beautiful surgical job that had been done on his eyelids, he responded that he wasn't so sure about the whole thing himself: "Now that I can finally see what the hell is going on," he lamented, "I want those eyelids down over my eyes again."

Meanwhile, in the election of 1966, Bill Petten passed me an envelope containing a cheque for $1,500 made out to me personally. It was to be deposited in a new account, to be set up in a bank in my district, and the account should be called something like the White Bay South Liberal Campaign. A trusted Liberal there was to be given signing powers, along with myself. The amount was designed to cover all my personal expenses in the campaign for three weeks—gas, food, lodging. All the other campaign trappings and accoutrements—posters, signs, literature, media ads, and the like—were supplied and paid for by the party.

I found out afterwards that the $1,500 given to me was very much at the lower end of the scale. In more problematic districts for the Liberals, the candidate was given double that and more. Bill Callahan said he got $4,000 for his campaign on the Port au Port Peninsula. All these cheques meant that just for the personal campaign expenses of individual candidates, the Liberal Party under Smallwood had ready cash of well over $100,000 for the 1966 election, an amount that would be equal to over $700,000 in today's money. And on top of that were all the other huge general party expenses. I wondered how much money the benighted PCs under their leader, Noel Murphy, had for their campaign.

I never even spent all my $1,500, even though I did my best to give it away by ten-dollar donations to the church of every clergyman I encountered. It would take me a couple of years visiting the district before I finally donated it all theologically and spiritually.

I kicked off my 1966 campaign by getting aboard my car in St. John's by myself and driving seven hours to a hotel in Baie Verte. From there I spent part of a day driving around and meeting with the half-dozen key Liberal kingpins in the district. If a Liberal Association existed, it was solely on paper. There was no such thing as an operating Liberal body of active members. These Liberal kingpins, who had seemingly occupied their informal positions as party operatives by divine right from time immemorial, were largely, I discovered, a time-consuming nuisance.

Some of them did genuinely help out by engaging some young fellows to distribute posters rather haphazardly and seeing to it that some signs were erected, but mostly their contribution consisted of merely being seen with the Liberal candidate as a prestige-booster for me. Their stature in the community was supposed to bring me votes. In return, I was getting disconcerting hints from some of them of the big favours they expected if I got elected.

Meanwhile, my campaign consisted of driving myself, alone in the car, to each individual community on the Baie Verte Peninsula and on the other side of White Bay from Hampden to Jackson's Arm—twenty or so places in all. In each community, I followed Joey's advice to knock on every door, and I had a short palaver down on the wharf. The weather was great. It was the most pleasant three-week period in my life, as enjoyable and rejuvenating, by and large, as a vacation. However, a few painful episodes did stand out.

Every community had its prizewinning insufferable sea-lawyer. Usually it was the local Tory shopkeeper. Selling Bull's Eyes and beans over the counter seemed to give him a notch up on the social scale, at least in his own mind, over his plebeian customers. If the people spending their money in his establishment were ragged-arsed Liberals, then he was, of course, the blue-blooded Tory merchant. Going into any such store, you got a long lesson from him in how to deliver a tedious and endless tale of woe, as he let loose the resentment stored up during his endless hours of "dealing with the public—it's something shocking, b'y. Wicked." In my first election in White Bay South, I learned that the encounters with the village Tory shopkeeper, heavy-going and even agonizing though they were, at least guaranteed you the votes of every unfortunate customer in the shop at the time, who had to listen to the shopkeeper's litany of moans and whinges.

The other painful encounters occurred in Westport and Hampden. These lovely communities contained the families of some of the loggers who had been caught up in the IWA strike seven years before. Their bitterness and resentment against Smallwood was very much alive, and their surly, abrupt, gruff, sometimes churlish attitude to me was all too palpable. One day I picked up a man hitchhiking from the TCH to Hampden. He was a friendly man and grateful for the lift until I introduced myself. Then he said he would not have gotten in the car if he'd known who I was. He'd rather walk on broken glass in his bare feet. I at least made him grin by saying I wouldn't mind slowing down to fifty miles an hour if he liked, so that he could jump out. At the end of the ride, when I dropped him off on his own doorstep, he said that I seemed like a nice fella but unfortunately he wouldn't vote for "Joey Small-Prick" to save his own mother's life.

There were some other examples of outspoken opposition to Smallwood, two of which were memorable. They made me wonder where people got the idea that Joey had imposed a monolithic dictatorship that permeated the population with fear and trembling from top to bottom. In one community, the foreman working for the Department of Highways in the area laced into me and Joey and the Liberals as useless, lying, crooked bastards. The community's Liberal kingpin, a member of the local roads committee, happened to be with me at the time, and when we got back in the car he said to me that he hoped I would see to it that, after I got elected, that fucker would be doing his bitching on welfare from then on. Thoughts of revenge momentarily existed, I must admit. After all, the guy was supposed to be a non-partisan public servant. But by the next community, I'd forgotten all about it.

Years later when it came back to me and I mentioned to Joey in passing the advice of the big local Liberal to get the fellow fired, Joey responded that we couldn't get into that with everyone who irritated us or was not slavishly onside. What did we want to do—turn this province into another Nova Scotia, where everyone with a pick and shovel digging a ditch was dumped and replaced from one government change to another? Besides, Joey smiled, if the fellow was detestable enough to make me dislike him intensely, you could be damned sure he had the same effect on everyone else, especially since he was a foreman. The man was my best vote-getter in the district. Leave him be.

Another example of outspoken opposition to Joey from right inside the dictatorship came as a big shock to me. I was in one community near the house identified to me as the home of the newly appointed chief returning officer for the district on voting day. I decided to walk by the house rather than risk having it look like I was fraternizing with the official who was supposed to be non-partisan and above the electoral battle. His job was to ensure, with fairness and objectivity, that all votes in the election were properly and legally cast and counted. But before I could get by, the man himself came out on his veranda and blared to me across the community for all to hear on this calm summer evening, "You've got a fight on your hands this election, my sonny boy."

He named my PC opponent, Cyril Pelley from Springdale, and continued that Mr. Pelley had lots of good friends on this peninsula and everyone believed he was going in this time for sure. At first I thought it was a misplaced joke by the returning officer, but then I could see that he was deadly serious. Having disgorged his political venom against me, he thereupon turned his back brusquely and stomped into his house. When I protested the outrage to some supporters around, one of them said, "Aw, that's just Caleb (pseudonym). Don't mind him." Evidently he was considered just a queer hand. So secure was Joey in the power of his own reputation and charisma that he didn't even bother to make sure that important election officials were non-partisan, let alone supporters. Great dictator.

*

AN EXCELLENT CONTACT and friend I made in the district was Tom Rideout. He lived in Fleur de Lys on the Baie Verte Peninsula. He was a young teenager when I'd first met him during a visit to his town one summer with my father. Tom's father and mine were great friends, and while they were talking, young Tom and I had a gab. To say he stood out like a sore thumb was an understatement. At fourteen or fifteen years old at the time, he was already keenly interested in and knowledgeable about politics. Whereas most boys his age seemed to be hanging around juke joints, he wanted to get involved in Liberal Party activities in the district and province. He was planning to become premier one day, he told me at our first meeting.

He gave me a hand in the 1966 election, and would act as my campaign manager in the next one, in 1971, when he was twenty-three. He had become a teacher by then and taught at a school in Baie Verte. At one meeting he told our group that he was so intensely involved in managing my campaign that, every morning when he got out of bed during that election, he would throw up. One can imagine the tasteless jokes everyone made about how far along he was in his political pregnancy. I would empathize with him because, back on the night of the returns of my first election in 1966, I myself had suffered a serious attack of nausea—idiot-induced nausea.

When the results started coming in on election night, the numbers showed me losing badly to my opponent, and at one point on television I was actually declared defeated. According to all the media, I had resoundingly lost one of the most Liberal districts in the province. I excused myself from my friend's living room, where we were watching the results, walked down the hall to the bathroom, closed the door, and threw up in the toilet. When I forced myself to go back out, the results had changed somewhat. Now I had resoundingly won, with nearly eighty per cent of the vote. The same delightfully daft returning officer I'd encountered on his veranda earlier in the campaign had managed for the first hour on election night to send the numbers in to head office completely reversed.

It was not long after election day that I learned the price of the support of a couple of the bigwig Liberals of stature in the district. One of them wanted me to immediately get his D8 bulldozer and front-end loader hired on by the Department of Highways. Another wanted me to have charges against his son for drug trafficking disappear. When I asked them, "Are you nuts?" and told them in both cases that regular legal procedures had to be followed, they couldn't believe it. Was it possible that I was refusing to deliver? Yes, it was exceedingly possible. Abruptly, they became my political enemies. One of them would run against me in a later election. He got some fifty votes out of the several thousand cast. His own extended family had more members than that. The other guy supported my main opponent, with no noticeable impact. So much for the stature in the community of the self-appointed Liberal bigwigs.

BACK TO THE 1966 election: Joey got thirty-nine of his forty-two candidates elected. When we all came together days later to celebrate at his family's restaurant on Roaches Line, he tried to look and sound pleased. But in fact he seemed strangely morose. I found out through later conversations that, rather than feeling ecstatic over the massive victory in the thirty-nine he'd won, he was hurt to the quick over the three districts he'd lost. He'd had his little heart set on winning all forty-two seats.

He couldn't stop talking to insiders about what "Rags" Murphy had done. This was John Murphy, the highly successful businessman (the Arcade chain of stores among other enterprises) who'd been the Liberal candidate in St. John's East Extern district. Joey would describe Rags as going around that salt-of-the-earth district in his expensive camel-hair jacket (sometimes in his telling it was expensive cashmere) and sporting yellow kid gloves and a cravat you'd wear at the Queen's garden party, and a long, Hollywood-style cigarette holder. "Can you imagine it?" Joey would ask us. "That getup in Torbay? In Logy Bay? In Flatrock? In Pouch Cove?" John Murphy had lost by only a handful of votes to Tom Hickey. He would try again for the Liberals in a 1970 by-election and lose. Thereafter he stifled his provincial aspirations in favour of municipal politics and would become one of the most successful, colourful, and popular mayors of St. John's.

EACH CANDIDATE IN the 1966 election had to pay a nomination fee of, I believe, $100 to the chief electoral office. The fee was refunded if the candidate got a certain minimum percentage of the votes cast. Every Liberal Party candidate received enough votes for a full refund. Thereupon, the Liberal Party whip, Gerald Hill, called us all on the phone with the "unprompted" suggestion that we pool our refunds as a gift, as a token of gratitude, to our esteemed leader. The pot amounted to about $4,000, worth in today's currency, after inflation, probably $30,000. That was gratitude.

The envelope of money was then handed over to Joey at our first full meeting of candidates after the election. The gift was intended to allow him, our Whip said, to make that trip around the world he'd been pining to make but couldn't afford on his modest income. Joey expressed complete surprise at the spontaneous generosity of his team of candidates.

In October, he took off from the St. John's airport on his trip, but within days he suddenly terminated it and came back. He was in Bangkok on his way to Japan on business, he told the media, when he got the telephone call of his life. We all went out to the airport to welcome him home as the conquering hero: the British-Newfoundland Corporation (Brinco) and Hydro Quebec had announced the signing of a letter of intent to proceed with the development of the Upper Churchill hydro development.

Could life get any sweeter for Joey than the happenings of that fall of 1966? His blockbuster election win; his pet Upper Churchill project going ahead after his years of dogged persistence in the face of failure; his new paper mill being negotiated with John C. Doyle; his big oil refinery coming to fruition with John Shaheen. When all our elected MHAs were being sworn in at the House of Assembly that fall, I looked around at my impressive, multi-talented colleagues, among them John Crosbie, Q.C.; Dr. Jim McGrath; Steve Neary; Alex Hickman, Q.C.; Ed Roberts; Aiden Maloney; Val Earle; Dr. Fred Rowe; Phil Lewis, Q.C.; John Mahoney, Q.C.; Clyde Wells; Captain Earl Winsor; Tom Burgess; Dr. Alain Frecker; Bill Callahan; Jim Chalker; Bill Keough; Nat Noel, Q.C.; John Nolan; Les Curtis, Q.C. . . . and on top of that, Joey's Liberal Party had the continuous financial backing of highly successful businessmen like Joe Ashley, Art Noseworthy, Bill Tiller, the Goodyears, the Lundrigans, the Crosbies . . .

Whenever the Tories would demand that Smallwood stop corruptly favouring these and other businessmen with projects funded with public money, Joey would respond that if a man exercised his democratic choice to be a Liberal supporter, it would be most improper to hold that choice against him in his dealings with the government. Who could have predicted, in the face of such success and self-congratulations and lording it over opponents, that within just one year the first cracks would appear in Joey's solid political dyke, and that a few months after that the whole solid structure would begin its inexorable crumbling, to finally collapse about his ears?

Certainly, no one would have predicted it to look across the House of Assembly at Her Majesty's Loyal Opposition. They were such a pathetic sight that perhaps Joey's hubris was understandable. Three seats containing three plucky little survivors: Gerry Ottenheimer, Ank Murphy, and Tom Hickey, all from the centre or east end of St. John's and environs. The recent new leader of the Tory Opposition, Dr. Noel Murphy, had been defeated by a close margin in Humber East by Clyde Wells, who'd been put over the top with a big boost from Joey's candidacy in the adjoining Humber West seat. Clyde Wells, despite the white-knight image he'd created for himself from the start, often found it a struggle to get personally elected under his own steam during much of his political career.

The hole at the top of the Opposition PC Party was now filled by Gerry Ottenheimer, who became its latest leader, with little fanfare or hope. Gerry was the grandson of salt fish magnate James M. Ryan, reputed to have been one of Newfoundland's wealthiest men. James was the brother of Dan Ryan, whose own wealth gave rise to the Newfoundland saying, "As rich as Dan Ryan."

Gerry Ottenheimer was a strange bird to be in politics. He was rumoured to be rich himself, but, more interestingly, he had made himself one of Newfoundland's most educated men, at least in the bookish sense. He had studied at the University of Rome, the University of Paris-Sorbonne, Memorial University of Newfoundland, and Fordham University, and later he'd go to Cambridge University. He was said to be the master of several languages. I heard him many times speaking French fluently, and he took his own cryptic notes, safe from prying eyes, by using the ancient Greek language in Greek script as his code. His later stage of university education—when he would study to become a lawyer—took place after he had been in the legislature for a few years, and was triggered by a ludicrous scandal.

Gerry seemed to have everything going for him in politics at first. If he didn't set the House of Assembly on fire with his orations, he did a fairly creditable job scratching away at the Liberal Government. Both publicly and privately, he spoke in soft, measured tones, invariably courteously, appealing to logic and rationality rather than passion and emotion. Once, after he'd made a rather intellectual speech to a mostly empty House of Assembly, I quoted to him the lines from Thomas Gray's *Elegy in a Country Church-yard*: "Full many a flower is born to blush unseen, / And waste its sweetness on the desert air." He responded immediately by citing the next two lines of the poem: "Some village-Hampden, that with dauntless breast / The little *tyrant* of his fields withstood." He smiled modestly, pleased that his quotation was so apt vis-à-vis the alleged little tyrant he faced daily. There were reports that outside the House he was quietly but effectively organizing the PC Party on the ground in rural districts.

Then, in November 1969, all of us in the House were surprised when Gerry suddenly resigned for personal reasons—allegedly to pursue studies abroad. Out of the blue, he felt an urgent need to top up his scholarly attainments with a degree in Law from Cambridge. We learned quickly the real reason why he was choosing to vamoose to England and bury himself in legal tomes. And it had little to do with higher learning. The police had raided a Montreal whorehouse and discovered Gerry inside availing himself of the services. Reportedly, they dragged him before the night court, where he was fined under the Criminal Code for being "found in" a common bawdy house.

The rumour around Newfoundland was that Gerry had been set up. For some reason, no one seemed to think that this highly intelligent man was capable of concocting a liaison with a whore without a sinister helping hand from someone else. The somewhat nerdy look and sound of him perhaps gave that impression.

At the time of the scandal, the blame for misleading poor Gerry into buying sleazy sex ping-ponged back and forth. On the one hand, Gerry's forced resignation cleared the decks for the election of a new and better PC leader, so some people suspected the Tory leadership hopefuls. Of the candidates who would obtain substantial votes at the Tory leadership convention the next year—Frank Moores, Hubert Kitchen, Walter Carter, and John A. Carter—only Moores, based on his later machinations and brilliant chicanery, seemed both connected and malevolent enough to perform such a deed.

On the other hand, a certain faction accused Premier Smallwood. This "blame Joey for Gerry's piece of tail" movement asserted that the feat had been accomplished either by promoter John C. Doyle or by one of Joey's German industrial associates formerly in Newfoundland but now operating a bar in Montreal. Joey denied the vile allegation and found it exceedingly distasteful. But that didn't keep him from regaling his inner circle with his lurid vision of Gerry Ottenheimer in bed with a whore: the fat, dumpy man humping away in all his flabby, pallid, jiggling, white-as-a-frog's-belly nakedness, with nothing on but his black socks, like a tubby stud in an old-time porn movie.

If in fact Doyle or the German friend had set up a trap for Gerry on Joey's behalf, then they ran the serious risk of hoisting Joey with his own petard: Ottenheimer had been no threat to him, but whoever took his place might turn out to be. And some of us told Joey so. Sooner or later, we said, his destruction of ineffectual Opposition leaders could lead to his own downfall. He had knocked off the feeble and alcoholic Malcolm Hollett by running against him personally in Hollett's own St. John's district and defeating him in 1959. When Hollett's replacement, Jim Greene, had retired from politics before the 1966 election and Dr. Noel Murphy of Corner Brook became PC leader, Joey had straightaway put the uninspiring Murphy out to pasture by becoming the candidate in the adjoining Humber West district and for all practical purposes running against him, too. Now the pleasant but lacklustre Gerry Ottenheimer had been ousted.

These leaders had been a major part of Joey's political arsenal that guaranteed him victory in election after election. By getting rid of them, we said, sooner or later someone was going to emerge as leader who might represent a real challenge to him. Joey remained unimpressed by our arguments. "And where is that great challenge going to come from?" he scoffed. "Frank Moores?"

*

I WOULD COME to the conclusion toward the finish of Joey's twenty-three-year reign that he had spent much of his political genius over that period unnecessarily undermining his own political capital and popularity, which had been so enormous that even the residue he still possessed at the end made him almost, but not entirely, impossible to beat as premier.

Meanwhile, Gerry Ottenheimer's vacant seat would be won in a by-election by his good buddy Bill Marshall, who would not prove to be an improvement in Smallwood's political fortunes. Marshall at once became such a fanatical chaser-down of alleged corruption by Joey that we in the Liberal Party dubbed him Witch-Hunt Willy. He was so zealous in his allegations that at one point in the future he would earn a good smack in the gob for his pains.

The Ottenheimer story had a sequel that subjected the family to further grief. Gerry would make a comeback with his law degree, get re-elected in 1971, form a partnership to practise law, become a minister in the provincial government, and Speaker of the House of Assembly, and a senator in Ottawa, and die of cancer at the age of sixty-three. His daughter would marry up-and-comer Ed Byrne, who would become leader of the PC Party and senior minister under Premier Danny Williams before going to jail for defrauding the government under the Criminal Code.

I FOUND, AS I was pulled closer to Joey over time, that his imaginative depiction of Ottenheimer in flagrante delicto with a prostitute was not an isolated story. He dearly loved to recount his tales of prominent Newfoundland men and their troubles with women. It must have been the journalist mud-raker in him.

One he related to me was the saga of two brothers, two big Newfoundland entrepreneurs. They used to travel to Montreal regularly for business and recreation and often to dry out. Part of their recreation and therapy during one visit entailed inviting two hookers to their hotel room for the night. Apparently, for the sake of economy, or maybe kinkiness, the two men occupied one room with two beds. After their lecherous activity, all four of them fell asleep. But then one brother woke up still frisky, looked over at his brother's bed, and took it into his head to engage with the woman lying there. Regrettably, his brother woke up and caught the interloper at it, and became infuriated at his sibling's trespass. A fist fight straightaway ensued, both brothers naked, pudgy, and swearing a blue streak, as they staggered, ducked, and weaved about the room. Their "dates" fled out the door for their very lives. After the two brothers had exhausted themselves and flopped down on their beds to recover, the one who had tried to encroach on the other's woman sobbed out broken-heartedly, according to Joey, "Jesus Christ, I never thought me own brother would begrudge me a lousy piece of tail."

Joey also told me of three laddios in Labrador West, whom he named, including two future politicians who were there working temporarily in the early days of the mining operation. The more naive residents were wondering why there was this big lineup of men around a trailer occupied by one of the young fellows. It turned out that the lads had flown in some ladies from Montreal eager to make money and were busy running a flourishing brothel. Joey reported that there was much grumbling among the disappointed clientele when the prissy Iron Ore Company of Canada closed the operation down.

AFTER THE ELECTION of 1966, I became a backbencher in the House of Assembly. Indeed, it would have been difficult for me to be more of a backbencher. My seat in the House—all seating arrangements had been made by the premier—was pressed right up against the rear wall of the chamber in the corner farthest from the Speaker. That was okay with me: I was articling with a great firm of lawyers and expected to practise law with them for many years to come. I remember one of the law partners guessing at my political career path. He figured I would become a minister in the government in about ten years. That would be more than soon enough, we both agreed, supposing I even wanted it then.

The next spring, when a number of us greenhorn lawyers were enrolled in the Supreme Court as barristers and solicitors, Chief Justice Robert Furlong gave a little courtroom speech of welcome and then, looking straight at me, intoned sternly that a lawyer ought to devote his full energy and intellect to the practice of law and not divide his loyalties. I said to myself, no worries there, Judge. Joey's cabinet was already top-heavy with young talent and several more were outside chomping at the bit.

Whispers described Ed Roberts as having been very disgruntled when Clyde Wells had been appointed to the cabinet instead of him after all Ed's valuable service as Smallwood's executive assistant. And Steve Neary was understood to be poisoned that Wells had been made minister of Labour instead of him in spite of his seniority and years of experience in the labour movement. In age and seniority, I was at the bottom of any list of potential ministers. Besides, I figured I had blotted my copy book with Joey, anyway.

When I'd given my maiden speech in the House soon after the election, I launched into an attack on the denominational system of education in our province. I mentioned my namesake from the early 1800s, William B. Rowe, an MHA and the first recorded head of the Law Society here, who'd been a strong proponent of separate schools by religion, and I pledged that I'd never follow in his footsteps. I didn't get the idea Joey liked my remarks. He didn't say anything directly to me, but I saw him looking at me askance a couple of times from his seat in the House as I held forth on the need to rid the province of the denominational education system.

Over the next few days, at least two representatives of the denominations approached me "by accident" in the lobby of Confederation Building to say they'd like an opportunity to sit down with me and explain a few things, since I didn't seem to fully comprehend the gravity of what I was suggesting. If they had contrived to approach me, I knew that they had certainly voiced their displeasure to Joey, and the last thing he wanted was a follower of his rocking the religious boat. Influential leaders in a couple of denominations supported Joey primarily for his unflinching support for their revolting little educational empires.

The next way in which I displeased our political lord and master happened when I appeared on a local public affairs television show that winter, where I was asked to voice my aspirations as a young, newly elected member. After it was aired on a Sunday afternoon, Joey called me up at home: "Mr. Rowe, this is Joe Smallwood." I was startled to hear his voice on the other end, and then delighted: the premier himself calling me directly! I waited for his words of praise for my performance. Two or three other generous persons had already called with their too-kind reaction to the show, and had turned my head a little. The premier, my leader, opined, however, that I should seriously consider never appearing on TV again. He was far from impressed with my piece, he said—in fact, he wasn't impressed at all. He didn't go into detail, and I was too stunned to ask him what he thought was so bad about it before he hung up.

I sat there perplexed. Obviously, the compliments of the other callers had been contrived so that I wouldn't feel too bad. And equally obviously, I'd better concentrate on practising law in the future if the great master of the media thought I was useless on television. A few minutes later, a hard-nosed, brutally frank friend of mine called. I'd been "okay" on TV, he said, but I'd only managed to get off one good line: that was when I'd stated that we in the new generation of politicians should move forward from the outmoded ideas of old-time politicians who were suffering from "hardening of the intellectual arteries." I needed to say more good stuff like that, he said, and establish a cutting-edge profile for myself.

Uh-oh, I thought. I had hardly noticed that comment myself as I'd watched the entire half-hour program—it was virtually a throwaway line—but obviously Joey had noticed it, and rather keenly, despite his "hardening of the intellectual arteries." Doubtless it was what had singularly under-impressed him. I was going to be in the rear of the peanut gallery of the House for a very long time by the way things were progressing.

But my fate was determined otherwise, because Premier Smallwood's clever political manipulations soon turned out to be more than too cute by half.

CHAPTER FOUR

The Advent of Frank

IN 1967, JACK Pickersgill retired as minister in the Government of Canada and from his Newfoundland seat in the House of Commons to become president of the Canadian Transport Commission. Joey made no secret of the fact to us in his caucus that he was taken by surprise, and dismayed at having lost his fixer in Ottawa. Before elective politics, Pickersgill had been a close adviser to prime ministers of Canada (federal ministers were told to "clear it with Jack") and a behind-the-scenes supporter of Newfoundland's Confederation with Canada leading up to 1949. As Clerk of the Privy Council Office, the top Canadian public servant, he had been the most knowledgeable and skilful mandarin in the country; he knew where all the skeletons were buried and the treasures hidden. So, he'd been a great catch when Joey persuaded him to run in Bonavista-Twillingate in the 1953 federal election.

Joey had joked that his biggest problem when he took Jack around the riding was trying to teach people to pronounce his unfamiliar name. Since then, except for the Diefenbaker interregnum, Pickersgill had been Newfoundland's powerful minister in Ottawa, and Joey had relied on him to obtain everything federal he wanted—from national parks to trans-Canada highways.

Reflecting on his contributions, Joey would tell me a couple of years later that he considered unemployment insurance for fishermen to be Pickersgill's great achievement. UI (now called EI) for fishermen was a progressive policy in that it helped bring an essential but seasonal industry above the subsistence level for some of its participants. I wondered if there was a dark side to it—the irresistible lure to many rural boys and girls to leave school without finishing and without further training in order to work for a few weeks in the fish harvest or a fish plant, and then heave off on the pogey for the rest of the year. I asked Joey whether it could be considered perhaps counterproductive and even corrupting in terms of the long-term well-being of our rural youth when they would become unprepared adults. The premier looked at me as if I was crazy and his response said as much. He wondered if I was getting too goddamned picky for politics.

Publicly, Joey always lavished praise on Pickersgill after his resignation, but he told me, and no doubt others, that Jack's retirement from politics was an entirely self-serving move, and that Jack had used his power shamefully to place himself in a virtual sinecure. Pickersgill's perspective may have been different.

I heard through the grapevine that, after fourteen years of it, Jack simply could not stomach the thought of trying to do Joey's bidding for one second longer. Whatever the case, the objective measure of Joey's loss was fully seen a few years later when Pickersgill was appointed Companion of the Order of Canada, the pinnacle reserved for those who have demonstrated the highest degree of merit to Canada and humanity on either the national or international scene.

Meanwhile, Joey felt he had to find a federal cabinet minister for the province to replace Jack. It never occurred to him to let the prime minister of Canada choose: lovable but politically naive Mike Pearson would only bugger it up. The two top choices were Richard Cashin, first elected in 1962, and Don Jamieson, elected in a by-election in 1966. Joey gave us the distinct impression that there was bitter squabbling and infighting between these two on who should get the appointment, but I never heard that from either of them during our many conversations. Whatever the case—probably Joey's fear of an emerging rival—he decided to run Charlie Granger in the by-election in Pickersgill's old seat. This notion was so convoluted and byzantine that there's no wonder it ultimately blew up in the premier's face.

Earlier, Granger had already been MP for nearly a decade, re-elected merely a couple of years before in the federal election of 1965. Then, just a year later, Joey cajoled him into resigning and running in Gander district in the provincial election of 1966, from which he was appointed to Joey's cabinet. Now, a few months later, Joey got him to resign from the provincial House and run federally again in 1967, whence he was appointed minister without portfolio in Ottawa. This tortuous scheme necessitated a provincial by-election in Gander district in October 1967. Unexpectedly, it was won by Harold Collins, the PC candidate. Only one year after Joey's near sweep of 1966, we saw the first fractures appear in his power.

LATER THAT SAME year, Prime Minister Pearson announced his retirement, and the federal Liberal Party called a leadership convention for April of 1968. Joey was now sixty-seven, and to show, perhaps, how young at heart, and cool, and "with it" he was, he decided to support Pierre Trudeau. I don't know who or what influenced Joey most to support someone so far removed from himself in style, but a number of us were in on it, including an enthusiastic Ed Roberts and Steve Neary. Steve was so keen about Trudeau that he named his own son, born around the time of the convention, Pierre. And I was certainly right behind Trudeau myself. I'd been very impressed with his positions as minister of Justice generally and liked the way he took on Quebec's Union Nationale premier Daniel Johnson, Sr., during the constitutional negotiations at the recent federal-provincial conference.

Also, Trudeau had liberalized our cruel and archaic divorce laws, and introduced the groundbreaking criminal law omnibus bill, which included the legalization of contraception, abortion, and lotteries, new gun ownership restrictions, and authorized Breathalyzer tests on suspected drunk drivers. I still recall my amazement at the guts of a minister of Justice defending on television his decriminalization of homosexual acts between consenting adults, with "there's no place for the state in the bedrooms of the nation." I didn't know at the time that he'd stolen the catchphrase from Martin O'Malley's piece in the *Globe and Mail*, but at least he had done what few other federal politicians had ever had the intelligence and courage to do.

Whatever got Joey going on PET, he was soon pronouncing him perfect for leader—a bilingual francophone Québécois who now, following Pearson, served brilliantly the Liberal Party tradition of alternating between English and French.

There was some dissension among our delegates at the convention about supporting Joey's incongruous choice of Pierre Trudeau. Many of our delegates wanted to support Minister Robert Winters, who had a strong connection with Newfoundland and Labrador as a former chief executive officer of Brinco. Joey harangued us in caucus on how Winters had first said he wasn't going to run before deciding too late to do so, and rhapsodized on the manifold virtues of Trudeau.

Most of the holdouts came over to Joey's position. My father, however, continued to openly support Winters on the first ballot. I remember John Crosbie, hove back on a bed in a hotel room at the convention, glass of scotch resting on his ample gut, humorously chiding Dad for sticking with Winters against our great leader's behest. John predicted catastrophe in store for Fred Rowe for breaking ranks with el supremo. You'd never have said there and then that, a few weeks later, Crosbie would be rebuffing, snubbing, and rejecting the great leader himself right in the middle of a federal election campaign, and be described for his pains by Joey as "a bagful of hate, a skinful of hate, two hundred pounds of vicious hate," and "a corrupt, diseased mind, turning the august House of Assembly into a beer garden."

But back to the Trudeau leadership race. Just before the convention, Martin Luther King was assassinated down in Memphis, Tennessee. I heard Trudeau making a speech about it at one of the venues that same night, and it was extremely moving. The next day Joey told us in caucus that it was the most affecting speech on a political tragedy by a politician he'd ever heard. If anyone had any doubts heretofore about Trudeau, he said, abandon them now.

Joey also found a way to demonize one of the leading candidates seriously opposing Trudeau. At a caucus of our delegation, he referred to the envelopes addressed to delegates by name that we had all found outside our hotel room doors that morning. They contained anonymous allegations that Trudeau was a rampant homosexual. On the envelope that one of our MHAs had received, Joey said, the MHA's name was spelled wrong—wrong in exactly the same way that it had always been spelled wrong on all envelopes the MHA had been receiving for years past from the office of Paul Martin, Sr., one of the leadership candidates.

WHEN TRUDEAU GOT elected leader on the fourth ballot against some eight other candidates, many pundits attributed a lot of his early momentum to Smallwood's support. Trudeau himself extended his gratitude to Joey for his backing at a crucial time. So, when Trudeau was sworn in as prime minister and quickly called a federal election for June 25, 1968, Joey felt exceedingly high in the PM's esteem and admiration. This was going to be great for Newfoundland, Joey told us, and—he didn't need to tell us—great for himself as premier.

Early in the federal election, Robert Kennedy was assassinated in

Los Angeles, California. On the campaign trail, Trudeau made another remarkably moving speech on the tragedy. I recall Joey wondering if Trudeau, with all the emotion, hype, and madness—the Trudeaumania—surrounding him, might be the next victim of some murderous lunatic. Trudeau's courage in facing the danger without qualm, Joey said, would elect him solidly, and should be especially effective here in Newfoundland, where bravery in leaders was so greatly appreciated.

Trudeau's display of courage reached a peak the day before the election. He was at the Saint-Jean-Baptiste Day parade in Montreal, when a riot of Quebec separatists broke out in front of the platform where Trudeau and dignitaries were sitting. Suddenly rocks and bottles came flying from the mob right at the seated bigwigs, who ducked and cowered and scurried off. All except Trudeau.

He stayed where he was and thrust his face at the rioters, ignoring the urgings of security to leave, and showing on TV to millions no fear whatsoever as the missiles and projectiles whizzed by his ears. I remember Joey being delighted. This display of guts and backbone would add to the Trudeaumania right across Canada, and the Liberal leader would have no trouble clinching the election win the next day. There'd been some ominous signs of softening support in Newfoundland, but Trudeau's demonstration of rock-hard bravery would sew up the seats for the Liberals here in Joey's bailiwick tomorrow.

EARLIER, MUCH TO Joey's chagrin, Frank Moores of Carbonear had won the nomination for the Progressive Conservative Party in the riding of Bonavista-Trinity-Conception, an area strongly Liberal since Confederation. Joey's attacks on Frank before and during the federal election were ferocious, both public and private. He launched print and radio and television and loudspeaker denunciations of Frank, condemning him for holding his nominating meeting in the Si Moores Memorial Stadium, named for Frank's father, and for buying his nomination out of his ill-gotten gains from the sale of his company, North East

Fisheries. He was a rich young man, said Joey—only twenty-eight when he came into his father, Si's, business half a dozen years ago—and he couldn't sell out to Birds Eye fast enough. He was said to have pocketed $2 million and did not invest any of the proceeds of the sale back into Newfoundland.

Frank's father, Si Moores, had died of a heart attack in 1962, and Joey had always considered him a good Liberal. Joey had claimed he'd tried to get Si to run for him, as well, improbably, as Frank's sister Megan Nutbeem, plus Frank himself. But when Frank now ran for the federal PC nomination, all Si's family suddenly became in Joey's election propaganda a "family of bloodsuckers." I had met Megan's husband, Bob Nutbeem, around St. John's now and then, and each time his conversation seemed to consist of criticizing and making fun of his mother-in-law behind her back. Joey was merciless in ridiculing in private the snooty but ignorant and ill-informed Moores family over how delighted they'd been when Megan married this guy Nutbeem with the oh-so-spiffy English accent before he turned out, under his put-on Oxford enunciation, to be a steward off one of those cruise ships for the love-lorn. (Nutbeem told me he'd been educated at London University and was chief purser for Furness Withy, a major British shipping line, when he came to Newfoundland around the time of Confederation.)

I ran into lawyer Tommy Williams, father of Danny and a good Tory, during that federal campaign, and he thought that we Grits were in for a big surprise with Frank Moores. He'd been a tennis champ, Tommy said, and he had a real gut desire to win. What we'd been hearing, though, was that Frank was dismayed by Joey's attacks on him and nearly gave up during the campaign. I never heard it from Joey himself, but some Tories mentioned to me that Joey had mixed some honey with his gall and had offered Frank a Senate seat to pull out of the race.

Certainly, the Tories I talked to were disheartened by Frank's lack of defence to Joey's attacks on him, or even more demoralizing, his complete disinclination to launch his own attacks on Joey. (I would find in the House of Assembly that he hardly ever responded to any of our Opposition criticisms, either. But I would also find that beneath his exterior congeniality lurked the stomach and heart of a cobra.)

In fact, Frank didn't have to be very critical of Joey. The premier himself had provided him with a slogan which rang true with the electorate and which the federal Tory candidate used with devastating effect. One of Joey's biggest, albeit unconscious, mistakes regarding Frank Moores stemmed from his love of Newfoundland's political history. This came back to haunt him in this federal election and later. Among Smallwood's favourite yarns, repeated over and over, concerned some genius in opposition to the government during his youth who, leading up to a general election, coined the simple, brilliant slogan for the Opposition party: "It won't be long now." It caught on so well, Joey would relate, that people would shout it across Water Street as a greeting to passing friends. Everyone was saying it to everyone else, with a wink and a nod: "It won't be long now." The result was that it became a self-fulfilling prophecy and led to the defeat of the government of the day.

By the 1968 federal election, Joey must have wished he had shut up about this obscure bit of Newfoundland history after Frank Moores stole those words from his tale and revived them as a fresh new slogan to be used with such demoralizing results in his campaign. "Ladies and gentlemen," went Frank's ballsy baritone over and over on radio and television with a built-in wink and grin, "it won't be long now."

Tommy Williams was right. Behind it all, Frank had a real gut desire to win, and he did win handsomely. He had won, Joey told us, because he had spent over $100,000 on his election. (If true, that was probably over $600,000 in today's money.) But generally the voters in all Newfoundland and Labrador seats were seriously underwhelmed by Trudeau's shows of courage or any other feature of central Canada's unbridled Trudeaumania.

The federal Liberal Party won only one seat here—Don Jamieson was able to hang on. All the other six ridings, some of them previously the most Liberal seats in Canada, went Tory. The extent of the disaster was clear from the fact that, in 1965, the Liberal Party, under lacklustre Pearson, had won all seven seats in Newfoundland and Labrador with nearly two-thirds of the popular vote and, now, just three years later, under the charismatic Trudeau, the Liberal vote here had dropped to well below fifty per cent. Whose fault could that calamity be?

Joey pretended not to be devastated by his ignominious failure to deliver for his hero, and he exercised his imagination, both privately to us his colleagues, and publicly, to try to shift the blame off himself. The Liberal debacle here, he told us, was owing to the underground sub rosa campaign by the Tories to push relentlessly and persistently the vile and odious rumour that Trudeau was homosexual. He even mentioned to some of us a foolish pun he alleged the Tories were spreading around: "There's talk that there's a homosexual at the head of the Government—is it true though?" (True though? Trudeau? Wink wink, nudge nudge, get it?)

Sometimes Joey also blamed it on anti-French, anti–Roman Catholic sentiments. If voters had realized what their prejudice was going to produce, he told us, they wouldn't have done it. He once or twice slipped and rued the day he had talked Trudeau into coming to the province a couple of times during the election. That was a mistake, Joey told some of us, because people could see in person how effete Trudeau was with his rose in his lapel, and wearing those sissy black loafers with the bows on top, often laughably up to his skinny little ankles in their silk socks in mud puddles.

To the public, Joey also partly blamed something he called "tight money," caused by the ongoing United States war in Vietnam. As a result of those global circumstances, the provincial budget of just three months before had been shattering, he said. Our Finance minister, Dr. Jim McGrath, had added taxes to gasoline, increased the retail sales tax, placed a tax on insurance premiums, raised liquor and beer prices, and sliced welfare and rural electricity subsidies and municipal subsidies, among the other shocks he delivered to the Newfoundland people.

Before that particular budget, Joey used to boast that he wrote every word of every budget speech. Once, when an earlier minister of Finance, Neddie Spencer, had been reading his budget speech in the House, and had commenced to weep, Dr. Jim McGrath was reported to have said to colleagues then, "You'd cry too if you were reading that stuff for the first time." I don't recall Joey claiming authorship, though, when it came to McGrath's bad-news budget speech, but it was a testament to the minister's grit that he managed to remain dry-eyed both while delivering it and then hearing his handiwork as Finance minister blamed for the near-total failure of the federal Liberals in this province.

We'd lost sight of the fact that other Atlantic Provinces also produced a dismal return for Trudeau: PEI elected four PCs and no Liberals, and Nova Scotia sent only one Liberal and ten PCs to parliament. Also forgotten was the fact that Newfoundland had sometimes bucked the national tide before in past federal elections, demonstrating, depending on whether your candidate had won or lost, either a sturdy Newfoundland independence of mind or the Newfie-joke cluelessness of being years behind the rest of Canada. The main blame for the present federal fiasco, however, both publicly and privately, Joey piled on John Crosbie and Clyde Wells.

IN THE MIDDLE of May, during the federal election, these two buckos had resigned from the government over the Come By Chance oil refinery scheme. Earlier, as ministers, they had agreed with and worked for months on the $200 million refinery promoted by John Shaheen. But now Crosbie and Wells claimed they could not stomach the last straw, the $5 million in interim or bridge financing, required by Shaheen. There was an unholy blow-up between Smallwood and Crosbie, with allegations of incompetence, corruption, lunacy, and all the trimmings, including a threatened defamation suit against Joey by representatives of the Crosbie family empire.

When John Crosbie had come into Joey's office to resign, the premier started to wave a letter of dismissal at him, but Crosbie was faster on the draw and pre-empted Joey's firing by barking "like fuck," and banging his own letter of resignation on the premier's desk. The contents of Joey's letter were more dramatic than John's, though. He claimed that Crosbie family members had tried to extort contracts from Shaheen, and from John Doyle's linerboard mill, and that Crosbie's obstinate blocking of the Come By Chance refinery project was all part of his family's shakedown and extortion. He told the media that John Crosbie's uncles, Bill and Percy Crosbie, and his brother Andrew, were the primary ones involved in the extortion attempts. Al Capone was a Sunday school teacher compared to Joey's depiction of the Crosbies.

When John's family members threatened immediate legal action against Joey for libel, he had to retract all his allegations in a humiliating climb-down. He told us in caucus that he had been led astray inadvertently by Shaheen and Doyle because, although what they alleged was absolutely true, it was their word against the Crosbies', and so, when it came right down to it, Joey and his henchmen didn't have the kind of "legal" proof that might stand up in a court of law.

He would tell me later, though, that Ed Roberts, his parliamentary assistant, had heard from his adjoining office John Crosbie clearly asking Joey for government business for the family without tender. When I inquired why he didn't just let the Crosbie family sue and have Roberts testify to the truth of his allegations in court, he replied that life was too short to open up that can of worms, and John Crosbie wasn't worth it: he was only a puffed-up bladder of piss and wind, anyway. When I asked why he'd raised all the fuss, then, to begin with, he said, "I'm a strange animal. When someone bites me, I bite back." No kidding.

*

IN THE HOUSE of Assembly, on the heels of the Crosbie and Wells resignations, the Tories brought in a motion of non-confidence in the government, and Joey kept the House open all night to bring it to a vote, claiming that this was an attempted coup by Crosbie to take over the government. Crosbie and Wells were painted as cowardly rats leaving a ship they feared was sinking: they had used the $5 million bridge financing as a lame excuse to scurry timidly away because they didn't have the guts to stay the course and help the government during these hard economic times.

The motion of non-confidence was voted down. Only two more Liberals would walk across the House, Jerry Myrden and Tom Burgess, but that was mainly because, it was rumoured, they felt slighted by the premier when he came to fill the vacancies in his cabinet. Meanwhile, Joey did win the battle: the "coup" attempt failed miserably, but it was the beginning of the ongoing savage war with John Crosbie that in a few short years would see a far different outcome.

WHATEVER THE REASONS for the 1968 Liberal election debacle in this province, not only had we turned Trudeau down just about flat, but the Newfoundland and Labrador Tories who went to Ottawa, the "Noisy Six," were the worst political thorns in Trudeau's side of all Opposition in the House of Commons. One of them, John Lundrigan, would provoke the normally rational prime minister into making the unorthodox debating point: "Fuck off." Ever the flexible linguist in both languages, Trudeau was able to translate those words for the media into "Fuddle duddle." But the extent of his exasperation could be seen from the fact that, apart from his "*Mangez de la merde*" ("Eat shit"), emitted at some pesky westerners, Lundrigan's provocation was one of the rare times, among many other provocations, that Trudeau was goaded into emitting indecent language in public.

*

FROM THE START of Frank Moores's political involvement, most of us, under the contorted guidance of Joey, treated Frank as a bit of a lightweight. It was only after seeing the television footage during and after the provincial elections of 1971 and 1972 that I would realize what a powerful character he was in the media. That deep baritone voice was a great asset. He seemed to be almost as much the master of the one-liner as a professional stand-up comic. And he turned his rowdy-man persona into an electoral plus.

But before the elections of 1971 and 1972, we treated him as little but a rich, boozing, womanizing playboy. He was that, all right, but more. Except perhaps for MHA Eric Dawe, who knew Frank and the area he lived in, we in the Liberal caucus treated Moores's election to the House of Commons in 1968 as a fluke. After all, as a result of the peculiar circumstances surrounding that federal election, five other Tories had also been elected, some in extremely Liberal seats.

AFTER FRANK MOORES made his maiden speech in the House of Commons, he was never heard inside its walls again, and rarely seen. He set a record for low attendance. Don Jamieson told us that there was a perfectly logical reason for Frank's absences from the House. He occupied an apartment in the same building as Don's, right next door to his, in fact, and if Frank wasn't often seen in the House pounding his desk, it was because he was too busy in bed day and night where he had help pounding the headboard against Jamieson's wall.

Apart from squeaking bedsprings and banging headboards, hardly a sound came from Frank's direction for months. Then he emerged to run for the presidency of the Progressive Conservative Party of Canada. A lot of people scoffed when he won. It was between elections, they said, and very much an off year for the party after the recent Trudeaumania. Plus, he was the harmless, innocuous nice-guy type of candidate the PC Party needed in the lingering civil war between the Dalton Camp crowd and the John Diefenbaker loyalists.

Back in St. John's, when the Tory Opposition in the House of Assembly tried to congratulate Frank Moores on his election as president of their federal party, Premier Smallwood jumped up and raised a point of order: Mr. Moores's election to a national party was not only a non-urgent matter but completely irrelevant to the provincial House, and should not be permitted any mention on its floor. The Speaker agreed.

BLUSTER ALL HE might, the fact was that, after the 1968 federal election, Joey suddenly found himself in an unaccustomed quagmire. Not only did he know that the Noisy Six were a constant reminder to Trudeau of Joey's failure on his behalf in Newfoundland, but the one Liberal who did get elected from here, Don Jamieson, felt that his political survival certainly owed nothing whatsoever to Smallwood. Quite the reverse: he'd gotten elected in spite of Smallwood. And that belief was on top of the resentment Jamieson harboured against him for having had Charlie Granger elected in the earlier by-election to become Newfoundland's minister in Ottawa, bypassing Jamieson. Thus, having helped make Trudeau prime minister in the first place, Joey was now seen to enjoy very small influence with him or with our new federal minister, Jamieson, who would present a dismal contrast to Joey's earlier man in Ottawa, Jack Pickersgill. Not only did Jamieson quickly demonstrate that he was completely his own man, he even went out of his way a few months later, as will be seen, to painfully embarrass Smallwood.

Meanwhile, back home, the Newfoundland Tories were buoyed up by the earlier provincial success in Gander, followed by the Crosbie-Wells ruckus, and then that huge federal election breakthrough here, and were now feeling exceedingly optimistic. Opposition MHA Ank Murphy even approached me, and no doubt others, with an official invitation to cross the floor and join his party with the assurance of my becoming a cabinet minister when they formed the government after the next election.

I declined the invitation on principle, naturally, but even if I'd been guided entirely by self-interest, there was no way in my wildest imaginings, or anyone else's in the Liberal Party at the time, despite our political calamities of the past year, that Smallwood's Liberals were going to be defeated by the Tories in the next election. Even Crosbie and Wells remained Liberal or Independent Liberal or Reform Liberal or something of that ilk, hedging their bets. Right after the blow-up, they had insisted that they didn't intend to cross the floor of the House at all, but planned to sit with the Liberal caucus in the House. However, Joey, in a fit of self-destructive vindictiveness, unilaterally ordered their seats to be carried across the House and bolted to the floor so that they couldn't come back, thus turning their mere opposition into bitter, long-term, and disastrous enmity.

CHAPTER FIVE

Joining Joey's Kitchen Cabinet

JUST TWO OR three weeks after the federal election upset, in the middle of July of 1968, Joey shook up his cabinet in dramatic fashion. I was relaxing one lovely summer evening at the country place of my in-laws not far from town. We were discussing the Smallwood-Crosbie squabble, which made our conversation interesting. On the one hand, I was their pro-Smallwood son-in-law, and, on the other hand, John Crosbie was their anti-Smallwood nephew. Now the telephone rang. My father-in-law answered it and seemed as flabbergasted as I was that, first of all, Premier Smallwood himself was on the other end and wanted to talk to me urgently, and that, second, he had known exactly where to find me. He certainly kept tabs on everyone, our looks said, even lowly backbenchers.

Without small talk, Joey queried me: would I be prepared to go into the cabinet as minister without portfolio, responsible for some important government programs? I forgot for the moment that I had only just reached twenty-six years of age, and I answered yes. In that case, he responded, I was to be in the cabinet room at a specified hour on a certain early date for the announcement. Meanwhile, I was to divulge the appointment only to close family on a strictly secret, need-to-know basis.

When I informed my wife and in-laws that evening and said it was confidential, they congratulated me, and my father-in-law issued a warning: Smallwood had good reason for making it confidential. He had invited my father-in-law out to Roaches Line one time years ago and asked him to accept some big prestigious appointment. The announcement was to come in the next week; meanwhile, he was to keep it completely quiet. And thank God he did keep it quiet: when the premier made the announcement, he appointed someone else to the position, not my father-in-law at all. And he never heard the subject broached again: Smallwood had evidently forgotten or become confused. That little anecdote gave me a suspenseful few days of waiting.

At the announcement, Joey appointed seven new ministers, including, as it turned out, me. To make room for us, he dumped three senior ministers, who, he said, were "retiring for health reasons." They were Max Lane, who had carried the can for him during and after the IWA crisis, Dr. Jim McGrath, who had just been forced to bring down one of the most difficult and unpopular budgets since Confederation, and Beaton Abbott. The three "retirees" first heard about their health problems when they turned on their radios. Two of them protested on the radio that their health was never better, but Dr. McGrath said, "That's all right, I'm sick enough for all three of us." However, Beaton Abbott was not amused. He would walk across the House in chagrin and join the Crosbie-Wells forces.

Dr. McGrath was cool with it, though, and even congratulated me by calling this year my *annus mirabilis*, referring to my marriage to Penelope Ayre, my admission to the bar, my appointment to the cabinet, and the birth of our son, Dorian, all in the space of about fourteen months. I was glad of his goodwill because I admired him a lot. Twice when I'd been studying in England, he invited Neil Murray and me out to dinner on his visits, once at the famous old Mitre Hotel in Oxford and once at a private residence. He was generous, knowledgeable, and humorous, and I always had an image of him as a modern Dr. Johnson. In the House of Assembly, he and I had some good discussions during dull periods over a book he was translating from the French. Once, when Dad mentioned to us in our caucus room that he was going off to play badminton after the House closed that afternoon, and asked Dr. McGrath what he did for exercise, McGrath replied, "Fred, I get my exercise acting as pallbearer for my friends who exercise."

THE ELEMENT OF the cabinet announcement that shocked me most when I saw the television news the same night was that I looked like a grinning, simpering, adolescent jackanapes. And I wasn't alone in my observation: I ran into a Newfoundland businessman I very much esteemed, the great Ken Goodyear, who had been badly wounded at Beaumont-Hamel. After he congratulated me, he leaned in close and added that I shouldn't smile so much when I was on TV.

When Liberal MHAs Jerry Myrden and Tom Burgess stomped across the House and joined Crosbie, disgruntled that they had been passed over for cabinet, I recall thinking to myself that I couldn't blame them—they'd watched a callow youth like me going in instead of them.

Joey was striving to give his cabinet a youthful look: the oldest ones, Captain Earl Winsor, Gerald Hill, and Steve Neary, were in their forties; John Nolan and Bill Callahan were in their thirties; Ed Roberts at twenty-seven was less than two years older than me. I believe they all received full portfolios. I, as a minister without portfolio but with certain responsibilities, soon realized why Joey laid on me this bunch of higgledy-piggledy tasks. Earlier ministers who'd had them couldn't get out from under them quick enough, and nobody else with any savvy would go near them.

First, I became responsible for the Housing Corporation, which Al Vardy had been using to execute his scheme for building Elizabeth Towers. This new apartment building was being depicted by the Opposition and the media as super-luxurious and designed solely to provide Vardy with his own penthouse suite and Joey's buddies with fancy digs. And at the same time, they said, the Housing Corporation had a waiting list of nearly 1,000 desperate families looking for decent subsidized rental housing. Answering those criticisms on top of the cost-plus construction overruns of Elizabeth Towers was no picnic in the House of Assembly.

Next, my responsibility was the federal-provincial household resettlement program, which many opponents and some St. John's and mainland media had already been denouncing as akin to the heinous forcing of people into concentration camps. Let me say that I grew up fast in those ordeals by fire in the House and the media.

I ran into Ank Murphy in Confederation Building a few days after the big cabinet shuffle. "You little shagger," he said looking up at me from about six inches below my eye level. "You knew you were going in the cabinet when I asked you." I assured him I knew nothing, but he didn't believe me. I had to have known. What other reason could I have had for turning down his magnificent offer?

I was now in cabinet with my father, and we sometimes found ourselves involved in minor arguments across the table. It must have been a father-son thing because I had no more difference in political philosophy with him than with any of the other old-timers. I often thought how painful it must be to work in the same business with a powerful father. Joey and some of the ministers seemed to enjoy our little altercations.

One of them was minister of Finance and president of the Treasury Board. I wondered idly to Joey and some new ministers in his office one time if there might not be an inherent conflict of interest in having the same minister holding those two offices: the minister of Finance was responsible for devising the budget, and the president of the Treasury Board oversaw all spending under that budget—two diametrically opposite and possibly conflicting functions. Shouldn't the two jobs be under two separate ministers at arm's length from one another? The minister concerned got wind of my conjecture and took umbrage, thinking it was directed at him personally. The next time I ran into him just before a cabinet meeting, he said angrily, "You and your hotshot buddies might think you're pretty smart trying to take over in here, but before you elbowed your way in, your father was way smarter than you are, and still is."

IT WOULD BE wrong to say that routine work never got done at a cabinet meeting when the premier was there, but it did proceed much faster in his absence, which unfortunately was not that frequent. He disliked being away from cabinet as he disliked being away from the House. They were the two places that had no telephones or supplicants but at the same time provided captive audiences to address on whim.

Often, in cabinet, Joey held forth for the two or three hours on items connected only tenuously to the agenda item under discussion. If it was a question of where the wood was going to come from for a new paper mill, then we might hear in journalistic detail how hard Sir Richard Squires fought to put the "hum on the Humber," with a digression on the drunken Sir Richard at cabinet meetings attempting to address politely his despised, but essential, political partner, Sir William Coaker, across the table—"Sh'Willyam."

If the issue of financing for John Shaheen's oil refinery was up for discussion, then we could very well listen to the particulars of John Shaheen's heroic exploits as an officer with the OSS, the Office of Strategic Services (the precursor of the Central Intelligence Agency) during World War II, in cahoots with the famous Canadian/British spymaster William Stephenson plus Roosevelt's man, the celebrated Wild Bill Donovan, and William Casey (much later the director of the CIA). "Were you aware, gentlemen," Joey asked us, "that in the movie *O.S.S.*, made by Paramount Studios just after the war, starring Alan Ladd and Geraldine Fitzgerald, Commander John Shaheen, yes, *our* John Shaheen, is listed as technical adviser?"

If a proposal for a potential industry came up for discussion, Joey loved to pronounce trippingly off the tongue some esoteric names of other companies he'd tried to attract here or had talks with: Pickens Mathers, Rio Tinto, Crown Zellerbach, Snia Viscosa, Schneider Creusot, Sumitomo, Siemens Schukart, and Thyssen, and Krupp, and Mannesman, and Humbolt-Klockner-Deutz . . . His list did go on.

And Joey would regularly talk about our "ancient and abiding inferiority complex" as Newfoundlanders. He thought Confederation with Canada would diminish and finally get rid of that trait over time because Confederation "is the greatest gift under God ever bestowed on our people . . . the greatest blessing, under God, next to life itself."

How Confederation would help us get rid of our "historic" inferiority complex when he was constantly insisting that we should fall on our collective knees and thank Almighty God for saving our sorry Newfoundland asses by granting us the "blessing" of Confederation was something I never quite got my head around. Nor did I see how our fawning, servile thanks for the constant flow of money from upalong, which made us the world's greatest welfare recipient, could be a source of self-esteem and pride. I told him as much in private conversation later and added that we would lose any inferiority we felt as individuals when we were among the best educated and trained and employed in Canada, and we would lose our *collective* inferiority complex when we became wealthy and self-assured as a people from our offshore oil and information technology. We'd lose our lousy weather then, too, I joked: just look at Calgary and Edmonton—among the coldest, most unpredictable climates in Canada, but who has complained about the weather there since the oil started to gush? Joey might smile indulgently, but he would never lose an opportunity in the future to rhapsodize about the advent of the union he was responsible for, and our resulting salvation. And after all, I thought, why would he?

His monologues were kind of interesting the first or second time—not so much, say, on the third and later go-rounds. As lunchtime approached after his soliloquy, Joey would ask if there was anything else that needed to be discussed urgently, and he'd pretend to go around the table from minister to minister. Naively, at the beginning of my tenure in cabinet, I used one such opportunity to try to bring up an important matter which I had placed on the agenda for this meeting, which we hadn't gotten to. As I began, Joey said, "Bill, Bill, Bill." I stopped and looked up, startled to see the premier pointing at something behind me. I looked back half-expecting to see someone with a shotgun trained on me, but saw nothing. I turned around again, perplexed. "Bill, Bill, the clock." I twisted around again and saw the clock high on the wall. It said ten to one. "It's lunchtime," he explained, and rose to his feet, whereupon everyone else gathered up their papers. Memo to self, I thought: either make anything important one of Joey's own pet projects, or just forget it.

OWING TO THE province's dismal financial condition, Joey led a delegation of ministers to Ottawa to plead our desperate case for more federal money. The group included, I believe, Ed Roberts, John Nolan, Aiden Maloney, and me. I have only a hazy memory of our other meetings in the nation's capital, but our get-together with our own federal minister, Don Jamieson, has stayed sharp because he played the role of a spider to us hapless flies. He invited us to his parlour, his own apartment, one evening, where spider number two, the deputy minister of Finance, was lurking and ready to ambush us.

Joey raised his arguments in favour of our receiving more federal money based on unfairness in the federal system and our consequent need for help in building basic services. The deputy minister greeted his points with a blizzard of paper—sheets of previously prepared graphs and statistics "proving" from a dozen different angles that, as a province, we were already getting much more than our fair share from Ottawa. His figures, grids, and tables established beyond all contention, he asserted, backed by our minister, Don, that Newfoundland was receiving as he spoke four dollars from Ottawa for every one measly dollar that Newfoundland contributed to Canada.

Joey then said that, after twenty years in Canada, simple fair play and equity required Canada to contribute to the basic municipal and provincial essentials required to bring our province closer to the standards that prevailed in other provinces. But the deputy replied that, although it wasn't his place to comment on matters within a purely provincial jurisdiction, in this informal, confidential setting, he perhaps wouldn't be faulted for observing that if certain provinces would only stop expending their tax dollars on lunatic industrial schemes, they would have more money to spend on their undoubted provincial responsibilities.

Jamieson jumped in: Constitutionally, he did not envisage his obligation as Newfoundland's federal minister to be the providing of federal money for purely provincial responsibilities. Moreover, politically, he deemed the Newfoundland people to have now grown far too knowledgeable and sophisticated to be bribed by a politician's promise to lay a pipe in a ditch to carry their shit to the sea.

Joey kept his cool, but he left Don's apartment that night, as did the rest of us, feeling humiliation and chagrin. That would change over the coming months to cynical amusement as we watched Jamieson looting the federal treasury for infrastructure in his own constituency—so much of it, the black jest would run, that the Burin Peninsula ran the risk of subsiding into the sea again.

WHEN I FIRST joined Joey's cabinet, he had a tremendous reputation throughout the land as an extremely hard worker, putting in exceedingly long hours—frequent eighteen-hour days, he'd say. Soon afterwards, I noted to my surprise what his "workday" in the office consisted of in the real world. He would arrive in his office at nine-thirty or later in the morning, driven there from Roaches Line by Nelson Oates, a nephew of his wife, Clara.

Before reaching his office, though, he would stop every morning at VOCM Radio on Kenmount Road, where News Director Elmer Harris would come out and interview him live. It was called *Conversation with the Premier* and it lasted for fifteen minutes, Monday to Friday, and it was a brutal onslaught against his political enemies. The segment was very popular, and to politicians and reporters, it was must-listen radio.

After John Crosbie became Smallwood's most ferocious opponent, John asked VOCM for equal time on the air. The radio station replied that they were not obliged to give him equal time but only "equitable" time as a leader, under some CRTC formula which was based on the number of his followers in the House. They concluded that whatever "party" John was leader of consisted of one follower: himself. On hearing him complain about that, Joey said on the air that Crosbie had all the traits of a natural-born leader, except the ability to attract any followers. Their "equitable" time formula allowed VOCM to offer John something like four-tenths of a minute—twenty-four seconds—of airtime any morning Joey was on.

Elmer Harris told me that every morning at VOCM they would watch for Smallwood's big Chrysler Imperial to drive up to the station. Thereupon, Elmer would go outside with his portable tape recorder and stand by the car door, as the premier rolled down his window. Then Elmer would conduct his "interview" by thrusting his microphone in the car window for the duration of the rant. Joey seemed oblivious to the weather from inside his car. So, whatever the conditions outside—driving rain, sleet, blizzard, hurricane, bitterly cold temperatures—Elmer would stand there by the car for the entire monologue every morning. Not once, during month after month of this routine, Elmer told me, did Smallwood invite him to get in the car.

Continuing the premier's "workday": once he was in his office, if there wasn't a cabinet meeting or an important visitor to meet with, he'd bring into his inner sanctum some of the scores of supplicants seated or standing in his anteroom waiting, one after the other, to have "Joey" fix their problem. And Joey would "fix" their problem by calling the appropriate cabinet minister or his deputy direct on his intercom, the dreaded "squawk box," no matter what important meeting he might be interrupting in the minister's office. He'd hale the minister up to his eighth-floor office to hear how this particular member of Joey's "ragged-arsed artillery" was being treated tyrannically by his department, and then he'd dump the poor visitor on the poor minister and send them out his door to have the problem dealt with down in the minister's office. When it turned out that the problem could not be legally solved within the rules—the usual outcome—the minister got the blame, not the premier. Joey had done *his* very best, but regrettably the minister was totally useless.

Those squawk boxes were controlled from Joey's desk and, reportedly, Joey could even use the device to listen in, unbeknownst to the minister or deputy, to whatever was being said in the offices. I would be lucky when I moved into my own office that, as a Johnny-come-lately department carved out of the bowels of the Confederation Building basement, there was no direct intercom from Joey's office to mine. Its absence saved me a lot of the "squawk box" grief I saw visited on other ministers.

EARLY ON, THOUGH, I got called up to Joey's office by telephone for an urgent matter. Just as I walked into the office to deal with whatever required my immediate presence, he first took a call from a clergyman in a rural community. The man of the cloth wanted to use his influence with God to make the government pave the gravel road to his church. This was a heaven-sent opportunity, he said, because the asphalt machine was just down the road paving the highway.

Joey pushed the button on the squawk box for the Highways minister's office and bawled out his name, "Harold." A few seconds later the minister's secretary's voice came through: the minister was in his district. Thereupon Joey pushed another button and hollered, "Clarence." Within minutes, the summoned deputy minister of Highways, Clarence Knight, arrived and heard the clergyman's request, seconded by the premier himself. Mr. Knight responded, "No, sir." The premier, with a pretense of astonishment in his voice, demanded, "No? *No*? Why not?" Because, said Clarence, it was against the law to use public funds to pave a private road.

Joey looked at him as if he had ten heads. But this was a request from a man of the cloth, he said, barely containing his biblical wrath, a man of God who had a congregation to serve in his church. It might not be a strictly public road, but it was not strictly a private driveway, either: it was certainly quasi-public, and that ought to be enough moral flexibility to allow the law to be bent so as to accommodate a man of God.

A deputy minister served at the Queen's pleasure—that is to say, at the premier's whim. But still Mr. Knight dug in his heels and persisted, until the premier finally gave up on him. When the deputy minister left, Joey complained to me about how contrary Clarence Knight was: "The man's obedience to the law is nothing short of an obsession, an absolute fetish." Anyone from the outside listening to Joey might wonder why, with that attitude toward Clarence, he kept him on in the public service so long as a top deputy minister. I think I knew.

In between listening to supplicants and summoning ministers, often at the same time, Joey would dictate letters to his sainted secretary, Betty Duff, mostly word-perfect from his mouth and her typewriter on the first go. At one o'clock it was off to lunch for an hour and a half, then back up to his office for an hour or so repeat of the morning until three-thirty or four, when he'd get in his car for the drive back to Roaches Line. On the days that he came in to his office, in my experience, Joey spent four to five hours there, tops.

AFTER A WHILE, following my appointment as minister without portfolio, I went to see Joey to tell him that, although I loved being part of his cabinet team, I would have to get out. The principals at my law firm were complaining about the half-assed job I was doing there because of the political demands on my time, and I was dissatisfied myself with the half-assed ministerial job I had. I was falling between two stools and I would have to resign to practise law more fully, while continuing to support the government from the backbenches as before.

Joey's response was to appoint me at once as a full minister over the fairly new Department of Community and Social Development. This was responsible for many federal-provincial agreements, including the upcoming multi-million dollar agreement with Trudeau's newly established Department of Regional Economic Expansion (DREE). Suddenly I was in the thick of negotiating with my federal counterpart, Minister Jean Marchand, the famous DREE program. It was the venerated Newfoundland journalist Albert Perlin who first pointed out in his newspaper column that, in Scottish, the word DREE meant "tedious, dreary; to suffer, to endure."

Federal governments during the past decade and more, whether Liberal or Progressive Conservative, were forever dreaming up some agency that was going to solve the lack of development in the Canadian boonies and backwaters, which included us. A partial list of earlier and current agencies of salvation were ADB—Atlantic Development Board; ARDA—Agriculture and Rural Development Act; FRED—Fund for Rural Economic Development; ADA—Area Development Agency; RDIA—Regional Development Incentives Act; and ACOA—Atlantic Canada Opportunities Agency.

One time in Ottawa I was meeting with the DREE minister, Jean Marchand, when I rattled off that alphabet soup of agencies to him and asked what was next—Program for Regional Incentive, Conservation, and Knowledge, to be known as PRICK? "How the hell did you find that out?" demanded Marchand with a straight face. "That was supposed to be top secret."

Seriously, though, it was excellent that Prime Minister Trudeau, and superb advisers like Tom Kent from the old Pearson days, had a broader view of what needed to be done in badly off regions of the country than did Don Jamieson and the Finance deputy he was enthralled with. Through the newly created DREE program, tens of millions of federal dollars were to be spent in our province, in Trudeau's battle against regional disparity, for building schools, municipal infrastructure, highways—all areas normally under purely provincial responsibility. (A small irony: in the early 1970s, Trudeau would name Jamieson himself as minister of the Department of Regional Economic Expansion.)

Meanwhile, there was a buoyant feeling in our caucus that this massive infrastructure program was going to ring the political death knell once and for all for John Crosbie and Clyde Wells and for the Official Opposition, all of whom had been scoring scathing points against Smallwood and the government in the House of Assembly.

Then, one morning while I was out of my office taking a few days annual leave, I received an urgent telephone call at home from the premier's office: there was an unscheduled, spur-of-the-moment cabinet meeting in progress, and the premier expected me to be there posthaste. No other information was forthcoming. What catastrophe akin to the end of the world had arrived? I got myself ready and went up.

When I arrived at the cabinet room on the eighth floor, the round table was fully occupied except for my seat. The air in the room already had the funk of a meeting that had been going on for some time. Sitting at the table were my deputy minister and assistant deputy, with huge piles of documents in front of them. It was highly unusual for officials to be at the cabinet table. I sat down mystified and waited to be told what was going on. Without preliminaries, Joey asked me where I'd been—they'd been waiting for me for an hour. I didn't answer that but told him, as testily as I could, that I had not been here earlier because I'd received no notice earlier of this impromptu cabinet meeting. That seemed to irritate him, and he proceeded to ask pointed questions about the DREE program—projects, times, dates, amounts. I responded with a question mark at the end of every answer, trying to sound as impudent as I could, as if to say, "Okay? Next stupid question?" Between myself and the officials, we established that all was going ahead according to plan and everything was well in hand. No other minister asked a question. Gradually Joey's tone changed from inquisitorial to calm and amiable. Obviously, some minister or ministers had approached him with the accusation that my department and I were buggering up the DREE program, and Joey had impetuously jumped on it.

After the cabinet meeting had wound down, and I was waiting for everyone to leave so that I could proceed with my intention regarding Joey, John Nolan came over grinning in his usual affable way and said, "I think some of the boys were getting worried, but I believe you laid any doubts to rest." I didn't reply except with a glower, and he stood there watching me as I headed for Joey's office right off the cabinet room. I opened the closed door without knocking and walked in. Joey looked at me somewhat startled at the intrusion. Les Curtis was there with him. "Sorry for interrupting, Premier," I said, "but just so we're absolutely clear—If anything like that is ever sprung on me again out of the blue, you can simply assume I'll be resigning."

Joey, unusually, said nothing, and he gazed at me coolly, rocking on his heels. "Saucy young bugger," muttered Les Curtis. "That's one easy way to get rid of him." Joey turned and glared at Curtis.

I said, "Thank you, Premier," and walked out. For the rest of my few days off I turned on his morning radio rant, half-expecting to hear I'd been let go from the cabinet. My secretary phoned me at home once to tell me that the premier's office had called to ask when I'd be back in my office. Maybe he wanted to fire me to my face.

When I did get back, there was a message for me to call Joey's assistant Miss Templeton as soon as I returned. I called and she said that, if I was free, the premier wanted me to join him for lunch in his dining room that day. Joey had a dining room off the lobby on the ground floor of Confederation Building with his own personal chef. After I'd been appointed to the cabinet months ago, Joey had asked me to come down for lunch once. There were several other ministers there, plus Al Vardy. I figured it was a revolving thing Joey had put in place to invite each minister down every couple of months as a display of camaraderie. I did notice that Les Curtis, Ed Roberts, John Nolan, and Vardy acted as if they were regulars there. Except for this second invitation today, I hadn't been asked back to lunch since.

When I went down today the same gang was there, and afterwards, Joey asked me to come there to lunch every day whenever I was around, if I was prepared to pay for it. The cost was not a token amount but it wasn't backbreaking either, probably about the same as lunch at A&W or McDonald's. And so, any day I was at Confederation Building over the next couple of years, I ate lunch with Joey as one of his regular half-dozen.

This must have been the kitchen cabinet deplored by Bill Callahan and some other ministers at the time, which they thought was capable of dire and heinous conspiracies and perpetrating fancy knife-work between the shoulder blades of unsuspecting colleagues. Callahan later described a conspiracy someone had reported against him. I never saw or heard any of that going on down there during my time. But like Callahan, I'd heard earlier that the attempted attack on me and my department over the DREE program had originated in the kitchen cabinet over lunch.

STRANGELY, I FOUND that Joey didn't seek to dominate the conversation entirely when only the regulars were present. Normally we talked about current happenings, not much different from a middlebrow cocktail party, with its highs and lows of conversational topics—pretty banal chit-chat generally, with the occasional reminiscence by Joey thrown in.

But it became clear that you absented yourself from lunch only at your own peril. Once when just Curtis, Vardy, Joey, and I were there for lunch—Roberts and Nolan were away—we got talking about World War II, and I recalled the old British song my war-veteran uncle had taught me, to the tune of the colonel Bogey march: "Hitler, he only had one ball; Göring had two but they were very small; Himmler was rather similar, and Goebbels had no balls at all." Everyone remembered it and all laughed at the memory. Joey's habitual laugh was peculiar. I never heard him make a sound. His face showed his enjoyment and sometimes his body shook a little, but in complete silence.

Then Curtis and Vardy had to leave early, leaving Joey and me by ourselves. Joey said, "Did you know that John Nolan only has one ball?" "No," I replied, "I didn't have any first-hand knowledge of that." Joey gave his silent laugh and went on: "I wouldn't put anything past him if I were you. He was the one who came to see me and whispered that you were buggering up the DREE program. He and Ed Roberts." Then Joey warned me to watch out for Ed Roberts even more than Nolan. Ed had been outraged at my appointment to the cabinet, Joey said, because I had taken away from him the glory of being the youngest cabinet minister ever appointed in the province, and possibly in the whole British Commonwealth. He hadn't seen Ed so infuriated, he said, since the summer of 1966 when Joey had appointed the young Clyde Wells to the cabinet instead of him. I recognized Smallwood's comments for what they were—part of his effort to try to divide and rule us ministers, especially Ed and myself.

At one lunch, leading up to a federal-provincial constitutional conference to be chaired by Trudeau in Ottawa, Joey designated me to make a presentation to it in front of the national TV cameras. It was a move patently designed to drive Ed nuts with jealousy. I didn't notice Ed eating his heart out in bitterness, though. As time went on I gathered clearly that Joey had fears of Ed and me working together in collusion to thwart some of his more lunatic plans. If so, his fears would prove to be entirely justified.

*

EVERY THIRD OR fourth day at lunch there would be a guest. Then, normally, Joey would come into his own and talk the table blind. There were only a few exceptions to his unrestrained holding forth that I can remember. One involved Peg O'Dea, the wife of former Lieutenant-Governor Fabian O'Dea. She put up with no crap whatsoever from Joey—took him on at every turn—much, I must say, to Joey's amusement. The big point she made was that Joey had let down Newfoundland at Confederation by not insisting that the head of state in the province should have been designated *governor*, not *lieutenant*-governor, which was an inferior status to the governor general in Ottawa. She had found her role as wife of a mere *lieutenant*-governor very demeaning when she'd been the chatelaine at Government House in St. John's.

(Not as demeaning as her husband's Royal Commission report was to Joey and some supporters after his resignation—a report which caused the policy governing such inquiries to be altered in order to prevent blatant findings of criminal misconduct with no safeguards for the rights of the accused.)

Another irrepressible guest I recall at the table, on a visit to St. John's, was the ambassador to Canada from the Soviet Union. He had a nearly perfect command of English and a great sense of humour. His eyes would twinkle with delight whenever Roberts, Nolan, or I—familiarity having brought us close to contempt—would poke fun at something Les Curtis or Al Vardy might say, or tackle one of Joey's pronouncements.

We got onto the subject of the English language and its difficulties for anyone trying to learn it. The ambassador said he still had problems with when he should pronounce the "h" at the beginning of words: honourable, house, hour, horse, herbs, historical. I told him it was even harder than he thought. For example, when Mr. Curtis went to his district of Twillingate, many people there would insist on pronouncing the "h" in "honourable" when they referred to him, as a mark of great respect. Someone else added that, however, they would drop the "h" as a sign of awe and admiration when they referred to the septuagenarian Curtis as the 'orny attorney. It was hard to keep up with these linguistic signs of esteem for Mr. Curtis, we said. Someone else added that, speaking of esteem, it wasn't a coincidence, surely, that they had named that huge erection over the Dildo Run the "Curtis Causeway." The ambassador had a great old laugh, as did Joey, especially when our remarks would elicit from Curtis, "Saucy young bastards. Joe, I don't know why you put up with the likes of them."

Often, when the ambassador was speaking, Joey would butt in as usual and try to take over the conversation, whereupon the ambassador would stop and say, "Am I interrupting you, Your Excellency, or are you interrupting me?" It had a strangely subduing effect on Joey, and he would back off. After the ambassador had left, Joey remarked that he'd been struck by the man's lack of obsequiousness or even respect for an authority figure. Since Stalin had died only in 1953, and the ambassador was old enough to have been a Communist Party functionary during the last years of that tyrant, Joey wondered, "How in the bowels of Christ did that man ever survive Stalin?"

Yes, Joey, the self-proclaimed last of the Wesleyans, often swore—"Christ," sometimes by itself, and sometimes in that phrase he'd borrowed from Oliver Cromwell. And often, too, he said the word "fuck." The first time I heard him use the F-word was when he was telling us of a candidate for the Communist Party he knew in his youth who had a hard time attracting even the votes of the proletariat. When Joey asked him what he'd do if the proletariat didn't elect him this time, the Communist candidate replied, "If the proletariat do not elect me this time, then I say fuck the proletariat."

Indeed, Joey, like the rest of us, often used foul language in the privacy of the dining room. He laughed when a citizen affected shock that an esteemed leader was reported to have cursed. One of his favourite bad words was "cunt," which he generally applied to a member of the male gender, either from the past, as in "Harold Horwood was only a cunt," or from the present: "John Crosbie? He's nothing but a cunt." The frequency of Joey's foul language increased with each glass of alcoholic beverage he drank.

What? *Each* glass of alcoholic beverage? But Joey was practically a teetotaller, wasn't he? Oh, perhaps an occasional small glass of wine for the stomach's sake, he'd say, but that was the extent of it. Charles, Joey's father, had been a drunken ne'er-do-well, he told us, and too many members of his extended family were alcoholic; hence, Joey would not touch hard liquor. Well, I never heard him acknowledge it, and I never heard anyone else say it at the time, but I soon realized that Joey could be one awful boozer.

This was his lunchtime guzzling routine: Before lunch was served, he would have at least two, and sometimes three, glasses of sweet Bristol Cream sherry. During lunch, he would have at least two glasses of red wine. Then after lunch he would have at least a couple of transparent liqueurs, usually those licorice-flavoured ones, Anisette or Pernod, and sometimes a Newman's Port. These "non-hard-liquor" libations all varied between ten to twenty to forty per cent alcohol. He got his refills by thrusting his empty glass without a word at Les Curtis or Al Vardy, who would thereupon hop to the sideboard to fill up his glass.

Joey told me that, in addition to his refusal to imbibe hard liquor, he had drunk beer regularly in his life during only one period. As a young man, skinny and apparently rundown, a doctor prescribed a case of two dozen dark beers—one bottle each night—to build him up. Joey dutifully followed the regimen, but it never worked—he stayed scrawny—and the habit never took. All his life Joey hardly ever drank anything alcoholic unless it was served in a sherry glass or port glass, or a tulip-shaped wine glass, or, if it was a liqueur, it could be in any container as long as the liqueur was transparent. But if the glass was the correct shape for the sherry, port, or wine, or if the liqueur was colourless, then, bejeezus, look out!

At lunch in the dining room, after his last liqueur, Joey would lie right back in his recliner, feet up, for a nap. The rest of us would gab away. We soon learned we didn't have to talk quietly. A trumpet blast wouldn't have awakened Joey before his half-hour snooze-time had expired. He could enjoy a solid nap on a pile of rocks in a sleet storm.

I don't know how much sleep Joey got in the nighttime, but he certainly augmented it during the day: that longish nap after lunch, and another nap of forty minutes to an hour in the evening, he said. And I was never in the car with him on the highway for a drive over a few minutes when he did not push the seat back and cover his eyes with his black Air Canada sleep mask for a siesta.

Whatever amount of sleep he got, it worked. No one I ever knew had more energy—on the stage making a speech, pacing in his office dictating, talking ad infinitum at a meeting, or knocking off a thirty-mile walk for charity in his late sixties without turning a hair, at the end of which he impressed the media who were waiting for him at the finish line by blithely walking an extra mile just for the hell of it.

I never saw him display any tiredness in any situation or anything less than abundant energy. He gave the impression of being able to go forever. He was proud of his limitless energy and he looked at me strangely one time when I told him that Prime Minister Benjamin Disraeli had made the remark that, unfortunately, it was all too easy to mistake great energy for genius in a leader. "Where did Disraeli say that?" he demanded. "I've never read anywhere that he said that." I couldn't point him to it, and I must confess that I haven't located it since. It was interesting, though, that he seemed to suspect that I might have been taking an indirect crack at him.

He told me once that as a teenager and young man he slept for twelve hours every night. When I reacted with disbelief—twelve hours sleep, night after night, it couldn't be, he must be making an error in his addition—he got half-angry at me. No, that was correct, he insisted, twelve hours a night, every night.

Certainly, Joey's metabolism seemed to be quite peculiar. I observed, in common with others, that he never seemed to be too hot or too cold, no matter what the temperature. Perhaps it came from years of withstanding, on the one hand, the infernal heat in crowded union halls and political meetings, and, on the other, of surviving the frigid cold at his Gander pig farm. Some mean-spirited people opined that the trait was genetic, and not in a good way: he was the human equivalent of a lizard or snake or some other slithering, cold-blooded creature. Indeed, Joey himself sometimes said, when he was professing to be coldly rational and logical on some subject, that ice water ran in his veins. He also made the same ice-water-for-blood comment about some enemy whom he might be accusing of plotting against him. The same physical attribute, metaphorically icy blood, made him a rationalist in his own eyes, while it made his adversary a psychopath.

On the subject of his pig farm, Joey often drew upon his experiences there to voice his view of his political opponents: he was well acquainted with both four-legged pigs and two-legged pigs, he would say, and he infinitely preferred the four-legged variety. I heard him charm a crowd once with a little self-effacing pig humour by purporting to quote Winston Churchill on why he liked four-legged pigs: "Dogs look up to us, cats look down on us, but pigs treat us as equals."

I asked Joey one time at lunch about his strange fascination with operating a pig farm when his great talents were obviously in the media—writing and talking. Joey replied that he was not religious or superstitious and did not believe in so-called destiny, but, still, there was something to think about in how everything came together for him, almost inadvertently, in the 1940s. On the one hand, if he hadn't become so well-known as the Barrelman on the radio from 1937 to 1943, promoting pride in Newfoundland's history and culture, he would never have been able to later become the leader of a great Confederation movement. On the other hand, if he had remained in St. John's as the Barrelman, there would have been no hope of his being elected to the National Convention from the anti-Confederate city as a Confederate.

But by leaving his acclaimed radio show in St. John's, against all advice, and moving to Gander to operate that pig farm at the Newfoundland Airport, he accidentally qualified himself for election as a resident of Bonavista Centre, where he did get elected in June of 1946, with nearly ninety per cent of the vote. Remember, now, he emphasized, he'd made his "foolish" decision to leave the Barrelman at the Broadcasting Corporation of Newfoundland and to live in Gander at a time when there was no thought of a national convention to determine Newfoundland's future or of any residency requirement for being elected to it. Each of his actions was an unconscious preparation for his political calling, as if—were he a religious man—his destiny had been directed from on high.

WHEN JOEY WOULD wake up from his habitual nap in the dining room after lunch, there'd be no trivial chatter from him. Usually, he'd grumble about something or issue a cantankerous bark. Then without ceremony he would trundle on out to his private elevator and up to his office. "Did you ever see anything so goddamned cranky and crooked as Joey when he wakes up from his snooze?" someone in our group asked. The consensus from the rest of us was, no, by Jesus, we did not. But we were quick to cut the premier some slack and make allowances for his after-lunch mood swing. After all, we didn't wake up at two-fifteen every afternoon hung over or still half-drunk.

It was when Joey was half-drunk from his fortified wines or liqueurs that he made some of his most egregious blunders. Three occasions come to mind.

In the summer of 1968, Joey invited American painter Rockwell Kent to a state dinner in his honour in St. John's. The event was supposed to commemorate Kent and to make amends for his claim that he'd been booted out of Newfoundland during the First World War because of his alleged sympathies with the enemy. He'd been suspected of espionage because of his walks on the cliffs of Brigus, where some observers contended he was sending signals to the German U-boats off shore.

Now, just before this big tribute dinner, I'd seen Joey guzzle down several sherries in the anteroom in quick succession. And during dinner he didn't hold back on the wine, either. Then he got up to speak. Somehow, in dealing with Kent's aborted sojourn here during the Great War, Joey referred to Vladimir Lenin as a great man, one of the greatest human beings of this century, and then added, in oratorical flight, that Adolf Hitler was a great man, too. I could see that what he was really trying to say was that Hitler was a genius—albeit an evil, malignant genius. But as he struggled in his mental haze to present that concept, he kept persisting that Hitler was a great man—oh, an evil man, a monstrous man, an atrocious man, to be sure, but a great man. A great man.

Afterwards, needless to say, the media and the Opposition had a field day with it, as did the Canadian Legion. He did seem to mollify the outraged veterans, at least on the surface, but I had my doubts about how placated they really were. The episode did not add to his statesmanlike stature.

Again, after a free-flowing lunch in our dining room not long before the 1971 election, he went over to the College of Trades, where he'd been invited to speak to the students. In the middle of his speech, which was apparently sensible and well-received, one of the students yelled out that he was a liar. Instead of ignoring it or dealing with it with wit or good humour, Joey stopped and demanded to know if they thought he was lying.

Getting no response, he kept demanding from the audience: "Are you calling me a liar?" And when he had finally goaded, prodded, and provoked that student and others to say, yes, he was a liar, Joey stomped off the stage in a huff. The utter ridiculousness of all this was captured on television for the entire electorate to see that evening. People who didn't know of his imbibing habits wondered if his grip on reality was becoming a bit shaky.

Smallwood's third drunken blunder nearly caused the death of himself and me and at least two others. It occurred in his car. It was the only time in my life that I witnessed drunk driving by someone who was not even behind the wheel. We were travelling up Kingsbridge Road in Joey's Chrysler Imperial toward the Newfoundland Hotel, where some afternoon function was being held. He was sitting in the front passenger seat as usual and a little woozy after his lunchtime sherries and liqueurs. His regular driver was behind the wheel. I was in the back seat with one or two others.

The car approached the traffic light at the intersection with Empire Avenue. Some distance away, our light turned yellow. When the driver slowed down to stop for the upcoming red light, Joey barked at him, "Drive on through." The man was now confronted with the dilemma of driving through a light he knew would be red at the busy intersection or disobeying his fearsome boss. Apparently he believed death by collision to be less terrible than the consequences of disobeying the Skipper, so he opted to follow his order and pressed on the accelerator to rush through the light. Cars were already starting to come east across Kingsbridge and two of them had to swerve and barely avoided hitting us. Others had to slam on their brakes. Horns blared and voices loudly proclaimed the absolutely obvious at whoever was in control of our car: you fucking idiot. That would have been Joey. But Joey continued with his discourse as undisturbed by it all as if he and the rest of us were normal.

ONE YEAR, DURING our last lunch in the dining room before that Christmas, Don Jamieson dropped in. He was back from Ottawa and Joey was leaving for Florida the next day, and both of them were scheduled to tape their traditional yuletide messages on CJON television that afternoon. Over the next hour or so, Joey got polluted on sherry, wine, and liqueur. He could scarcely walk when the time came to go to the station. Four of us helped him to the door, and then he had to be literally propped up by John Nolan on one side of him and Jamieson, John's old chief, on the other, as he wended his way across the lobby, out of the building, and down over the steps to his car. I stood there with someone—Ed Roberts, I think—both of us dumbfounded that the premier was going before the cameras plastered.

But when Joey's Christmas message did appear on TV, I was equally amazed at how good his presentation turned out to be. His reserves of bullshit had overcome his inebriation except for some laboured enunciations—once I'm sure I heard him say "occifer" instead of "officer"—but only my mother seemed to know for sure. I happened to drop in on her as it was coming on after the news, and we watched it together. I didn't say a word. She looked at me: "I thought Smallwood said he didn't drink. He's sitting there right on television, drunk as a lord." I merely grinned at her as she shook her head. Still, amazingly, he performed so well that I heard only one or two other spectators mention that if they didn't know that Joey was a teetotaller, they might have suspected he'd downed a few. For the rest, no one else ever said a word, unprompted, about Joey's pickled state.

CHAPTER SIX

Waiting for Chairman Mao

FOLLOWING THE DEFECTION crisis of John Crosbie and Clyde Wells, Joey called a big renewal meeting of the Liberal Party in Grand Falls for a weekend late in September of 1968. Similar get-togethers were planned for that same fall in Corner Brook and Clarenville. He also announced a leadership convention for the fall of 1969 where, he promised emphatically, unconditionally, and categorically, he would resign and allow delegates to elect a new leader in his place.

At the party revival meetings, Joey asked several ministers, myself included, to speak to the assembled Liberals as if he was auditioning us for the prize leadership role. Before one of the evening speech sessions, I had made the mistake of dipping into the first edition of *Smallwood: the Unlikely Revolutionary* by Richard Gwyn that had just come out. I recall how hard it was to get up there that night and wax enthusiastic about our fortunes after having just read Gwyn's take on Newfoundland's $40 million surplus from Commission of Government days disappearing down a sinkhole from Joey's hare-brained industrialization schemes. Luckily, the human mind is so resilient that my gloom soon passed as a result of ambition, team camaraderie, and the contagious, still-eager passion of the audience of party supporters.

My father told me at one of the meetings that Joey had fervently encouraged him to run flat-out for the leadership and to count on Joey's active support. I told Dad what I now suspect he didn't want to hear: I did not believe for one second that Joey had any intention of actually giving up the leadership or the premiership.

Also, at one of the renewal meetings, in either Grand Falls or Corner Brook, a new president of the Liberal Party was to be elected. Joey's choice was Grant Chalker, a good party loyalist and hard worker. But a dissident group, loyal to the party yet independent-minded and spearheaded by engineer Dunc Sharpe, decided to persuade former MP Richard Cashin to run. They pulled off a bloodless coup and got Cashin elected as party president.

Some deduced from their success that Joey was slipping. But this kind of miscarriage had happened to the great dictator before. A few years earlier, Clyde Wells had pulled a similar stunt in an election involving the young Liberals. What it did show, though, was that the party was not a monolithic structure controlled from top to bottom by Joey, but a very loose, segmented, fragmented, and ad hoc group commanded by nobody, really, except in a most wobbly and whimsical sense. I learned later that John Crosbie had been greatly encouraged in his leadership aspirations by the fact that Cashin had taken on Joey's man and beaten him. What Crosbie should have been more wary of was the universe of difference between someone beating one of Smallwood's minions and someone trying to knock off the man himself.

IN THE HOUSE of Assembly during this period, I watched John Crosbie transform himself, politically, from a sow's ear into a silk purse. His speaking style as minister under Smallwood had been monotonous, flat, whiny, and boring, and delivered with his eyes closed tight. People laughed at his pronunciations—instead of pronouncing Hebrides with three syllables, he would say HEEbrides with two syllables, as if he was talking about men in wedding dresses; he'd say high-tee for Haiti, and whereWITH'l for wherewithal, and high-per-bowl for the four syllables of hyperbole. He had a reputation for having been a brilliant student at university with his nose always buried in a book where he absorbed his arcane, hit-or-miss pronunciations from the look of words on the written page rather than from hearing them pronounced by knowledgeable human beings in conversation. Then he retained Howie Young, a Dale Carnegie course instructor, to guide him on how to speak effectively in public.

Howie helped change John Crosbie from an inert slug to a stinging wasp. John kept most of his mispronunciations and his flat St. John's accent—some things turned out to be impossible to alter—but he livened up his content and delivery and added humour until he got the reputation for being the most entertaining, if sometimes off-colour, politician in Canada. I remember when he was guest speaker at a convention of eye doctors one time and, as he walked to the podium, he noticed a big blown-up picture of an eyeball on the wall behind him. He turned to the audience and said, "Thank God this is not a convention of gynecologists."

Crosbie became so effective at needling the premier and government in the House that Joey started calling him "Bullyboy." I was also guilty of helping to bring the tone of the House down to the kindergarten level. At one point in the House, as Crosbie was complaining about something the government was doing wrong, I called him a big sook. Joey picked up on this children's street usage and gave wide and common currency to a term normally employed as an insult from one kid to another. Crosbie became "The Big Sook." But he always gave as good as he got or better. And with Crosbie and Wells together, Joey, the master of the House of Assembly for the previous twenty years, had met his match.

But not all of the damage to the Liberal Government was done by that duo. We were very capable of shooting ourselves in the foot. Before the House started one day, the kitchen cabinet was talking about the media at our routine lunch. A reporter at the local CBC station had said something that we perceived as anti-Liberal, and one of us said that he got the impression there were a lot of Tories at the CBC. Al Vardy piped up. "It's all Tories over there," he said. "Tories and queers." Les Curtis, the son of a famous Methodist clergyman, cast an eye around, saw that there were only Protestants by birth present—John Nolan was absent—and said, "Yes, nothing but Tories, queers, and Catholics." Joey looked at me and chortled silently. He was always amused and delighted by the viciousness of his long-time comrades.

That afternoon in the House of Assembly, the Opposition mentioned the CBC, taking comfort from the same story that had raised our ire at lunch. I leaned over to Steve Neary, who sat next to me, and whispered what seemed to be a pretty good line in those insensitive days: "The CBC? Vardy says that place is full of Tories and queers." I left out Catholics in deference to Steve's own faith. I saw the light go on in Steve's head and, without any dawdling, he jumped right up to ask the Opposition member then speaking if he would yield for a question. When the member courteously obliged, Steve inquired, "Mr. Speaker, would the honourable member not agree that the CBC is full of Tories and homosexuals?" Steve's toning down of the wording from queers to homosexuals availed him nothing. The proverbial hit the fan, with demands that Neary apologize, that he be expelled from the House, that he have the guts to utter that defamation outside the House, and the like. Steve did apologize under orders from Joey, who, when his eye caught mine, displayed, I couldn't help noticing, none of his earlier amusement in the dining room. You idiot, his eyes said. Didn't you remember when someone had told Neary that lawyers charged too much and he had caused such a fuss that the government had to appoint a Royal Commission into lawyers' real estate fees? Hadn't Joey told me before how he'd hesitated long and anxiously before appointing Neary as minister because he could be such a loose cannon?

THE PREMIER ALWAYS seemed to have a Royal Commission on something or other on the go. In 1968, in the House, Smallwood lambasted the report of the Royal Commission on the Economic State and Prospects of Newfoundland and Labrador. Back in 1965, his own Liberal Government had appointed the commission, chaired by Gordon Pushie, one of his own economic development advisers. The report recommended the need by the government for more cost-benefit studies for new industries and greater planning of fiscal resources—pretty tame stuff. But Joey called the document ninety per cent bunkum. He dismissed it out of hand, claiming that most of the members who signed it, some fourteen in all, had never even read the report. I remember thinking that it was dangerous to be a close acquaintance of Joey and risk being appointed by him to anything: besides Pushie, the members included Art Lundrigan, Doug Fraser, Albert Martin, Frank Moores, John O'Dea, Albert Perlin, Ches Pippy . . . all well-known and prominent in their own spheres, many of them good friends of the premier himself.

Frank Moores was singled out for special treatment: he had neither contributed to the report nor read it, according to Joey, and his participation in the report involved borrowing someone's pen and signing it, without so much as a glance at the text, and then pocketing the borrowed pen. Looking back, it was not really surprising that Moores, after defeating Joey's man in the federal election that year, seized the leadership of the provincial PC Party a couple of years later and—probably motivated by Joey's affronts—spearheaded a frontal attack on the premier that, in focus and energy, belied his previous image as a lazy, booze-swizzling, fornicating playboy.

IN MAY OF 1969, a headline in the St. John's *Evening Telegram* read: "Churchill Fall's Deal: Everyone's a Winner." At long last a power contract had been signed between Brinco's Churchill Falls Labrador Corporation (CFLCo) and Hydro Quebec to develop the Upper Churchill Falls hydroelectric site. Joey would often tell us of his twenty-year dream and acrimonious battle to get that project going. Canadian Lord Beaverbrook had set up a meeting at 10 Downing Street in London in the early 1950s between Sir Winston Churchill—his wartime boss—and Premier Smallwood. It was just after the great man had been re-elected UK prime minister, bouncing back from his party's electoral defeat following the Second World War.

Everything went swimmingly at the beginning. Churchill was immediately interested, proclaiming it a great imperial concept but not imperialistic, and he arranged for the de Rothschilds, his renowned merchant banker friends, to become involved in the Hamilton Falls development. (On Churchill's death in 1965, the river and falls were renamed in his honour.) The British Newfoundland Corporation (Brinco) was formed by the de Rothschilds and the other investors to pursue the deal. But then everything started to go sour. Quebec stood in the way. Or as Quebec saw it, Newfoundland was trying to develop a resource on their territory, since Quebec had never reconciled itself to what it considered Newfoundland's judicial theft of Labrador.

When the firebrand René Lévesque was minister of Energy in the early 1960s in Jean Lesage's Liberal Government of Quebec, before he started his separatist party, he was asked about the possibility of Newfoundland being granted a power line from Churchill Falls across Quebec. Lévesque said simply, "The people of Quebec would not allow it to stand." Whether that statement was a threat or, as Lévesque himself claimed, just a prediction, Joey told us that it was no different from a shakedown by the Mafia. Surely the great Government of Canada was not going to be intimidated by gangster-like threats of violence.

Carrying with him an order-in-council from the Newfoundland government requesting the Government of Canada to declare the development of Churchill Falls to be in the national interest, Joey flew to

Ottawa. There he went to see Prime Minister Pearson to obtain federal authorization for a power line across Quebec. He was prepared to argue that what he was asking for was only what the earlier Liberal federal government under Prime Minister St. Laurent had been prepared to stand or fall on—a natural gas pipeline across western Canada. But Pearson met him with a request of his own: Please, Premier Smallwood, don't even ask. If he did ask, then the feds, constitutionally, would have to act. But that would mean having to deal with an earlier question to the prime minister from Lesage, echoing Lévesque: who was going to protect from sabotage a hydro line of hundreds of miles across the Quebec wilderness carrying power that the Eastern Seaboard would be depending on? Like a good English-speaking Canadian, in the face of the Quebec reality, Premier Smallwood didn't ask Prime Minister Pearson, the Nobel-prize-winning mediator, to enforce our rights as a Canadian province under the Canadian constitution.

As a result of those long years of difficulty with our neighbouring province, Joey was accused of pissing on Quebec. Literally. He did this, allegedly, before Premier Maurice Duplessis died in 1959 or during Jean Lesage's premiership from 1960 to 1966, or both. The story was that he stood on the Labrador side of the Quebec border during the Upper Churchill Falls battle and urinated over the border onto Quebec territory. But did he actually do it?

Well, Joey told me in the late 1960s that he'd been praised or blamed for many things he'd allegedly done or said. And he took full credit for four.

One: describing Newfoundland as "this poor, bald rock." Two: inventing the term "British union" to help counteract the "Economic Union with the United States" mantra that gave the Responsible Government gang such a boost during the Confederation battle. Three: inventing the description "the little fellow from Gambo" for himself in the self-effacing way he knew audiences loved to hear when he was clobbering some high and mighty bigwig. (The concept would be borrowed by Jean Chrétien as "the little guy from Shawinigan" to great success in his political career.) Four: inventing the slogan "jobs, jobs, jobs" for campaigning in Newfoundland. (Which Joey would live to see Tory PM Brian Mulroney filch and use to win his 1988 federal election on free trade.)

But there were these four other things, Smallwood insisted, which, despite what some alleged, he never did or said. One: he never became friends with Maurice Duplessis, the fascist premier of Quebec, just because, as alleged, Duplessis was the one premier of Canada who was an inch shorter than Joey. Two: during his great industrialization leap forward in the 1950s, he never said to fishermen, "Burn your boats." He credited the Tories with attributing that catchphrase to him, and he admired it. Imagine, he told me, being able to come up with a beautiful piece of deceitful propaganda like that as a party and still being unable to win more than a handful of seats. Three: he never invented the term "Anglo-Saxon route" to describe the possibility of undersea power transmission of Churchill Falls power. That was concocted in Hydro Quebec as propaganda against *les maudits Anglais*; he disliked it intensely, he said, and never used it. Four, and finally: he may or may not have wanted to, but in fact, "I never pissed over the Labrador border onto Quebec." Many remained unconvinced on all four counts. And, indeed, on one of them, Joey would later recant: yes, it was possible that his bladder had become short-taken one time and he'd been forced to make his water, inadvertently, onto Quebec territory.

THE FIASCO THAT the Upper Churchill later became in everyone's eyes in hindsight was far from everyone's thoughts in July of 1967, when Joey turned the sod on site. Eddie de Rothschild and Winston S. Churchill (Winston Churchill's grandson) were at this groundbreaking ceremony, as were most of us in Joey's caucus, plus dignitaries and reporters from both sides of the Atlantic. I recall hearing Donald Gordon, Brinco president, muttering to someone as we all trudged along a fairly short path to the falls, swatting blackflies, "We're getting too damned old for this." In less than two years he was dead.

At the falls that day, Joey thundered out his notorious speech that was filmed and would be seen and heard throughout Newfoundland and the world without let-up for years into the future: "This is our land. This is our province. This is our river. This is our waterfall . . ." As events turned out, without any escalator clause for us in the contract for the rising price of power, and with Quebec consequently getting as much revenue as they would have received if they had owned the resource outright, poor Joey's rant would be perceived as the biggest piece of cockeyed bullshit ever orated by a political leader in the history of Canada.

In his own defence, Joey would always argue that he did not negotiate or sign the Upper Churchill deal. That was technically correct, but, of course, the real truth was even worse: he had fought tooth and nail for years to get the project going, and he had provided the opportunity and means for Brinco to virtually give away this vast provincial resource to Quebec.

But all that would arise in the years ahead, when Moores and Crosbie would demonize Joey for everything from Churchill Falls to our cruel spring weather. Back in May of 1969, with the hydro deal at last signed, Smallwood was riding high. And since he had now realized the final great dream of his life, he reiterated that he would be resigning as premier and leader when the Liberal leadership convention was held that fall, and he would not be running. To prove it, he was setting off on a trip around the world. For company, he asked me to join him.

First we had to fly to Europe for some meetings in connection with the Come By Chance refinery, and then we'd proceed on his planned global trip at our own expense. My father had already announced his campaign for the Liberal leadership, and was running, he said, only because the premier wasn't. Smallwood had told him he had absolutely no interest—zero interest—in contesting that upcoming leadership thing.

His disappearance from the province on his trip like this for a longish period of time, Dad thought, confirmed Joey's stated intention to retire. I told him I still had my grave doubts that he was truly out.

After Joey and I finished our work, his son Bill joined us, and we set out for Asia. Flying over the Mediterranean toward the Middle East, we passengers were unnerved to suddenly see fighter jets on either side of our aircraft. The captain came on to say they were Israeli planes, here to escort us over their territory in safety. I told Joey that although this was only a couple of years after the Six Day War, while the simmering War of Attrition still continued below, I felt secure surrounded by the armed Israeli war machines. Joey looked at me as if I had just confirmed that the sun comes up in the morning, and said that this was the safest part of the flight. We passed over that boiling cauldron without incident, dropped down in Karachi for fuel, and flew on. By the time we stopped in Calcutta, I was starting to think that when he had talked about flying around the world he meant it literally, non-stop.

We stayed a few days in Calcutta. Joey said he liked to pitch down there whenever he could in order to reaffirm his socialist background and beliefs. He thought the only hope for India was communism, as existed in neighbouring China. He told me he had been talking to an international banking executive recently, an American, who agreed with him on that. I told him I hoped that guy would enjoy his international posting to Greenland.

We checked into the Oberoi Grand Hotel, which billed itself as the top hotel in Calcutta and where a seven-foot-tall doorman in a turban guarded the entrance. I didn't get the impression it was a hotel where the Socialist Party held its conventions. Then we strolled about the city and were immediately beset by tenacious beggars of infinite varieties of demeanours and presentations: young, destitute mothers with babies at their breasts; twisted and contorted and blind children; adults crawling along on all fours; people sitting catatonic on the sidewalks, obviously gravely ill, some unto death.

Joey said he'd been shocked when he'd first come here that some of the people he'd been forced to step around on the sidewalk were in fact dead—the bodies would be picked up by the sanitation department every morning. I told him that I didn't like this at all—strolling around among some of the most wretched of the earth—especially since the nutrition and health problems of India and all other Third World countries were well within the resources of the rich counties to resolve. My lack of joy surrounded by this brutal but remediable human desperation made Joey say that he hadn't realized before that I was so delicate—I should enjoy being exposed like this to the authenticities of life.

The next authenticity of life occurred while we were being pulled through a slum in three rickshaws. Joey got it into his head to stop his rickshaw, jump out, and order his mystified driver to climb up into his place so Joey could pull him along instead. This had to be taken, I surmised, as a gross mockery by the hundreds of people around us. There had been communist-inspired riots and violent deaths reported in the papers here a few days before we'd arrived, and, judging by the nasty looks around us now, I fully expected to be soon numbered among the dead as a result of this travesty. But then I noticed that a lot of people, especially the kids, were starting to grin and point delightedly at Joey striding along and at the driver sitting up in the rickshaw like a *maharaja*, with Joey's camera slung around his neck. Pure dumb luck, or an unerring instinct for what appealed to humans everywhere in the world? I couldn't decide, but I was glad when we got the hell out of there.

The day we left, Bill Smallwood and I picked up what we self-diagnosed as the Calcutta scutters. Joey did not contract the ailment, even though we'd all eaten more or less the same food from the same source. I could only conclude that he possessed by nature, or had developed over the years, a cast iron gut to go with the brass face. He did tell me, though, that he had caught some sort of intestinal worms during his long-ago travels that had to be combatted most aggressively by doctors when he got home.

From Calcutta we flew to Hong Kong, skirting Vietnam. When the pilot announced that his flight plan would bring us wide of the war raging down there, I thanked the premier for having staved off economic union with the United States twenty years before, since it would probably have led to actual union by now, and Ed Roberts and I were just the right age to have been brought home from below in body bags. Bill Smallwood said, "You, maybe, but Ed would still be alive—he would never have passed the physical." Joey gave his silent laugh. It was the first time I'd seen him show any appreciation for anything said by his son.

From the airport, we drove to the world-famous, top-flight Peninsula Hotel. This looked like yet another socialist hangout, I said, to Joey's amusement. At the desk, they told us they were completely full and had no rooms. Joey managed to talk them into renting us a loft-like suite next to the roof with one bedroom and a couple of cots in an outside anteroom for Bill and me.

Joey said he missed having Al Vardy along in situations like these. He recalled a time somewhere in Asia when they had arrived without reservations and no rooms were available at the top hotel. In his pipe-organ voice, Vardy proclaimed that Joey was a prime minister from Canada—which, conveniently enough, was misconstrued as the prime minister *of* Canada—travelling incognito. They ended up with the presidential suite at no cost. We agreed now that those were the good old days, when no one outside Canada knew the prime minister of Canada's name, let alone what he looked like—Pearson, St. Laurent, Mackenzie King. Nowadays everyone everywhere would recognize the charismatic Trudeau, thanks to Joey having put him over the top at the convention.

No sooner had we entered our accommodation than a knock came on the door. Outside stood a well-known Chinese restaurant owner from St. John's. He was back to the old country on a short visit and word had reached him from the airport immediately on our arrival to this crowded city of several million that Prime Minister Smallwood was in town. He invited us to dinner that night and Joey accepted. Bill and I were in no condition or mood for a big Chinese meal, not having recovered from our collywobbles, but we went. The dinner consisted of thirty-seven dishes—small courses, like the two tiny birds on a plate with their feathery heads still on, and the miniscule hearts of some diminutive mammal. Despite our malaise, the meal was delicious.

The next day Joey took us to his tailor and shoemaker. He instructed us to just give them our suit or shoes for a day, and the next day we could pick up an identical outfit and footwear. Make sure you pointed out to them, he advised, any defects or damage in the cloth or the leather you didn't want copied, because otherwise when you picked up your newly made items they'd have the same rips or abrasions as in the originals. He also got from the cobbler a vial of Chinese medicine—the very best—guaranteed for sure to cure the Calcutta scutters. I wouldn't drink any of it, but Bill Smallwood did when we got back to our room, and he had to rush to the bathroom and throw up violently.

The next day he accused the cobbler of trying to poison him. But this gentleman took no offence. A modern renaissance man, combining in one head, the latest shoemaking techniques with ancient and profound medical wisdom, he patiently explained that Bill's violent reaction was in accord, of course, with the age-old method of re-establishing the yin-yang in the body, which had become so dreadfully unbalanced by the culinary atrocities forced on us in India. Not being entirely convinced by his reasoning, I abstained, but I did observe Bill recovering from his condition a day or two faster than I did.

The next day Joey pursued his real reason for being in Hong Kong. He wanted to get into Red China. On the flight he had finished a book he was reading and passed it to me. I believe it was called *Mandate of Heaven*. You should study up on that, he said, for when we tour China. I opened the book at random and my eye lit upon a paragraph where the western author was saying that he was amazed, after coming to China, at how little he had earlier understood the concept of shit. You only fully comprehend the whole notion of shit, he was now able to write, when you witness with your own eyes an aggregation of human feces bigger than a three-storey house floating placidly down the Yangtze River.

We went to the office of the Hong Kong representative of Communist China. Behind the desk sat a man whose head did not move, nor did any facial muscle so much as twitch, for the entire half-hour we were there that morning. Off to the side in the corner sat his equally impassive note taker. After we had been motioned into our chairs—I don't recall any greeting—the communist rep's opaque eyes rested on Joey without expression throughout his spiel. The thought that came into my mind was how blood-curdling it must be for a person confined to a tiny cell to see this guy coming through the door every hour to continue his "interrogation."

Meanwhile, Joey was talking about his great admiration for China and the 1949 communist revolution—the same year, he said, that he'd led his own county into Confederation with Canada—and his esteem for Chairman Mao. He'd always been a fervent socialist, he revealed, and had been prompted in his days as a leader in Canada to follow many of Mao's initiatives. His industrialization program had been based on Mao's great leap forward.

I noticed that he didn't mention any examples—for instance, his rubber plant in Holyrood. Joey had already told me that half the problem with that initiative was the rumour someone started that it was going to actually make rubbers, that is to say, condoms. The parish priest out there went nuts and his campaign against it led to its failure. I told Joey that it was probably a good thing the plant did not make condoms, since the rubber boots it produced for fishermen all leaked. Joey had to laugh in spite of himself. Now, in the rep's office, he did not go on to say, either, that his great leap forward had been generally just as disastrous as Mao's, albeit on a smaller scale and with fewer people actually starving.

I did half-expect him to say, though, how much he admired Mao's "re-education" program. He had "jokingly" told me en route that he wouldn't mind making it part of the higher education curriculum in Newfoundland. He thought that all his wrong-headed opponents and hostile commentators in urban Newfoundland would benefit greatly from being sent to farms in the countryside and required to shovel fresh pig manure against a strong wind sixteen hours a day for twenty years.

After half an hour, during which the Chinese guy said nothing, he held up his hand. Joey and the note taker stopped. "Come back tomorrow," he said in perfect English, bowed, and left. The next day, back we went, and the Chinese government man indicated that Smallwood could resume his speech, which he did. After many minutes more, the soundless, motionless Chinese man held up his hand and said, "Come back tomorrow." And so it went, day after day, for a week.

Meanwhile, we wandered about observing the frenetic activity of Hong Kong. Many people sought us out, including eminent Canadian journalist Bill Cunningham, who was covering the Vietnam War for the CBC. He interviewed Joey and shot footage of us, with the result that our images and "story" appeared on the national TV news in Canada.

My best memory of our encounter, though, was hearing Cunningham's explanation of something called the pucker factor. Journalists who regularly flew in and out of the Vietnam war zone by small aircraft described how the reports from Saigon each day determined how tight your anus constricted at the probability of being hit by ground-to-air fire. A high-number pucker factor, reported to comrades, indicated just how terrified they should be on a flight.

Some businessmen approached Joey to talk about Hong Kong investments in Newfoundland. One of them was involved in putting up high-rise buildings in the city and told us his mortgage financing took only eight years to be paid off entirely from the revenues. Joey was fascinated. He marvelled over the transformation he thought would take place in our province if a million people from Hong Kong were to come to live and work in Newfoundland and Labrador.

AS JOEY AND I meandered about the city—Bill was being fitted by the tailor that day—we laughed about the offer made by the taxi driver who had taken us from the airport to our hotel on our arrival. He knew of a wonderful live sex show we three men would surely enjoy, he said. Very explicit, but very tasteful. He could take us to it and introduce us as soon as we had checked into our hotel. Joey did his silent laugh now at the utter absurdity of any such concept even existing, let alone his attending and looking at it. He told me that he'd lost all interest in sex during the hurly-burly of the Confederation battle in the 1940s, and it had never returned. He quoted Lord Chesterfield's pronouncement on sex: "The pleasure is momentary, the position ridiculous, and the expense damnable."

Knowing that Joey's lack of interest in sex had nothing to do with any lack of energy, I replied that the great energy possessed by many successful leaders in politics and business seemed to turn some of them into sexual athletes. He said he believed that to be true sometimes. For example, David Lloyd George, Kemal Ataturk, Joseph Kennedy and his son John, and Si Moores and his son Frank did come to mind as sex maniacs. But Joey felt that he was not alone in his own attitude, because the very best, the greatest of them all, were not sex mad at all—for example, Mahatma Gandhi and, of course, Winston Churchill, who was throughout his married life a model of sexual propriety. Certainly, it helped curb Churchill's urges, said Joey, that his brilliant father, Lord Randolph, had died in his prime, a raving lunatic, from syphilitic paresis of the brain, picked up young and drunk from a bawd.

Whatever the cause of his propriety, I had never heard even a hint of sex scandal involving Smallwood. No doubt it was part of the secret to his political longevity. It had allowed him to get away with a notion he sometimes expressed to his audience: that he was as devoted to Newfoundland as if he was married to her. This had led one wag to bawl out in a crowded hall that he sincerely hoped Joey *was* married to Newfoundland, because he'd been fucking her for twenty years.

Joey's general attitude to women was interesting. He was almost painfully polite around them. I never heard him addressing any woman but his wife and daughter by her first name. And I never heard him seriously contemplate the idea of his party running a woman for the House of Assembly. Even his hero Sir Richard Squires had arranged to have a female candidate elected to the House of Assembly, albeit his own wife, but Joey only enlisted the "Liberal Ladies" to stuff envelopes, and get the women's vote out, and "man" the polling booths at elections. And that was more or less the limit of their participation. (He did mention an offer he said he'd made to Megan Nutbeem to become his candidate, but I had the feeling he'd only made that up to show the family's ingratitude to Joey when her brother Frank Moores turned Tory.)

Al Vardy told me once that, after Greg Power and Joey had fallen out, Greg had characterized Joey's attitude to women as the outer manifestation of an inner sexual malaise, to wit, psychological impotence triggered by possession of a small member. And Harold Horwood had also told people, Vardy said, that that was the cause of Joey's preoccupation with upwardly thrusting phallic structures like Confederation Building and the Sir Richard Squires Building, and his spurting fountains at the Colonial Building and in Pippy Park. It was all an expression of penis envy in the diminutive little man.

If any of that was so, Joey certainly had a healthy sense of humour about it. He regaled a number of us once about a straitlaced member of his cabinet who had made the mistake of using the urinal next to one being occupied by a backbench colleague who was reputed to be "the best-hung man east of Montreal." The backbencher was so well-endowed that he was afraid to go in the woods, Joey said, ever since the time he'd been having a leak behind a tree and a hunter, who only saw his organ, mistook him for a bull moose and nearly shot him. In any event, the straitlaced minister at the urinal next to him was soon seen staggering out of the washroom muttering maniacally, his eyes out on stalks, "My God, did you see it? My God, my God, did you see it?" The backbencher was also a great ballroom dancer, which he would exhibit at any opportunity. He was extremely successful with the ladies. But, although he always wanted very much to go into the cabinet, Joey would never put him in. One of our colleagues said that if he was as well-endowed as the backbencher and could dance as skilfully, he wouldn't be worried about going in any goddamned cabinet.

But I think it would be safe to say that Joey himself was not all that interested in ballroom dancing. Nevertheless, at one Liberal ball, not long after my wife, Penny, and I were married, we succeeded in cajoling him into starting off the dancing by going out on the floor alone with Penny. Now Joey was pushing seventy, attired in his rumpled black suit and skewed bow tie, and shorter than his partner. Penny was in her mid-twenties and looking fit and lovely, and clad in a low-cut gown that she wore to excellent advantage. Just the two of them out on the floor waltzing by themselves caused a lot of photos to be taken, some of which unerringly found their way to the newspapers the next day. One caption under a snapshot of Penny and Joey said, "Beauty and the Beast." The description of the picture that most people liked best, though, was the one by Ray Guy: "The Naked and the Dead."

Joey told me in our wanderings about Hong Kong that he believed he was descended from central European Jews. His physical appearance pointed to it, he said, as did that of some of his siblings and forebears. His mother's maiden name was Devanna, which people often think is a Huguenot name but might be Jewish. He also said that, during his early years in New York, everyone, even many in the Jewish community, automatically thought he was a Jew, based on his appearance. He hobnobbed with them, speaking all the time at their rallies. Many told him he looked like a Jewish intellectual. He even had a Jewish girlfriend and said that he nearly passed himself off as a Jew in front of her parents. But he tripped up on some point and was kicked out of her life for his scam.

He'd been three years old, he told me, before he spoke a word, and he knew of only one other person of consequence like that—Albert Einstein. I didn't tell him that Vardy and Curtis, having heard this before, kidded to me that there was one big difference between Joey and Einstein: after Einstein did finally start talking, he would occasionally shut up between brilliant insights.

I told him that a Jewish background would be a wonderful intellectual heritage to possess. Many individuals who were or descended from Ashkenazi Jews seemed to be the most brilliant people on the face of the earth, excelling in everything—science, mathematics, literature, business—as evidenced by the disproportionately high number of Nobel Prize winners they produced compared to their percentage of the population in North America and Europe. Joey said that Valdmanis had told him exactly the same thing, and that his surname, Smallwood, could well be a translation. The Central European Czech name "Hayek" meant "a small wood or grove," and was probably Jewish in origin.

Valdmanis had intended all that as a great compliment, of course, said Joey, which was proof that he wasn't an anti-Semitic Nazi, as some had viciously alleged. Later Joey would tell me that, during one of his early trips to Germany with the same Valdmanis, the Latvian had met for days on end with the industrialist Alfried Krupp in the prison to which Krupp had been sent as a Nazi war criminal for employing slave labour in his factories during the Second World War. After each visit, Valdmanis would report back to Joey on possibilities for the Krupp empire in Newfoundland. I didn't have the heart to ask Joey who had suggested that Valdmanis go to see Krupp in the first place or how he happened to have such easy and welcome access to the Nazi war criminal.

Joey told me, wandering about Hong Kong, that he didn't so much conceive the ambition of becoming prime minister when he was a young boy, as some have reported, as realize at an early age that he possessed the gifts of eloquence, persuasiveness, energy, single-mindedness, memory, leadership, and the like, which he knew could take him anywhere. He repeated that he did not believe in the concept of destiny for himself, but he did wonder why his grandfather had ended up in Newfoundland. Joey felt he himself would have been much happier in a farming province like Prince Edward Island, where his forebears had come from. He didn't like the sea very much and he could never stay away from farming, which seemed to be in his genes. He had not been able to resist, for example, the chance to drive cattle down the Burin Peninsula, which everyone had laughed at as preposterous, but which had been one of the happiest days of his life.

His father was a Methodist and his mother a Catholic, a highly unusual matrimonial union in Victorian-era Newfoundland. And just as unusual in those days of peer pressure and authority-driven religion, both his parents were lapsed from their birth religions. His mother later became a zealous Pentecost, and Joey told me that, as a child, he loved going with her to evangelical prayer meetings and sitting there awash in the clamorous and repetitive orations and sermonizing.

He often said he was a Wesleyan—the last of the great Wesleyans, he called himself—and he had scores of books on John Wesley and the movement. In reality, though, he said, he was agnostic or simply indifferent. He invoked the name of God and the concept of Christianity for rhetorical purposes. In his speeches, his province was forever full of "God-fearing Newfoundlanders" and it was always "this Christian province" that the Godless IWA or some other nefarious villain had dared to affront.

He told me he didn't mind spending money but that he could never galvanize himself into any interest whatever in the actual possession of it, or to do something he didn't want to do in order to earn it. And he was not in the least attracted to the idea of surrounding himself with extravagances. He restricted himself to a recliner chair in the corner of the living room of his elaborate house on Roaches Line, which some contractors had built for him after Diefenbaker had booted him off Circular Road. He slept in a simple single bed with a light on the wall above it that he could reach up and turn off and on for reading.

And his living room often looked like a storage room. Former St. John's councillor Dave Barrett, who'd gone out to visit him one time, was so impressed by the sheer amount of rubble—books and files and knick-knacks and artifacts—lying around the living room floor at random, he told me, that he'd asked the premier seriously if he was moving house. Joey looked at him in surprise, having no idea what he was talking about.

The builders of his house had taken it upon themselves to install an indoor swimming pool. But after a first dip or two, Joey had lost interest in it. Whenever I was in the house and happened to glimpse the pool, it appeared to have gone to rack and ruin, and the water in it was covered with algae.

In school at Bishop Feild, he told me, his report card one year had awarded him a grade of nine per cent for character. In the eyes of the teachers, he said, a student of good character was one who sat down and shut up and mechanically did what he was told. There were no marks for speaking up before being spoken to, or for feisty independence of thought, or for any display of energy unless you were on the soccer pitch. In other words, there was no encouragement of any of the characteristics that a boy would need for later success in life. He left school at fourteen through pure discontent and became for the rest of his life an autodidact. But his self-teaching was extremely haphazard, he knew, and there were, on the one hand, great gaps in his knowledge, and, on the other, a tremendous concentration and focus on some narrow areas.

For example, leading up to the Confederation battle he acquired a knowledge of Canada and the Canadian system of government and its policies and programs second to no one else in the entire world. And he attained an encyclopedic knowledge of the British parliamentary system. He employed the same technique all his life. On some particular issue that he wanted to master for political purposes, he would, like a lawyer with a brief heading for the Supreme Court of Canada, acquire full knowledge so he could dominate in debate or conversation any audience, discerning or ignorant, with facts, figures, and names and backgrounds of corporations and principals. He figured that, with training in the law, he would have made a top barrister.

Unfortunately, his facility with the language and his overriding ability to dominate in talk, in his early days, led him to stray into areas of unawareness and inexperience that made him look foolish and ignorant in the eyes of the more discriminating and knowledgeable. He told me that this feature of his makeup was what had made it so difficult for him to be taken seriously as a leader in the referendum battles, or to be considered credible, by the more learned and discerning in society. Listening to him, I thought there might be another side to this, too: his zeal in amassing debating points and his brilliance in articulating them perhaps led him sometimes to ignore the basic question of whether a particular project he was proposing was fundamentally sound or simply lunatic.

I asked him if he regretted his lack of a university education. He didn't give a definite yes or no. He replied that he would not have become premier if he'd gone to university. He pointedly disparaged some politicians whose scholarly training in an academic ivory tower had divested them of the common touch. He especially complained about the classroom persona in some politicians, not because of their training as teachers but because they hadn't altered their old habit, in making a speech, of boringly lecturing down to their audience as if they were students.

He seemed to like it a lot when I described one of his opponents as "educated way beyond his intelligence." That was exactly what he meant, he said. But, if he never told me outright that he regretted his lack of higher formal education, it was clear to me he felt it. His actions regarding Memorial University spelled it out. His desire to have a great university with scholarships and low tuition—even student salaries—and a magnificent campus, was, I have no doubt, spurred by his desire to make sure that no young person was ever again deprived, by untoward circumstances like his own, of an opportunity for higher learning.

At a floating seafood restaurant in the floating fishing village of Aberdeen in Hong Kong, we gazed out over the many houseboats on the harbour where whole families lived permanently and struggled desperately to survive. Viewing the scene, Joey waxed nostalgic, and sometimes rather gloomy, over pre-Confederation Newfoundland. He said he had learned from one of his heroes, Sir William Coaker, the slogan so appreciated by his more impoverished outport supporters, that he'd "make the grass grow on Water Street." And he got his "develop or perish" slogan from another of his heroes, Sir Richard Squires. These two heroes of his, he said, hated each other's guts. But that didn't stop them from joining forces in a government to stave off the Opposition, or keep them from sharing in the spoils of victory. The two leaders divided up a million dollars one time between their respective parties, he said. Where had that phenomenal sum come from? Joey was not perfectly sure. He thought it had come from the railway or the paper mill on the Humber, or some combination of both.

It was the inability of even those two veritable political geniuses to stop, or even resist, the corruption and instability of Newfoundland politics, Joey told me, that converted him strongly to the opinion that we needed a long rest from elective, partisan politics, and he welcomed the advent of the Commission of Government. The curse of Newfoundland politics, Joey said, was everyone's overweening personal ambition—including those who were incurably mediocre—for the top job, and their greed for money. Even the men in the Responsible Government movement, including the twenty-nine dictators they'd elected to the National Convention, were split and in conflict before they even tasted power. Could we imagine what state Newfoundland would have been in again after a few years if that gang had assumed absolute power under a return to Dominion status and Responsible Government?

Smallwood told me that someone had worked out how much he was on his feet at the National Convention and it turned out to be over eighty per cent of the convention's time. That wasn't all speech-making but also included his numerous and frequent points of order. He was forever jumping up to shout, "Point of order, Mr. Chairman." Then, when he'd go around Newfoundland campaigning, he recalled, people would say to him, "My son, that gang in there is so crooked they won't even give you a drink of water." Many listeners to the broadcast of proceedings had thought he was shouting out, "Pint of water, Mr. Chairman."

He knew, though, that many intelligent listeners of his speeches found them repetitious and tortured, but he lived in unholy fear, he told me, that there was one person somewhere, perhaps Bill Keough's "last forgotten fisherman on the bill of Cape St. George," who did not quite grasp his point, and that was why he repeated it in a dozen different ways.

Joey dismissed the conspiracy theory of Confederation that had been given such a boost by the powerful rhetoric of Major Peter Cashin, snatches of which were engraved on his mind: "a conspiracy to sell this country to the Dominion of Canada;" "attractive bait which will be held out to lure our country into the Canadian mousetrap;" "their flowery sales talk that our only hope, our only salvation, lies in following a new Moses into the promised land across the Cabot Strait."

Joey told me he only wished there *had* been a conspiracy between London and Ottawa to drag Newfoundland into Canada; unfortunately for him, however, there was none. But, I asked him, wasn't there a long-standing official colonial policy in London encouraging the federal union of all British North America? There was such a policy, he told me, but he received hardly any encouragement from Great Britain or any of the British government's representatives in Newfoundland. He didn't know if that was because he was not a credible leader in the eyes of the British government or because the empire politicians and bureaucrats had learned through bitter experience that too much of a hands-on policy was counterproductive and tended to blow up in their faces.

But hadn't his Confederate movement connived with the Commission of Government or the British governor to have the debates of the National Assembly broadcast throughout Newfoundland? Joey replied that he had no idea where that decision to broadcast had come from, and he himself had no more to do with it than the man in the moon. Besides, it was only in retrospect that the broadcast seemed to have favoured him and the winning side. At the time, it was a neutral decision that both sides in the convention could have taken equal advantage of.

Then what about the British government's decision to place Confederation on the ballot, overriding the decision to keep it off by the National Convention, whose judgment the Brits had promised to honour? That, said Joey, was only elementary democracy in action, and the maintenance of democracy was a higher principle than anything else for the Mother of Parliaments. The bully-boy tactic of keeping off the ballot a legitimate option because the majority cabal didn't want it on was proof positive of the democratic need to place it on. And there was absolutely no truth, he told me with a straight face, that a substantial number of the tens of thousands of names on the petition to have Confederation placed on the referendum ballot came off gravestones.

As for Canada supposedly helping the Confederate movement with money—absolute poppycock. He had found it exceedingly difficult to get a red cent out of Canadian sources even though Water Street money and the rich Catholic hierarchy in St. John's were dead set against Confederation. And far from Canada being part of a conspiracy, many in Ottawa were more of a counterproductive nuisance than anything else. Take Lester B. Pearson, for example. He was at the highest level of the civil service as Undersecretary of State for External Affairs at the time, but he was naive enough to play right into the hands of the anti-Confederate, Responsible Government movement. Pearson made a statement in the middle of the battle that Canada would prefer to deal with an elected government on the question of Newfoundland's future, which was the very thing that Cashin and Ches Crosbie and all the other anti-Confederates of every hue were saying.

Oh, Pearson would go on to win a Nobel Peace Prize over the Suez Canal crisis, and would be very helpful to Newfoundland as prime minister in the 1960s, but at the time of the great Confederation debate, this top public servant had no idea whatsoever of the hidden agenda of the anti-Confederates in Newfoundland. Pearson was more of a political problem child than a sensible help. Conspiracy in Canada to force Confederation? If so, it was a conspiracy conceived by the Three Stooges, and executed by the Keystone Cops.

The biggest help, outside of his own Confederate movement, Joey thought, had arrived from whoever had originally dreamed up the idea of placing on the referendum ballot the option of a return to Responsible Government "as it existed prior to 1934." The addition of those words reminded ordinary voters that Responsible Government would be a return to a corrupt, self-serving enemy of the people. Whoever had come up with that phrase to go on the ballot was a genius, even if he didn't know it.

Joey disdained commentators who described the result of the second referendum in 1948 as narrow: 52.3 per cent voted for Confederation versus 47.7 per cent for Responsible Government. That was not narrow but decisive. It would have produced a massive majority for any government. When Prime Minister Mackenzie King expressed doubts over whether it was a sufficient mandate for the Canadian government to proceed with union, Jack Pickersgill had to remind King that he had never received a popular vote himself that high to form a government, and yet he had felt possessed of enough authority as a prime minister to make crucial decisions, including life-and-death decisions during the war.

*

JOEY LOVED TO call his administration, tongue in cheek, Her Majesty's Outport Government. But seriously, he told me, he was glad that the vast majority of his caucus, wherever they may have originated, lived now, and had for years, in St. John's. Thank God, he said, because anyone with any ambition and ability will soon gravitate to the centre of the action. He told me that the UK government's insistence on a two-year residency requirement in the districts electing delegates to the National Convention had been based on the well-meaning theory that this would keep the St. John's elite from dominating the election. Perhaps it did, but in practice it also guaranteed that most of those elected from around the country were mediocre and run-of-the-mill or worse. Take Clyde Wells, Joey said. He always made a big deal about living in Corner Brook, but just watch him as soon he got a better law practice going and felt he had become important enough: then, he'd move to St. John's.

SMALLWOOD'S PERSONAL DISTASTE for religion in general extended especially to the hierarchy of the Catholic Church. He told me his attitude was exacerbated during the Confederation struggle as a result of the enmity of Archbishop Roche. When Prime Minister of Canada Louis St. Laurent, who was a prominent Catholic, visited St. John's after Confederation, Joey said, Archbishop Roche point-blank refused to meet with him. Joey could not comprehend how there could be so much loathing in a Christian. And hadn't one of Roche's own, Bishop Michael O'Reilly of St. George's, actually favoured Confederation?

He contrasted the democracy and the freedom of thought and the rule of law of Protestant nations versus the tyranny of Catholic countries. What about Germany and Nazism? I asked. That country was only about one-third Catholic. Yes, but Hitler had been brought up a Catholic, he replied.

He told me he once listened to my father and Greg Power talking about religious idiocies and arguing over the relative merits, if any, of various religious denominations and sects. My father, who Joey figured was at least an agnostic and perhaps an atheist, was arguing that some religions were more rational than others, more secular than others, less dangerous than others—the all but secular United Church of Canada, for example, compared with some primitive, brain-dead cults. And Fred made the point that any religious denomination that was closer to secularism and science, and freer from superstition, and had less control over its adherents, was better than the others. Greg Power made the point, however, that all religion was all absolutely unalloyed horse manure, and just one step along the religious route was as bad as a mile. I asked Joey what his own opinion was. He thought my father was right politically and economically but that Greg was right theologically and philosophically.

Greg was an out-and-out atheist, said Joey, but a flexible one when it came to politics. His atheism didn't stop him from convincing Joey one time in Rome that they seek an audience together with Pope Pius XII. There Greg drew attention to his good Irish Catholic surname, and had the pope bless a satchel of beads and crucifixes so that he could later distribute them among the voters in his district, most of whom were good Catholics. Joey was clearly in awe of what he saw as his old friend's cynical brilliance.

I told Joey I never knew Greg Power. I could remember meeting him only once, casually and accidentally, but I'd been very impressed by him in the space of a few seconds. I was in a bookstore looking at a book on the problems of Middle East countries and I heard a voice behind me: "I would guess that when it comes to religion and rational thinking they are about where we were in Europe in the ninth century." I turned around and was surprised to recognize Greg Power. Before I could say much beyond hello, he smiled and nodded and walked on. I told Joey I wished I'd known at that time of my dad's theological argument with him because I could have said to him, "Then you do agree with my old man after all."

Joey wouldn't hear of the opinion that his Confederate comrade and former great friend Power had resigned from his cabinet over a squabble about their competing chicken farms. He told me Power had resigned because the income tax department descended on him with a claim of a quarter of a million dollars, which, Joey said rather disdainfully, Greg had no trouble whatever paying.

The tax problem did not account, however, for the vitriol with which Power later attacked Joey in his newspaper column, and when I asked him about it, Joey had no explanation. All he would say was that Power was very Machiavellian. He would have been right at home in renaissance Italy under the Borgias. He would have gone around wrapped in a cloak with an open stiletto dagger concealed underneath, ready to plunge it into the guts of an unsuspecting enemy.

Greg Power had invented the term "Comic Union," for the Economic Union with the US Movement that threatened to derail the Confederation campaign, and came up with the name "Sitting Bull" for Ches Crosbie, which, Joey said, fit like a glove. He'd always thought that Greg had also stuck the name "Donald Duck" on Don Jamieson, too, but Don himself said it was his mentor Ches Crosbie who coined the name because Jamieson waddled along like a duck, with that fat arse on him. That would explain, said Joey, why Ches's son John was so nasty to people who had helped and befriended him, like Joey himself. John had come by his malicious, malevolent nature honestly.

JOEY HAD A reputation for not being fond of travelling in boats or of being on the water at all. When I asked him about it, he said it was because he was a farmer by nature, not a sailor. But it was dislike, not fear. He told me one of his brothers used to call him a landlubber and laugh at his squeamishness about going on boats. One time when Joey had to campaign from a small boat with a cabin on it before Confederation, they encountered a big blow. His brother asked him afterwards what he thought of the gale. Joey said, "What gale?" His question was sincere, said the skipper of the boat: he had slept right through it in the cabin.

I believed it, I told Joey. My father had recounted a time he and another man were up in a small single-engine aircraft with the premier when they encountered a severe storm that buffeted the plane about like a leaf. The two other men held on for dear life, occasionally looking at each other to confirm by the fear in their eyes that they were going to die. Joey was lying back in his seat the whole time, sleeping like a baby.

That got him started on some comical stories about flying around Newfoundland and Labrador in small aircraft. He could only remember being frightened to death once in a plane, he said. He and the pilot had taken off in a one-engine seaplane when suddenly they heard these great whacks and thumps somewhere on the outside of the plane—"whack whack whack," said Joey to me, slapping his hands together. He looked at the pilot for reassurance. But the pilot was already looking at Joey with a terrified look on his face, and shrieked at him: "What the fuck is that?" (They found out, after putting down again in a panic, that the end of a paddle had come loose from its ties and was flapping against the pontoon.)

Joey told me that, because of a certain pilot he used in one campaign, he got to know some Newfoundland communities better than he needed to. After they'd been in a settlement for an hour and Joey wanted to leave for the next place, this pilot would sometimes go outside in the dead calm with the sun splitting the rocks and perform an elaborate ritual—wetting fingers and thumbs with spit and thrusting them up into the air, aiming his nose at all points of the compass and loudly sniffing into the air, throwing handful after handful of grass above his head in several directions and watching the blades fluttering down as if his life depended on it. Then he would finally conclude in a grave tone that there was a big storm about to hit, and, for safety's sake, they had no choice but to spend the night there in that community. In such fashion, Joey told me, he got to know intimately every place in the province where the pilot had a girlfriend.

The premier got a great kick out of Ted Pearcey, the pilot of the government aircraft who became the first director of the provincial government's air service. We both remembered the time we were settling in for takeoff and Ted asked the premier and the rest of us if we'd like a coffee when we were airborne. We all said yes. Then he joined his co-pilot in the cockpit. After we were airborne, Ted came out into the galley and began preparing the coffee. Turning to us he pointed to the co-pilot inside and said, "He's too stupid to make coffee, so I've got him flying the plane." Joey shook with his silent laugh.

My father had told me of another time when he and Joey had flown into a tiny community with no roads out and had ended up being stormbound there for several days. It was an evangelical place where even a little wine for the stomach's sake was strictly taboo. They had absolutely nothing to drink, even in the privacy of their own rooms. Finally, a weather window arose where the pilot figured they could get out. But in the course of taxiing out on the harbour to take off, the pilot noticed that a pontoon had somehow gotten damaged. It had to be fixed, he said. It was not safe to rev up and take off like that. However, Joey said, "Go. Go. Take off." The pilot said there was probably a fifty-fifty chance that the plane would tip over on takeoff or that she'd go bottom-up when he was trying to bring her down in the next harbour. Joey looked at the pilot and bellowed, "Take this goddamned plane up." He'd rather die than go another day without his sherry.

I didn't repeat that one to Joey, but I did enjoy telling him exactly what I thought on most topics that came up, and rationalized my pleasure at his sometimes pained reaction as the brutal honesty of a faithful adviser. When he wondered what his legacy would be after he left politics permanently that coming fall, I told him that he should be prepared for his own de-Stalinization that would probably take place. The same process that Khrushchev had applied to Stalin to turn him into a diabolical monstrosity might be applied to Smallwood by those who came after him. There was no comparison between him and Stalin, of course, I added, but my point was that the process could likely be the same. I don't think Joey liked that prospect very much, even though I said that he could rely on his friends to fend off a lot of his de-Stalinization, and it seemed to set him thinking pessimistically, perhaps with consequences unintended by me.

Joey also asked me what I thought of the alleged dramatic decline of people's satisfaction with him in the political polls. I told him the problem was that he was being compared with perfection. In other words, he was being compared not with another human being but God Almighty, and in such a contest, naturally, God won. It would be different if he was being compared to a mere mortal—say, the Tory leader. He seemed to like that prospect better.

I fear that my answers may have been an incentive, if he needed one, for Joey to stay on in politics. On the one hand he wanted to hold off his post-politics days of de-Stalinization. On the other, he wanted to measure himself—not against the perfection of God, but against a couple of fiendish devils: the one in the upcoming leadership race and then the one in the next election.

AFTER DANGLING US for a week in Hong Kong, the Chinese government representative told us that it was not likely we would get visas to visit mainland China during this trip. For the first time he smiled and indicated that if it had been up to him he would have arranged the visit. He had obviously been captivated by Smallwood. He urged us to try again in the future when, he intimated, His Excellency (Joey) might have better friends in his own country.

We found out later that, in spite of assurances to the premier by the Department of External Affairs in Ottawa that they'd do everything they could to smooth his entry, they had, in fact, put the kibosh on it. Trudeau was in the process of establishing full diplomatic relations with China, which did take place within two years, and the last thing he wanted in the meantime, we heard, was any Canadian, more particularly a madman from Newfoundland, in there stirring up the *merde*.

And so Smallwood's intended great coup at the end of his political career of visiting China while he was still premier—of being one of the very first western statesmen to do so—came to nothing. And the failure would have far-reaching effects back home. Early the morning after the Chinese had denied his request, Joey came out of his room to the anteroom where Bill Smallwood and I were asleep on our cots. It was about 3:00 a.m., but that didn't stop Joey from turning on the light and pacing vigorously about. He could not sleep, he said, because he was haunted by the fear, by the veritable nightmare, that the Government of Newfoundland was going to fall into the "wrong hands."

The wrong hands belonged to John Crosbie. None of the leadership candidates now in the race, like my father, and none of those considering it, like T. Alex Hickman, could beat Crosbie, he feared, with the millions of dollars Crosbie would receive from his rich family and his rich backers. And Joey well knew how rich they all were, he said, because they had all made their millions from his government, the ungrateful bastards. This line of thought, plus his desire to avoid de-Stalinization and his certainty of victory in the next election once people started comparing him with some imbecilic whoremaster of a Tory leader instead of with the perfection of God Almighty, went on for an hour, while Bill and I tried to stay awake and swivel our eyes to match Joey's walkabout. Then, thank a god, perfect and benevolent, he went back to bed.

Before eight that morning, though, he was on the phone making reservations to fly to St. John's. He had to return immediately, he told us, to save Newfoundland. Then, abruptly, he left for the airport and, from what I could gather later, he flew virtually non-stop back, coming down to earth only long enough to make his next flight, punching in about twenty-four continual hours of flying and sitting up between connections in airports.

Meanwhile, Bill Smallwood and I wended a more leisurely way back via Taipei, Tokyo, Honolulu, San Francisco, and New York to hear the news on arrival in St. John's that—surprise, surprise—Joey had thrown his hat in the ring. He was afraid for our beloved province, because he didn't think anyone else had the resources or organization, he said, to prevent the government from falling into the wrong hands of John Crosbie.

I wondered whether, if Joey had not been kept out of China by his good friend Pierre Elliott Trudeau, he might have stayed clear of the leadership race. Then, John Crosbie might have been elected Liberal leader, and he and Wells and Hickman and others would not have spent the next two years undermining Joey's government but instead might have gone to the people fairly quickly thereafter, before the PCs had a chance to get organized under a leader like Frank Moores, and the Liberal Government might have remained in power for years to come. But that's a huge "if" and a lot of "mights." Maybe Joey, as I'd told my father at the beginning, was going to run for the leadership no matter what, and the same bizarre scenario that actually happened would have spun itself out.

CHAPTER SEVEN

The Wrong Hands

THE LIBERAL LEADERSHIP convention was announced for Halloween of 1969, and the predictable back-from-the-dead jokes and zombie gags flew. In all, counting elected delegates, district executives, and ex-officios, there would be some 1,700 delegates. It would be the biggest political convention in our history. Crosbie claimed that the number of delegates was so much larger than normal in order to allow Joey to control the outcome, owing to his superior organization in the districts: it was out-and-out bias on the part of the party, John alleged, which was patently favouring Smallwood.

Clyde Wells came out for Crosbie, of course, and in the middle of October, just a couple of weeks before the convention, Alex Hickman announced his candidacy, having been deluded into thinking a pygmy could go up the middle between the two fanatical titans.

Joey asked me to be treasurer of his campaign funds. Cash flowed in like manna from heaven. During the course of the campaign, many hundreds of thousands of dollars were passed over to me by Joey himself in cash and cheques and I deposited the money in the "Action for Joey" bank account.

One afternoon, I came home from the doctor with a diagnosed strep throat and a prescription for antibiotics and bedrest. Penny was at her office, and a mature babysitter was downstairs. I went to bed and dropped in and out of high-temperature, semi-delirious sleep. Suddenly, I suffered what I took to be a horrific, fever-induced nightmare. Joey Smallwood's face was looming over me. There was no escaping his image even in my sickbed.

I opened and closed my eyes a few times, but the hallucination would not go away. Then I saw the babysitter behind him. "Here," said Joey. "For the campaign." He stretched out his arm, staying as far back as he could, and gingerly passed me a thick envelope. Then he turned around and left my bedroom. I hadn't spoken a word, although I did have a thought: "You can run—Christ, you can die—but you can't hide." He had sweet-talked or brazened-faced his way into my house and up the stairs, and he'd opened the door to my sickroom and barged on in. I looked in the envelope. The wad of money inside amounted to over $8,000. I had to roll out of bed, dress, go to the bank, and deposit the sum in the campaign account. When I was up and about in a couple of days, I told Joey we needed two at this treasurer job, and he appointed John Nolan to share the burden.

DURING THE LEADERSHIP campaign we developed the slate system for getting Joey's delegates elected. Slates of delegates for leadership conventions are commonplace everywhere in Canada now. But they were a new thing at that time, at least to me, and also, I do believe, to Newfoundland and the Liberal Party generally. The novelty of slates here may simply have been because there had been no such thing as a real, competitive, viciously fought, wide-open leadership convention involving more than one candidate before. I recall the essence and potential of the slate system being outlined to Joey by Eric Dawe, one of the canniest politicians I've ever encountered.

Eric—often called Eck or Eckie by us in deference to the absence of the "r" sound in his hometown, "Bay Wobbitts"—was dismissed as a simpleton by some who contrasted his unassuming and apparently artless nature to the brilliance of, say, an Ed Roberts. Indeed, the contrast in learning and intellectual appearance between him and Ed could not have been greater, but Eric himself got to the heart of the issue and the fallacy of outward appearances when he told me one day with his characteristic laugh, "Ed Roberts might know a lot more hard words than I do, but I'm twice as cute." Eric's essential modesty was encapsulated there, because, as will be seen from his political judgment later, he was in fact twice as cute as all the rest of us put together.

Our slate strategy required organizers for Joey to hand out a sheet of paper to everyone at the door of a meeting to elect delegates. On the paper were the names of the delegates to be elected at that meeting to support Joey—no more, no less. All of them had already committed themselves to vote for Joey at the convention. Any person at the meeting who supported Joey would simply vote for that entire slate of delegates whether the voter knew them all or not. Any delegate on the list who brought a load of supporters to the meeting would instruct them to vote for, and only for, himself and the other Joey delegates on the slate and no one else.

To ensure that the entire Joey slate would be elected, our organizers merely had to bus in enough supporters to form a majority at the meeting. It took a fair amount of hard slog and organization on the ground, but it worked with a vengeance, and I believe considerable time passed before Crosbie's campaign cottoned on to it and started to fully utilize the slate system as well. The fact that all the Liberal MHAs were out in their districts organizing for the slates was a tremendous leg up for Joey and a terrible handicap for Crosbie.

One of John Crosbie's main men in his campaign was Rob Parker, at the time a son-in-law of a Liberal senator appointed at Joey's behest, Eric Cook. Rob lived a few houses up the street from me, and had been employed in some way by John Crosbie, when he'd been Joey's minister of Health, to help usher in medicare. (Later Parker would become a media personality, a short-term MP, and a creepy spokesman for the tobacco industry.) Now, he asked me for a meeting, and I went along, mostly out of sociability and curiosity.

With him was some fellow from the mainland hired to help run Crosbie's campaign. Both of them tried to persuade me to defect from Joey's camp and join John's. My wife, after all, was Crosbie's first cousin, they urged in support of their argument. Why didn't we join our own kind? Now, I liked John, but these two Upper Canadian types, with their contrast between the "low-lifes" supporting Smallwood and the "better sort" behind Crosbie, made it easy for me to say no. Later I learned they were telling people that they didn't mind their failure to recruit me, because they didn't think I was all that bright, anyway. No argument from me on that score, but still, for the hell of it, I thought I'd show them that, in fact, they just might be even less bright than me.

I travelled to my own district of White Bay South and dug in. Success there was by no means assured. Crosbie had some good workers in the area who were very actively organizing on the Baie Verte Peninsula. Brian Peckford, the future premier from Green Bay next door, for example, was certainly no slouch, and he and others like Bill Eaton, mayor of Baie Verte, were vigorously creating Crosbie slates. It was a hard-fought battle. Future premier Tom Rideout became a tremendous help in Joey's cause. In the three or four meetings held in my district, we elected every single delegate on our Joey slate.

Proof of how easily we could have lost some or all delegates to Crosbie came from the adjoining district of White Bay North. There, MHA Ed Roberts, who was also organizing for Joey, lost several delegates to Crosbie. Apparently, that happened because Peter Gardiner, head of Chester Dawe Limited, which had large lumber-woods operations up there, was working to elect delegates for John.

Whatever the reason for the loss of delegates, Joey never stopped blaspheming and denigrating Ed Roberts to me about it. Joey characterized Ed's district to me as the most Liberal district on earth, containing the greatest percentage of Smallwood supporters in the entire world, and yet Ed . . . the contrast between me and Ed, according to Joey, was very evident. Oh, Ed was exceedingly intelligent on paper—a near genius—but he possessed utterly no street smarts, and was completely devoid of practical political sense, and was to the nth degree unpleasant and disagreeable. He'd had a real dilemma with Roberts when he was his executive assistant, the premier told me: because by his intelligence and knowledge Ed had made himself indispensable, but by his arrogance and nastiness he had made himself insufferable. Joey solved the predicament, he said, by giving Ed a good slog in the arse, metaphorically speaking, every couple of weeks.

From those descriptions, I had a pretty good idea what Joey must be saying about me to Ed and others whenever I displeased him or refused to go along with some lunacy. But whatever he might say now or in the future about either of us, or whatever wedge he tried to drive between us, it did not prevent us from combining to take him on over the oil refinery and the linerboard mill and his wholly unwarranted clinging on to power two years later.

But the real coup in my contest with Crosbie's two mainland organizers over who was stupider—them or me—occurred in the Tory district of St. John's East. This was the veritable centre of the Crosbie universe. The hordes of Crosbie supporters there were buttressed by the many Tories who would join his forces in any effort to oust Joey. It was also where my wife, Penny, and I happened to live—just down the street from Crosbie's man Parker.

At the time, Penny was at least seven months pregnant with our daughter, Toby, but that didn't stop her from becoming a human dynamo in organizing for the election of Joey's slate. I remember John Crosbie and his wife, Jane, and their retinue coming into the hall with such confidence at the beginning of the meeting to elect delegates, and I watched their self-assured demeanour gradually changing to that of a person clobbered across the head with a crowbar as the evening's results unfolded. Penny and her team won nearly all the delegates for Joey in St. John's East.

The Crosbie organizers were gobsmacked and shell-shocked. Some of the more genteel supporters of Crosbie, members of the St. John's east elite and professional classes, muttered that Penny Ayre (Rowe) had betrayed her heritage and dirtied her hands by associating with such low-life types as those supporters of Joey. We had such a great laugh I forgot to ask Parker and his Ontario pal who they thought was stupid now.

We heard through the grapevine that Crosbie's disastrous delegate meeting in St. John's East was the greatest morale destroyer for him and his gang in the entire campaign. Joey himself was stunned by the outcome. Earlier, he had been so skeptical of any success there that he had offered a beautiful silk carpet he had bought on our trip to Hong Kong as a prize if even one delegate, just one single delegate, was elected for him in St. John's East district. He was as good as his word. He put the lovely carpet up on tickets for a draw and it was won by a woman delegate on York Street.

During the lead-up to the convention, Joey occasionally invited some supporters to lunch with our usual crowd at his dining room. When Joey was with you by yourself, like during the trip to Hong Kong, he was soft-spoken, and a good two-way conversation could take place. But when others besides the usual familiars were present, he went from Dr. Jekyll to Mr. Hyde. That was even more so when a woman was present, especially one of his colleagues' wives. Then he tended in a forceful voice to cut his comrades off or interrupt us far more than normal, particularly the husband, exercising a little man's need to assert himself as the guy in charge in front of the females. I couldn't help thinking how hard it was for anyone to remain on a friendly basis with the old fart and what a strain he continually placed on your loyalty and camaraderie. Just about everyone he was ever close to, ultimately and inevitably, became estranged from him.

Some came back later, but only when he was no longer in a position to dominate or humiliate them.

Joey was always talking, in print as well as conversation, about this good friend and that old friend, but in fact I don't think Joey had, when I knew him, anyone who could be considered a friend. He had thought that Greg Power was his best friend until their long, hostile gap of enmity began after Greg had left the government in the late 1950s. Joey told me that he and Greg had been so close in the old days the rumour was spread that they were homosexual. But that was a common accusation in Newfoundland politics, he said. Sir William Coaker and Sir Robert Bond had been subjected to it, but with perhaps more reason. I asked him if he and Harold Horwood had been good friends or merely colleagues during the Confederation battle. Never close friends, he replied.

Joey had considered Valdmanis a good friend until shortly before the economic saviour went to jail. (Anyone I talked to who'd seen Valdmanis around Joey considered Valdmanis's relationship to be that of an obsequious, sly, ingratiating, heel-clicking ass-kisser.)

As a young man Smallwood had naively thought Ches Crosbie was his friend, especially when Crosbie invested in his *Book of Newfoundland* project, but he learned over the years that Crosbie essentially considered him an amusing, occasionally useful buffoon.

The closest anyone ever came to being friends over the long haul, in my observation, were probably Al Vardy and Les Curtis. Vardy had sold ads in Joey's *Book of Newfoundland* on commission in the 1930s and made pretty good money with his big voice and his big brash face, and they became friends from that, plus their involvement in radio. What was surprising to me during my time was that, on the surface at least, he'd apparently forgiven Vardy for treating him with contempt during the late 1930s and early 1940s.

Joey told me how, anytime he had bummed a cigarette off Vardy to feed his three-pack-a-day habit, Vardy would throw his pack on the floor, forcing Joey to get down and pick it up and remove a cigarette. Some of us didn't think Joey's modern attitude to Vardy was so much forgiveness as convenience—he found Vardy's flexible morality very useful in his various dealings.

Joey's original two volumes of the *Books of Newfoundland* had failed to sell well and mostly stayed in storage until the Canadians and Americans came here during the war and bought them all up as collector's items. But his later four volumes, published when he was premier, were successful immediately. They were reputed to have made him $100,000. I heard some representatives of businesses and organizations muttering that Joey, through Al Vardy, had twisted their arms to force them to advertise therein. I remember Joey sitting in the House of Assembly through tedious debates, giving every impression of loving the democratic process for its own sake, while he proofread pages of his books day after day, away from the phone and nuisances of the office. And as far as friendship was concerned, the relationship I saw between Joey and Al was more like master and menial servant as Joey waved his sherry glass at him for a refill and Al heaved himself up, po-faced, and trudged over to oblige.

One time, in the premier's office, Joey, apropos of nothing related to our discussion that I could see—purely on a whim—went behind his desk to his intercom, pressed a button, and bawled, "Al, are you there?" The reply came that he was but that he was in the middle of an important meeting. "Al, come up." Vardy said he would finish there and be up as quick as he could. Joey's voice rose in volume: "Come up, Al." He walked around his desk resuming the discussion that had nothing to do with Vardy. And when Al's presence outside was announced a couple of minutes later, he was made to cool his heels in the anteroom for a good ten minutes. I guessed that pal Joey's loyalty to dear friend Al entailed a repayment many times over for those cigarettes thrown to the floor.

Attorney General Les Curtis was the only person I ever heard calling Smallwood "Joe," except for Geoff Stirling. Joey always said that Les's sole job was to keep him out of jail. That was a full-time occupation, said Les. Once I told Les that his name Curtis probably came from the French word *courtois*, meaning courteous, polite. "That makes sense," said Al Vardy with a smirk. "A couple of weeks ago when I was introducing him to a group of Japanese businessmen, Les said to me in front of them that there was no point giving him their names, since 'those slitty-eyed bastards all look alike to me.'"

"What nonsense," said Les, unconvincingly.

Les Curtis was the MHA for Twillingate district. When ten years later I would become the member there, I found that it was well-known by everyone in town that he would prepare like a doctor for the operating room in the Twillingate hospital and go in and watch operations. Evidently he considered it to be one of his perks as the member for the district.

Once, Ed Roberts, Les, Joey, and I were in New York on something Joey was cooking up for the province. Whatever it was, it required a pledge or earnest of tens of thousands of dollars by way of a guarantee in order to keep it alive. Normally, this would be a government guarantee okayed by an order-in-council passed by the cabinet. But for some reason—probably it was a weekend—such a backing was unobtainable at that precise time, and Joey suggested that we all put up our personal guarantees, just as his hero Sir Robert Bond had done, until it could be replaced in a day or so by the government guarantee. Everyone agreed to it, except for Les Curtis. He refused and his reason was so compelling we couldn't argue against it: he was the only one among us who had the money to cover the guarantee if it was ever called.

One morning at a Liberal Party convention in Ottawa, some of us sat at the same table as Les and Mrs. Curtis for breakfast in the dining room of the Château Laurier. When Les left his chair for a few minutes, Mrs. Curtis loaded up her purse with packets of sugar, marmalade, salt, jam, coffee cream, and pepper from the table. I later expressed my surprise to Joey at what I'd seen, and he replied that she had no idea whatsoever that Les was wealthy—worth millions—and the pinching of the condiments was her contribution to their economizing for this trip.

When Steve Neary and I were waiting to go into Joey's office one afternoon, we saw a man coming out of Les's office close by. I could hardly believe my eyes. The man looked like a replica of Les, thirty or forty years younger. He and Steve exchanged greetings in passing and Steve told me he lived on Bell Island and was a big Liberal organizer there. Giving me the man's name—it wasn't Curtis—Steve said, "He doesn't look half-bad like Les, does he? He was in to get some money."

Relaxing after lunch one afternoon, Les told us that in his late twenties, when he'd gotten married, he'd been forced to get a circumcision. Up to that time, every erection he had was so painful that he was still a virgin at twenty-nine. Well into his seventies by the time of this post-lunch reminiscence, and known as the Horny Attorney for his active extracurricular sex life, he now brought a sad and wistful expression to his old face. "It breaks my heart," he said with great poignancy, "whenever I think of all that time I wasted."

Having spent three years nearly every day eating lunch with him in the dining room, and attending various meetings, and travelling with him, I happened to spot Les Curtis at a function at Government House a few years after he'd retired from politics. He had physically and mentally deteriorated and was sitting on a chair on the lawn when Penny and I approached him. I said, "Hello, Mr. Curtis," but he looked at me blankly. He didn't know who I was. Then he looked at Penny standing next to me. Penny had spent perhaps a few hours in total in his presence stretched over the years. But immediately, upon seeing her, he turned back to me and said, "Oh—hello, Bill." He knew me, his long-time colleague, only by the sight, and his fleeting memory, of my wife.

PEOPLE SOMETIMES CALLED Joey a dictator. I found that he did run a one-man show, but it was not your typical tyranny. It was too loose for that. I would describe him as a despot by whim. He knew nothing about team leadership. There would be long periods of Joey not interfering at all in what you were doing, but suddenly that would be interspersed with hands-on interference and the expectation, when he had some brain wave, that you must hop right to it. But other than that he left you alone.

One time, after I mentioned to him that I needed a couple of days of peace and quiet to review some hefty documents in connection with the DREE program, he suggested that I use the government fishing cabin on the Gander River that summer weekend. I had never been there before and I never went there afterwards. During my one and only two-night planned visit to the cabin, he tracked me down by two-way radio on the first night and asked me to come back to St. John's immediately for an emergency meeting on an urgent matter. Whatever the urgent matter was, I now have no memory of it or any idea whatsoever of what it could have been, except perhaps some leadership issue. I do recall concluding later that it had only been a capricious exercise of his authority.

I remember another occasion shortly afterwards when Penny and I had a bridge foursome at our house on a Friday night. When the telephone rang, I made the mistake of answering it. Joey himself was on the other end. He needed me urgently up at his leadership headquarters. He didn't ask what I was doing or if I was occupied—I just had to come immediately. I told him I was occupied entertaining some friends, and having received that intelligence, Joey described the matter at headquarters as urgent and crucial and my personal presence became absolutely essential at once.

Leaving my guests startled and wondering, I departed, with my apologies, for his headquarters. There, eight or ten other ministers and members were standing around a table busy at something. The urgent need turned out to be counting and sorting the hundreds of applications for Liberal Party membership his workers had brought in from outlying districts, and making sure that each one was accompanied by the required one-dollar membership fee for delivery to party headquarters the next day. It would have been a nice piece of weekend work for a few high-school students to make a little pocket money.

I joined in for an hour of counting and sorting, while my guests and my wife at home sat on their hands waiting for their fourth player to come back. I knew Joey's campaign was not that badly organized, so I figured he must be doing this to test the depths of loyalty in his colleagues, or maybe there was just no concept in his head that he might be imposing on others by such a total lack of consideration. I watched for my chance and made my escape. Needless to say, I never answered the phone at home again while Joey was premier if I was engaged in anything I didn't want to be dragged away from.

Joey smarted, however, under the accusation, constantly thrown at him, that he was a dictator. Later, while writing one of his books, he twisted the arms of many of his former colleagues into composing denials that he was in fact a despot. I had to laugh when I read all the disclaimers, including one from me, because it was a little like each of us playing the role of an army private saying to a tyrannical drill sergeant, "No, sir, it's just as you say, sir: you are not a dictator, sir."

AT LAST, THE Liberal leadership convention at the stadium started that Halloween, 1969. Smallwood billeted many of his delegates on the Marine Atlantic ferry, the *William Carson*, then in St. John's harbour. Remarkably, having survived that event, the *Carson* would swiftly sink eight years later, in 1977, after striking a small iceberg off Battle Harbour. All passengers and crew by luck and skill would survive.

Crosbie organizers at the leadership convention claimed that Joey was confining his delegates in the ferry and in railway train cars to keep them from defecting to John's side. A strong but forlorn hope was evident among the Crosbie-ites that many delegates committed to Smallwood were going see the light on the floor of the convention and switch over in their hundreds to John as their messiah just as soon as they got a chance to cast their ballots in secret.

Clyde Wells did his best to continue his role of courageous fighter against tyranny. As one of Crosbie's chief organizers, he or someone in his retinue sent word ahead that he was coming to the convention despite Smallwood's stated opposition to his presence. Joey now rose to the bait. He told us that Wells did not have the proper credentials to attend—he had not indicated that he was a supporter of the party and the leader as required—and that the party officials must be advised of Smallwood's implacable opposition and Wells must be kept out of the stadium. A follow-through on Joey's instructions, of course, would have garnered Wells all the publicity he craved, and would have shown Smallwood and his gang in the usual very poor light. Two or three mainland journalists at the event had already asked me why two "intelligent and educated" young men like Ed Roberts and myself were "heavies" for the oppressor Smallwood.

Ed and I told Joey not to be so foolish about Wells. What an uproar such an action by the premier as leadership candidate would have caused. And to what end? If Wells was allowed in without protest, it would be a non-story. Finally, Joey, who had become a classic case of someone preferring to do himself untold damage than suffer a perceived indignity to his honour or authority, very reluctantly agreed with our argument. Wells came in without any of the fuss that had been expected from the entrance of the white knight.

The famous convention itself had to be the least exciting leadership process in the history of Canada. The speeches were uninspired and the voting dragged on and on because of the number of candidates, but because the decision took only one ballot there was no buildup of suspense. The Smallwood delegates and supporters on the floor and in the seats were rather subdued, which may have given hope to the Crosbie supporters, many of whom appeared to be young non-voting observers caught up in their own hoopla.

I recall only one mildly humorous incident. A co-chairman of the convention was Herman Batten, former MP for Humber-St. George's-St. Barbe. An Ottawa journalist who was there, to report knowledgeably on the convention, read from a note on Batten's career, and said to me, "Oh, right, he's the former MP for Humber Street, George Street, Barbe."

When the result of the voting was announced, Joseph Smallwood had received 1,070 votes, John Crosbie 440, Alexander Hickman 187, Randy Joyce thirteen, Peter Cook three, and Vincent Spencer one. Many of the Crosbie and Joyce supporters instantly went nuts with disappointment and grief at Smallwood's victory. They screamed, cried, threw their placards and paraphernalia to the floor, shouted insults at the winner, and swore their heads off.

Randy Joyce set his Liberal membership card alight and burned it. Some followers of the losers gave the Nazi salute and chanted "Sieg heil" over and over, which was portrayed by various media, not as a misguided trivialization of the actual horrors of Nazism or a desecration of the memory of those who had suffered under Hitler, but as a legitimate reaction against Smallwood's "dictatorship."

Alex Hickman joined the winner up on the stage to congratulate him, and Joey then issued to "Mr. Crosbie" an opportunity to come up and make his election as leader unanimous. I could see much agitation in the Crosbie camp. Jane remained calm, though the strain and frustration were etched on her face. Crosbie was being barked at by those around him, especially Clyde Wells. Karl Wells told me at the CBC station much later that, at the time, he had been standing right in front of the Crosbie platform. Clyde Wells was beside himself with rage, his face red as a lobster as he screamed at the still-seated John Crosbie. He seemed to be trying to stop Crosbie from going up to the podium to join Smallwood. Crosbie had to actually jerk his arm away from Clyde's viselike grip. Karl said he heard Clyde say, "No, John, don't give the old bastard the satisfaction."

Crosbie at last got away from the enraged Clyde Wells and went up to congratulate Smallwood. After Crosbie arrived on the podium, Joey pointedly ignored him and kept talking to those around him. Crosbie and Hickman both looked about as comfortable up there as a couple of clergyman at a strip joint. When Smallwood did deign to notice Crosbie, he shook his proffered hand as if it were a dead rat, and turned his back again. On the surface, Clyde had been right. It must have been galling for Crosbie to give the old bastard the satisfaction of going up there and be humiliated, but for him not to have gone up would have been characterized as the action of a graceless lout. And besides, if revenge was any consolation for Crosbie, that would be only a couple more years in coming.

A LOT OF money was spent on those leadership campaigns. John Crosbie said that he went through over half a million dollars on his effort—in other words, over $1,000 for every vote he received at the convention. His brother Andrew told me afterwards that John owed over a quarter of a million to the Bank of Montreal. He said John paid off the debt by selling to Andrew his shares in Crosbie companies. I found that surprising because I had clearly understood John to state that he'd sold all his shares in the family companies before joining Smallwood's government in 1966 so that he would not be in any conflict of interest.

How much did Joey spend? At least a million dollars, also about $1,000 a vote for the 1,070 votes he received. Alex Hickman went into debt, although his campaign was very short. He had presented himself as the sensible compromise candidate, a posture rejected by all but 187 delegates. The Bank of Nova Scotia, whom Hickman had acted for as a lawyer before politics, was more co-operative. To the raised eyebrows of many, there was a report that the bank forgave Hickman's large loan after he became a Supreme Court judge.

RIGHT AFTER THE convention, Joey gloated that he had made good on his promise to bury Crosbie ten feet deep. He had beaten Ches the father during the Confederation battle, he said to some of us, and now he had trampled and buried John the son.

Understandably, in the future, Crosbie and Wells increased the ferocity of their attacks on Joey in the House. They called themselves Reform Liberals and the media loved them. One of my university friends, who was reporter sitting in the press gallery every day, told me he thought Crosbie and Wells were absolutely brilliant in their questions and debates, and their savaging of Smallwood. Most members of the media, he thought, shared his view.

Besides being knowledgeable and articulate on government issues, they also needled Joey mercilessly, giving him, for the first time in his political life, better than he threw out. I recall one time Joey used the word "indubitably" and Wells slapped it back at him, articulating it in the most precious way possible, making fun of Joey and his fancy words: in-dew-bit-ab-lay. It was a small matter, miniscule in importance, but it signalled a complete change in tone in the House—a reversal—someone poking fun at Joey wherever he turned, and on every level. They even referred to the premier now and then as a "crackie"—the little yapping St. John's mutt.

At some point during all this, Smallwood made a deal with New Brunswick oil magnate K. C. Irving for the building of a string of Irving service stations and restaurants across Newfoundland. Grants of land from the government were involved, including, unbelievably, lovely Shell Bird Island on the Humber River near Corner Brook. In the legislature, Clyde Wells was able to tear political strips off Joey's hide at the very notion of defiling that beauty spot with a gas station, and the premier had to retreat from that part of the deal in total disarray.

With their professional training Crosbie and Wells easily caught Joey in an illegality when he neglected to table guarantee agreements in the House within the fifteen-day legal requirement. There was no penalty, but the lapse was widely remarked in the media and certainly embarrassing for the premier: was the tough old parliamentary pro losing his grip?

One time Crosbie and Wells saw that the House was without a quorum and, acting quickly, they forced the Speaker to adjourn the House, catching Smallwood, as one Opposition member elegantly phrased it, "with his drawers down around his ankles." During the ensuing hullabaloo in the legislature, Joey accused Crosbie of forcing his way into the Speaker's office and physically threatening the highest official of the House. I didn't hear Crosbie denying it. Whatever happened in the Speaker's office, the Speaker disobeyed the premier's arguments for probably the first time since Confederation. Rumour had it that His Honour didn't relish the thought of being thrown bodily out of his ninth-floor window. Agreeing with Crosbie's position on the rules of procedure, he kept the House adjourned. It was the first of some very traumatic moments for Joey.

Soon after the leadership convention, meanwhile, Hickman and his supporter Val Earle left the Liberal Party—some would say they were shoved out, since Smallwood kept them out of the cabinet—and they joined the Tory caucus. In just three years, from 1966 to 1969, Joey had succeeded in growing the Opposition to his government in the House from only three members to eleven, some of whom became very effective in their attacks on him. And we kids in our twenties and thirties were now the senior ministers.

CHAPTER EIGHT

The Decline of Joey, the Rise of Frank

AFTER THE 1969 leadership convention, Ed Roberts and I ended up carrying the government slop bucket for John Shaheen's Come By Chance refinery and John C. Doyle's Stephenville linerboard mill. We began to develop an appreciation for what John Crosbie and Clyde Wells and Alex Hickman had gone through. The departments we were responsible for had nothing to do with those two developments, but Joey started to include both of us, and to a certain extent John Nolan, in discussions and negotiations and travels involving the projects.

Lest we got the idea that this was caused by Joey's admiration for our superior abilities, Les Curtis put forward at lunch one day in Smallwood's absence his theory for the inclusion of Ed and myself: as Lyndon Johnson said about J. Edgar Hoover, the premier would rather have us two pigheaded know-it-alls inside the tent pissing out than outside the tent pissing in. Whatever Joey's reasoning was, Ed and I spent much of the next two years flitting about from St. John's to London to Paris to New York sticking our fingers in the holes of various government dykes.

During one of our visits to London, Edmund de Rothschild invited the premier, Ed, and me to lunch in the dining room at N M Rothschild & Sons. Joey's office had booked us at the Savoy Hotel and Joey got the concierge there to order a burgundy-coloured Bentley, complete with liveried driver, to drop us off at the de Rothschild premises in the city. Ed and I looked at each other: our boss was certainly a socialist with panache.

This was the second time I'd had lunch with Eddie de Rothschild. He'd been a principal in Brinco, struggling to develop Churchill Falls, when he'd invited me, as a Newfoundland student in England in 1964-1965, to lunch at their head office. When Smallwood introduced Ed Roberts and me now, I mentioned the earlier visit, and de Rothschild surprised me by saying, yes, he remembered it. The firm had been at temporary premises at the time while renovations at headquarters were being effected. I was impressed by his memory, but then he astonished me by recalling that we'd had a rather lively discussion back then about a book I'd recently read by Frederic Morton on the de Rothschild dynasty.

"Yes," I replied. "You said at the time that the book was full of inaccuracies."

"And it's still full of inaccuracies," laughed Eddie. Then he said we'd also talked about a play in the West End, Iris Murdoch's *A Severed Head*. He recalled it because at that time the title was an accurate prediction of his own future if he didn't soon get the Churchill Falls development up and running.

And that was the last conversational exchange I remember during this entire lunch, because the only voice I heard for the next two hours was our premier's. I could have been back in my family living room with Joey and his entourage when I was in my teens. I would confirm to myself at lunch this day that never in my life had I been in the company of anyone who was able to hold court, and hold attention, and monopolize conversation in any group, high or low, like Joseph R. Smallwood.

There were ten or a dozen people at the table, all men. Ed Roberts and I were steered to the bottom of the table, well below the salt. We were joined there by a couple of other young men who looked like they might be interesting to have a chat with, but we didn't or couldn't converse, because our attention was riveted on what was happening at the head of the table. Eddie de Rothschild sat in the middle. To his right, the place of honour, he had placed Premier Smallwood. On his left sat Sir Alec Douglas-Home, the former fourteenth Earl of Home and a former prime minister of the United Kingdom from 1963 to 1964. To Joey's right sat Ted Heath, former high-ranking cabinet minister, now leader of the Conservative Party, and soon to become prime minister of the United Kingdom. To Douglas-Home's left sat Baron Philippe de Rothschild of France, a banking magnate, a former Grand Prix race-car driver, a writer and producer of plays and movies, and a grower of some of the world's top wines in Bordeaux. In other words, Smallwood was up there surrounded by four of the most interesting and insightful men in all London that day. But they divulged little of interest or discernment over the next couple of hours. Joey held forth non-stop for the duration.

He ranged from the mighty Churchill Falls and Sir Winston's "grand imperial concept—imperial, not imperialistic," to his first time in London as a young man haranguing the multitudes on socialism at Speakers' Corner in Hyde Park, which evoked chuckles at the table now over one's charming, juvenile idealism, and he passed on to how, some argued, his intervention had made the great intellectual and former socialist Pierre Trudeau prime minister of Canada. He touched on how Newfoundland had won the First World War owing to Prime Minister Lloyd George's adaptation of Newfoundland's ancient convoy system to allow ships to cross the Atlantic in relative safety and thereby loosening the German U-boat stranglehold on Britain. He reminded everyone that

Newfoundland had won the Second World War because, in Churchill's earlier words during the first conflict, Newfoundlanders were the best small-boat men in the world.

Some of this was taken as tongue-in-cheek hyperbole, of course, but Joey was so glib, so ready with the right word, so confident of his vocal powers, and so assured of his own quick and easy recall of experience and knowledge of any subject he broached, that this exalted company were as dwarfed as his own ministers from the 1950s would have been sitting around this table now in their oversize homburgs. Even the two leading Conservative statesmen were reduced to elegant grunts. When one of them tried to jump in with a sentence of his own, his contribution seemed ponderous and pathetically inadequate.

Joey next gave Baron Philippe de Rothschild, the top Bordeaux vineyard owner, some tips on wine. He had told me long before this that Valdmanis had started a wine cellar back home and tried to make him a sophisticated oenophile. Some of us would joke among ourselves that most of Smallwood's wine knowledge came from leafing through a *Time-Life* picture book on wines of the world one day while getting a haircut in his office. But no one here at this lunch could interrupt the flow of words, the authoritative delivery, the embellished truisms, the misconceptions presented in a way that allowed the listeners to take them as jests. For example, Joey said that Dr. Jim McGrath, one of his colleagues and a magnificent gourmet, had told him that immersing your fingers in a glass of water and then flicking a few drops of the water into your glass of vintage wine was a good practice. Philippe de Rothschild replied that he was sure it *was* a good practice—good for the fingers. Then he laughed, not at Joey but with him, as if they had collaborated on embellishing Dr. McGrath's amusing story.

At length, after two hours of it, Eddie de Rothschild rose and said that this was the first occasion since the last visit to this dining room by Sir Winston Churchill himself that the designated time for lunch had been exceeded at all, let alone by a full hour like today. As everyone made their way to the door, I heard former prime minister Douglas-Home stage whisper to future prime minister Heath: "A most remarkable man. He is said to have read forty thousand books in his life." Heath replied, "Quite STROdnry." That exchange started me wondering how come Britain's Conservative leaders seemed to be too dense to master elementary arithmetic.

As long as I'd known Smallwood, he kept saying that he had read 40,000 books in his lifetime. So, after the Rothschild lunch, when he brought Ed Roberts and me to some antiquarian bookstores near our hotel, I couldn't help myself: I raised what Douglas-Home had said and I started computing out loud the mental math that Joey's feat of reading required. At the time he was about seventy years old; *ergo*, if he'd been reading seriously for sixty years, that would allow just over 20,000 days in total for reading, which meant that he had read nearly two books a day every single day of his life since he was ten. I didn't draw the obvious conclusion, to wit, that his claim was utter bullshit. I did notice, though, that he bristled at the time and stayed irritated at me for most of the trip, but the next time I heard him mention his life's reading total to someone, it had dropped to 20,000. Now he had read "only" one book a day, every single day of his life.

Joey did have a great collection of Newfoundland books, paraphernalia, and gewgaws at home. Whenever he was in London, he would drag whoever was with him during off hours to stores up and down Charing Cross Road, and in Chelsea, and further afield, seeking to add to his several thousand items. (I was able to pick up a Cook map of the west coast of Newfoundland, containing my mother's childhood home of Bonne Bay, under his guidance.)

Another time in London he took Ed Roberts and me down to a bookstore in Guildford, over an hour away, because he'd learned that a particular Newfoundland book was for sale there. He told us he was collecting for the Newfoundland and Labrador people, and he considered it a crime, if an old book from or about our homeland was for sale, to permit it to be bought outside the province. He was going to turn his entire collection over to the Newfoundland archives.

OUR REASON FOR visiting London on this occasion was the oil refinery. One of the few redeeming features of the Come By Chance enterprise was that, from the start, it was an out-and-out scam at the expense of the federal government. The refinery was a provincial crown corporation, which gave it tax-free status. The feds would lose taxes on the output and export of the refined oil. Pleased with ripping Ottawa off on the taxes, Joey also shamed them into a commitment to build a huge $23 million wharf in Come By Chance entirely at federal expense. I sometimes wondered whether Trudeau ever asked himself at any point if it had really been worth it to win the Liberal leadership with Joey's support.

Dealing with John Shaheen was like no other experience on earth, except for dealing with John Doyle. But we'll come to Doyle. I'd first heard of Shaheen when I got a summer job with a survey team connected with the construction of a small refinery for Golden Eagle in Holyrood by Shaheen Natural Resources. If I'd known that the success of that operation would help lead to the Come By Chance refinery and that, less than a dozen years later, I'd be experiencing a wild ride on the government roller coaster regarding that project, I might have been tempted to sabotage some of my survey readings in Holyrood.

John Shaheen was a great operator. He had a management scheme cooked up with the provincial government which paid him an income as if he was CEO of a private corporation, plus he had an option to purchase the refinery for next to nothing down the road. He had hired Richard Nixon as his US lawyer before Tricky Dick became president. That gave him cachet among certain business types in North America. And over in England he hired Lord Arnold Goodman to deal with the Export Credit Guarantee Department (ECGD) of the British government in connection with the refinery. Goodman, a life peer, was the leading lawyer in London at the time, being solicitor and political adviser to the likes of Prime Minister Harold Wilson. Over there they called him "Wilson's Mr. Fix-It."

On one of our visits to London, Shaheen told us before we were ushered into the lord's presence that Goodman was famous for his brilliance and memory. He cited some local legal lore that His Lordship had listened just once for fifteen minutes to a financial presentation from a corporation at a meeting recently, and then dictated it all back to his secretary word for word, and word-perfect. I don't think I endeared myself by saying, "Impressive parlour trick, but someone should tell him about the invention of the tape recorder."

I must have inherited a certain gene from my mother because, when I met Lord Goodman for the first time, what came into my mind was, "bloody phony—big, bloated, loudmouth phony." But not everyone agreed with that appraisal, judging by his appointments, past and future. He held some nineteen national chairmanships, from the Arts Council of Great Britain to the Newspaper Proprietors Association, plus untold directorships ranging from the Royal Opera House to governor of the Royal Shakespeare Theatre and Senior Fellow of the Royal College of Art. Shortly after our dealings with him, he would be appointed as a Companion of Honour, an Order personally headed by the Queen herself.

I was glad to see at the time, though, that the satirical British periodical *Private Eye* was not in awe of him. They referred to him as Lord "Two Dinners" Goodman—a reference to his girth—and portrayed him as a sinister power behind the throne who exerted excessive influence on the British establishment. According to a television documentary I heard about after his death called *The Gangster and the Pervert Peer*, Goodman was one of the chief parties responsible for suppressing information gathered by journalists that uncovered how his friend Lord Robert Boothby, "the pervert peer," was responsible for protecting from justice the Krays—the murderous London gangsters—among whom he had a lover.

In any event, Goodman was Shaheen's London lawyer, and he helped induce Smallwood to pass secret "comfort letters" to ECGD and to the historic merchant bank Kleinwort-Benson, giving the impression that the Newfoundland government would stand behind the refinery's financing. Ed Roberts and I were not one bit happy about that when we learned about it. After ascertaining from our Justice department that the letters would have no legal effect if anyone ever tried to enforce them, which kept us from resigning on the spot, we nevertheless told Joey that we would not tolerate any repetition of such crap, but would quit forthwith.

At the Savoy Hotel, where we were staying in London, one of Shaheen's henchmen just happened to encounter me in the corridor outside my door that same evening and engaged me in a little chat. He spoke with a New Jersey accent, which I wouldn't hear in its full glory again until I watched the Mafia series *The Sopranos* on TV over thirty years later. Shaheen's henchman made some comments about Mr. Shaheen and Mr. Smallwood not being very pleased with Roberts and me, and that the project would be going ahead whether we were alive on this earth or not. No one was indispensable. I laughed in his face and went on into my room. Listening to Tony Soprano holding forth murderously years afterwards, though, I was kind of happy I hadn't heard him before that long-ago chat in the corridor of the Savoy Hotel.

On another trip we all ended up at the famous Hôtel de Crillon on Place de la Concorde in Paris as Shaheen tried to raise money or get the backing of French government agencies there. I'd been away so much from home that this time my wife, Penny, came with me. (I'd been in British Columbia when our daughter, Toby, was suddenly born—after midnight in Newfoundland, before midnight in BC, so that I have always wished her happy birthday the day before the actual anniversary of her birth.) Our full entourage to Paris included Shaheen's people, together with Joey, Les Curtis, Ed Roberts, John Nolan, and me. Freeman White of CJON television news also travelled with us to report on our doings. We seemed to spend a lot of time being dragged around to nightclubs and supper clubs like Le Crazy Horse, Moulin Rouge, Scheherazade, the Lido, and the like, where we were supposed to ogle rigid bare breasts and where waiters gave us cheap champagne with swizzle sticks, which, because we were vulgar North Americans, we were expected to use to get rid of the very raison d'etre of champagne in the first place—the bubbles.

One day all the rest of the group except for Ed, Penny, and me took off to Amsterdam because some possible financing prospect had arisen there. In an amateurish game of cloak and dagger, no doubt an echo of Shaheen's spying days, we three were left behind as decoys, intended to fool the French government people into thinking that Shaheen wasn't trying to two-time them.

Meanwhile, a big dinner had been arranged at the celebrated Maxim's restaurant for that night, since all the others in our party were due back early that evening. Reservations had been made there for some twelve people. While Ed and Penny went on over to Maxim's as an advance guard at the appointed time, I tried to contact our absent members to see exactly when they would be arriving back. I discovered that they would be delayed until very late and would miss dinner.

I had to trundle on over to Maxim's with the bad news. On entering I saw our big table set for a dozen right in the middle of the restaurant, with Ed and Penny looking a little anxious as they waited in the bar. The table was covered with fresh flowers, and bottles of champagne had been placed in buckets, chilling, all around it. Diners at their nearby tables were looking expectantly about for the entrance of some big celebrity megastars.

I broke the sad tiding to my dinner companions, and informed the maître d'. You never saw anyone as fast on their feet as those waiters. The Kirov Ballet troupe had nothing on them. Within thirty seconds, all flowers were whisked off the table, the table dismantled, the champagne made to vanish, and we sorry three were placed at a small table next to the swinging doors leading in and out of the kitchen, where we had to fight to get noticed all night.

Another evening we were taken to a starred Michelin restaurant where our dinner companions now included some Parisian merchant bankers. One of them was a one-eyed Austrian duke sporting a black eye patch, who was as ancient and ugly as sin. They seated him next to Penny. Despite the fact that I, her husband, was sitting across the table from him, Cyclops the duke spent the night calling Penny "Ma Belle" and inviting her to go to bed with him for the time of her life. Either he thought Penny and I were more sophisticated, in the European mode, than we strictly speaking were, or he was too inbred and stupid to learn his lesson from having already lost one eye though amorous adventure. However, there was no way I was going to shut him up, because it was worth the cash just watching Penny struggling all night not to burst out laughing every two minutes.

BACK HOME TO St. John's again, and in response to the constant demands from the media and the barrage of criticism from Crosbie and Wells regarding the Come By Chance oil refinery, a cocksure Smallwood brought John Shaheen and a minion onto the floor of the House to answer the questions and comments of the Opposition. Joey always said that John Crosbie had gone into his government fully intending to use the refinery after a year or two as an excuse to break with him and take him on for the leadership. Well, this live appearance of the refinery principals in the House, all televised across the province, Joey confidently predicted, would shut both him and his lapdog Clyde Wells up, once and for all.

Across the province, on every TV set in the land, Crosbie and Wells made mincemeat of Shaheen and company. For nearly a week of sittings, day after day, the whole province watched the annihilation of the refinery concept and the massacre of everyone associated with it. At one point the premier complained that Clyde Wells saw Shaheen as virtually a criminal; well, said Joey, the president of the United States, Richard Nixon, most assuredly did not. (A few years later, the same President Nixon would insist, equally ineffectually, about himself, "I am not a crook.")

To dampen the onslaught of John Crosbie and Clyde Wells, Joey kept the House open afternoon and night, putting an intolerable strain on their ability to research and debate day after day and night after night. Wells was also trying to keep his law practice going way over in Corner Brook, and the upshot was that he resigned his seat during the last year of the session and went back home to tend to his clients. He and Crosbie together had inflicted great damage on Joey's credibility and standing, and now Crosbie and the Tory Opposition kept it going.

IN THE FALL of 1970, four years had passed since the last election. By now, or earlier, the old, confident Smallwood would normally have called a new election. But that summer he had convened a meeting of the caucus to hear the results of a survey done by renowned Toronto pollster Martin Goldfarb on the popularity or lack thereof of Smallwood as premier and of the Liberal Party. The survey results showed that, although the party and Joey had gone down drastically in popularity, we could still win an election that fall. A spirited discussion followed.

In retrospect, it became clear that Joey had lost his nerve that summer of 1970, and he led the discussion away from a fall election. He argued that after another year of DREE spending on schools, sewers, and roads, plus the culmination of the oil refinery and Doyle's linerboard plant, the party's fortunes would have gone up by next fall, in 1971. I recall only one voice dissenting, that of the member for Port de Grave, and a successful businessman in his own right, Eric Dawe.

Eric, as I've said, gave the impression of being naive and unsophisticated, but in fact was one of the shrewdest people I'd ever come across in politics. He argued now that we should go to the people that fall of

1970. Next year would be, he said, too late. Part of his reasoning might have been based on his better knowledge than the rest of us of Frank Moores, since both of them had deep roots in Conception Bay North. And Eric had seen up close Frank Moores's election as an MP in 1968, and how effective he was campaigning in person.

We tended to treat the newly elected PC leader Moores as nothing but a partying, hard-drinking playboy. "A whoring womanizer," Joey would call him. "His cerebral hemispheres hang between his legs." Someone added that there was more intelligence in his bellhead than in his real head, to which the premier responded, "And he takes his orders from the head below." All of that might be true, Eric countered, but people did like him a lot and he was therefore a dangerous man. In one of the formerly most Liberal ridings in Canada, he'd gotten himself elected as a PC MP in 1968. Then his election as president of the PC Party of Canada had to mean he was held in some esteem by intelligent party insiders. But Joey refused to countenance any of that as an indication of Frank's abilities. "It was an off year," said Joey: there was no federal election in the near future, so a lightweight like Frank was acceptable to the party as president. That was why they had let a small fry like him take the presidency.

AFTER THE OTTENHEIMER-AND-THE-WHORE debacle, the provincial Tories had set their leadership convention for May of 1970. Frank Moores threw his hat in, joining half a dozen other candidates, including stalwarts like Dr. Hubert Kitchen, Walter Carter, John Carter, and Hugh Shea. Frank clobbered them all. He won on the first ballot with over 400 votes, more than doubling all the other candidates combined. The closest was Kitchen, with fewer than a hundred votes.

Concerning the placards containing Frank's leadership slogan, "Frank's the Man," Smallwood said in private, "Yes, if having four testicles, each the size of a grapefruit, makes you a man, then Frank certainly is the man." John Nolan and I started referring to Moores, because of his reputation as a good-time stud, and especially because of his penchant for fornicating with young ladies of all estates anywhere, anytime, just like Frank Sinatra, as "Frankie Baby." It wasn't long before that was Joey's main term for him, privately and in public.

After the PC leadership convention, we in the Liberal Party heard reports of serious disgruntlement, especially from the old-time dyed-in-the-wool St. John's Tories. Some of them resented the success of Frank Moores, this Johnny-come-lately dilettante, who was opportunistically taking advantage of the political situation they had created, they said, by their two decades of hard work. But, in fact, the only open rift with Frank came from a Tory from outside the overpass, Hubert Kitchen. He must have been getting bored by defeat at Moores's hands. He'd run against him for the PC nomination in the federal riding of Bonavista-Trinity-Conception in 1968, and lost. Smallwood rubbed his hands with glee at lunch: Kitchen had met with him "secretly" after the PC leadership, he divulged, and was considering Joey's offer to take him into the Liberal Party.

Soon the Tory bigwigs got wind of Kitchen's meeting with Joey and kicked him out of the party, whereupon he did join the Liberals. Tories I knew were outraged at him. I recall being at some function at the time where a former newsman of my acquaintance, now turned Tory organizer for Frank, regaled his companions by maliciously mocking Kitchen. He walked with a deep dip at each step across the floor, mimicking Kitchen, who had a pronounced limp. This former colleague of Kitchen's had it down to a tee. He must have practised it assiduously for the vicious entertainment of his buddies.

While Smallwood hunkered down in the House of Assembly—escaping from reality and wasting his time, some of us thought—Moores was out pressing the flesh "around the bay," and recruiting candidates. He batted away Joey's offer of a free seat into the House of Assembly from Ottenheimer's old district. He knew it was a poisoned chalice. Joey only wanted to get at him. Meanwhile, the premier didn't put much stock in what was happening outside and away from the legislature where, for the first time, the Tories were getting well-organized in rural districts.

The height of Smallwood's rationalization could be seen in his continued denial of any significance in Moores's overwhelming election as party leader. In his mind, that was only clear evidence of a party wallowing in desperation: If the Tories honestly thought there was a chance of their winning the next election, he kept saying, Alex Hickman would have run for the leadership, or John Crosbie would have joined them to take over as leader. All he needed to do now was give Frank Moores enough rope to hang himself before he called an election next year.

But Eric Dawe turned out to be absolutely right. The two big projects, oil refinery and linerboard mill, far from gaining kudos for Joey, continued to undermine his credibility and popularity as the onslaught by Crosbie and the Official Opposition went on. No amount of spending by DREE on infrastructure could stop the slide. And Frank Moores was turning out to be a natural politician province-wide, with his big ballsy voice and his sense of humour and his sunny, winning, larger-than-life look on TV.

AN EXAMPLE OF what the House of Assembly became during 1971, as the forced election loomed, was seen from the uproar following an assault by Bill Smallwood. Bill was the member for the district of Green Bay. As Joey's son, he had a lot to bear. He was a lawyer, having graduated from Dalhousie law school, but some lawyers whispered that he had never really passed his law exams. He was too stupid, they said. But, because the Smallwood government funded a certain number of places for Newfoundlanders at the law school, which was a lucrative source of money for the university, spiteful tongues alleged that Joey was able to strong-arm them into awarding Bill a law degree which he'd never earned.

Back in October 1967, Bill had been involved in a nasty custody battle with his estranged wife. I had been told by a senior lawyer that his wife had combed Duckworth Street looking for a lawyer to represent her, and only with great difficulty did she find one to accept her case. I never believed that, and considered it to be the usual St. John's gossip about how frightened everyone was of Joey Smallwood. Such so-called "fear" never stopped Tory lawyers from taking Joey on in everything else, including running as candidates against him.

The House of Assembly had been sitting in 1967 when the *Evening Telegram* started reporting on those custody proceedings in court. No intimate, private detail of the lives of Bill Smallwood and his wife, no matter how shocking or gruesome, was omitted from the newspaper's pages. As a result of allegations in court of Bill's adultery, dutifully reported in the paper, people started referring to him, in a double-punned recognition of his district, as "the Green Bay Packer."

It seemed clear that if Bill hadn't been the premier's son, none or few of the salacious "facts" or allegations would have been blazoned across the newspaper. In the House of Assembly, Joey even referred to the contrast between Bill's case and the many other domestic cases in court that went largely unreported in the media. The scandalous sensationalism involved in media reporting of the Smallwood litigation was probably the greatest force for changes in Canadian law which would severely restrict the public reporting of evidence and testimony in divorce and custody cases.

Now, less than six months before an election had to be held in 1971, poor Bill Smallwood became the centre of a sensational physical assault drama right on the floor of the House. Sparked again by his being the son of his famous father, it was the only example of actual fisticuffs I witnessed in the House of Assembly. The year before, Tory Bill Marshall had been elected in a by-election in the St. John's East seat vacated after his good friend Gerry Ottenheimer had been caught in the brothel. Now, on a spring evening of 1971, Marshall stood in the House and quoted from a journal alleging that Premier Smallwood's wife, Clara, the owner of some downtown property, was a slum landlord. Thereupon Bill Smallwood stood up from his seat on the Liberal side and declared that he wasn't going to put up with that. He lunged across the House with amazing speed, coattails flying, and pasted Bill Marshall in the face with his fist.

All hell broke loose. The Speaker called a recess of the House to allow tempers to cool and for the parties and members to sort out their positions on the "outrage." In our caucus room, Joey argued for forgiveness for his son because of Bill Marshall's intolerable provocation. He was a son defending the honour of his mother: "What young man is going to just sit there," he demanded, "and listen while his own mother is being slandered and defamed?" In fact, he was astonished, he said, at Bill's moderation under such insufferable goading. What red-blooded son would not have roundhoused a good clout to Marshall's obnoxious mug?

Now, normally Joey gave the impression he didn't derive a great deal of joy from his son Bill's existence. But he always stood up for him when it came to a matter of pride. He knew that any attack on Bill was in reality meant as an attack on himself. It was almost as if he considered Bill to be part of himself—perhaps a wart or a carbuncle, but part of himself nonetheless—and as such, therefore, to be treated with respect. I remember being present when Joey objected to some words or action against Bill—the details are gone now—by declaring, "He is a lawyer—a piss-poor lawyer it may be—but he is a lawyer and he is my son."

On the question of an appropriate penalty for one MHA who had clocked another MHA in the kisser, a number of our caucus members, including me, argued that there simply had to be a serious punishment of a member who committed an act of violence on the floor of the House of Assembly. Anything less in this case, we said, would be, and would appear to be, preferential treatment of the premier's son. Apart from the question of the need for a severe sanction for the sake of justice, too mild a punishment would hurt Joey and Bill and the rest of us in the party in the eyes of the public. If I remember correctly, the Opposition wanted Bill to be expelled from the House permanently for having committed that unprecedented atrocity in "this august chamber."

The upshot was that Joey finally agreed that there would be a motion from our own House leader, Les Curtis, to suspend Bill for, I believe, a week. Still, the Opposition went off their heads at the favouritism they alleged was being shown to Joey's son. In fact, though, it was mostly bluster. Much later, one of Bill Marshall's colleagues present during the assault disclosed to me that their biggest problem had been resisting the desire to egg Bill Smallwood on to clobber Marshall again, instead of stopping at one smack. "Bill Marshall," he said, "was not a lovable guy."

On the radio, however, Joey repeated his reasons for wanting to pardon his son's violence; hence several members of the Opposition wanted to condemn the premier in the House for breach of privilege. When the Speaker declined to hold Joey in contempt of the House, John Crosbie called the Speaker a tool of the government and, as a consequence, Crosbie and some other members who supported his words were suspended for a few days as well. Then, in a show of solidarity, the whole Opposition upped and boycotted the House, whereupon Joey took advantage of their absence to have the House pass every piece of legislation on the order paper—scores of bills—in just a few minutes without one word of debate.

The whole sorry episode, including the Opposition's attention grabber of being booted out of the House, raised their public profile, and Smallwood and our party continued the inexorable decline down a popularity sinkhole.

WHAT I'D DISCOVERED in the past of Smallwood's state of mind, his relationship with his family, his reminiscences, and his general psychology, always a tad peculiar, seemed to intensify during this period.

In later life, Joey would develop a reputation for being a doting, indulgent, loving grandfather and great-grandfather: Poppy, they called him. His affection for his family seemed to have skipped a generation because I never saw any of that in his relations with his wife and children. Even as a student in school, whenever I used to observe Joey at speech nights and prize-givings—premiers and ministers and lieutenant-governors used to attend those functions in those days—he would always be barging ahead of Clara and she'd be trotting behind, trying unsuccessfully to keep on a happy face. I never saw him show the least attention or consideration to her in public. After a while, I noticed that she seldom appeared in public with him at all.

During the five years or so that I was relatively close to Joey, if I saw Clara at functions or over at their house, I can't say that I was ever able to exchange more than half a dozen words with her in total. Usually, if she was sitting in their living room when you arrived with Joey, he would peremptorily dismiss her with, "Clara, give us the room." Once, latterly, when two or three of us had been talking strategy for half an hour there, we heard a rustling in the shadows of a corner. Joey bawled, "Is that you, Clara?"

"Yes, Joe," came the meek reply.

"Clara, give us the room. Give us the goddamned room."

She slowly rose, and, in her own good time as Joey twitched and fumed, walked out. She tried hard not to look completely humiliated.

His daughter, Clara, seemed to have something approaching a reasonably normal relationship with Joey—fairly civilized, and business-like in the way of families, though rising sometimes to some rather feisty exchanges in which the daughter gave as good as she took from the father. On occasion, she filled in as his chatelaine at some functions and then she would show attention and affection to her dad. But in his dealings with his son, Bill, everything seemed to be a matter of Joey issuing orders and Bill querulously objecting to them before reluctantly complying.

During 1971, Joey and I dropped into his house on Roaches Line on our way to a meeting farther along the TCH. He wanted to pick something up. Bill was there and came out into the living room to greet us just as the power failed and the lights went out. In the dwindling twilight, we found ourselves able to see only with difficulty, and an exchange like this ensued between father and son:

"Bill, telephone Newfoundland Light and Power."

"What for, Pop?"

"What for? To find out what's wrong."

"It's a power outage, Pop."

"I can see that it's a goddamned power outage. Call them and find out when they'll have the power back on."

"I'm sure they're trying to get the power back on as quick as they can."

"Bill, just telephone the goddamned power company and find out."

Bill made a big production of looking for the number in the phone book, twisting and straining to see in the dim light, while Joey stood over him, glaring at him as he searched. Then Bill punched in a number and got someone on the other end and entered into a palaver about the outage. Joey stood there, three feet away from him, looking on in supervisory mode. As Bill spoke he would allow the receiver to drift away from his mouth. There was no indication that the person on the other end couldn't hear what Bill was saying, but Joey would step toward Bill and with one finger, his index finger, he'd push the receiver back toward Bill's mouth. Each time he did this, Bill would look at Joey flustered, lose his train of thought, and falter in his conversation. After being subjected to several such pushes on the receiver by Joey's index finger, Bill turned away from his dad, whereupon Joey also moved around and pushed again, barking in the middle of Bill's sentence, "Speak into the goddamned mouthpiece."

Bill's voice was high at the best of times. Now he let out a ferocious squeak, "Lord Jesus, Pop," flung the receiver across the room, wires and plug trailing, and he stomped out the door. I don't know what the person at the other end was thinking by now, and Joey didn't seem to care. Silently and matter-of-factly, he picked up his stuff, and he and I walked out to his car. And we drove off to our meeting as if we were normal.

DURING THESE STRESSFUL days for Joey, he began reminiscing even more than usual about the old days. At least once, a big multitude of us crowded into his office on the eighth floor to commemorate some occasion—perhaps an anniversary of Confederation—and Joey began to read from the eleven letters or articles he had sent to the newspaper in the late 1940s to kick off his Confederation campaign. And he read and he read. And then he read some more. None of us looked at each other, but only, I'm sure, because our eyes were glazed completely over or rolled back in our heads. Joey stayed oblivious or indifferent to the roomful of pain.

JOEY HAD A certain fondness for talking about Peter Cashin. He told us at lunch that Peter was excellent at bringing together lynch mobs. He'd been responsible for assembling several such hordes, including the riot at the Colonial Building that nearly murdered Prime Minister Sir Richard Squires. He'd also gathered a rabble outside Joey's big rallies at the CLB Armoury during the Confederation battle that all but assassinated Smallwood himself. To prevent Joey from being killed, his bodyguards had been trained by Irving Fogwill and Harold Horwood in the proper use of Communist Party subduing tactics, perfected in revolutionary Russia.

For example, Joey told us, to remove a troublemaker from a rally, the bodyguards were instructed never to strike him or break his bones or draw blood. Instead, two or three hefty guards would simply carry the mischief-maker quietly out while one of them surreptitiously reached down and squeezed his testicles hard, which caused him to draw in his breath sharply and stay very silent. Squeeze his nuts properly, they were taught, and you could end the man's family line right there and then, and pre-empt the risk of revenge from a later generation. Al Vardy, who was listening to this depiction of security by Joey in the dining room, said that they must have practised the technique too much on Horwood himself, judging by his high-pitched little voice.

Neither Joey himself nor anyone in his old-time retinue liked Harold Horwood much after he'd left the party. He was good during the Confederation battle, they said, especially the way he dragged religion into the campaign and helped win the second referendum. Apparently the *Sunday Herald* had reported that the Catholic Archbishop, who was zealously against Confederation, had released nuns and brothers from their vows and allowed them to vote in the first referendum. Harold Horwood sent the page of the *Herald* containing that story to every Orange Lodge in Newfoundland. The famous Orange Letter, very favourable to the Confederation cause, resulted, galvanizing Protestants to vote "the right way."

A dozen years after Horwood stopped writing his nasty pieces against Joey in the *Evening Telegram*, the mere mention of his name still brought comments from Joey like "Horwood lies," or "loathsome scavenger." Les Curtis said he was a "flaming homosexual." Vardy extended his sexual predilections to "he liked preadolescent boys."

Joey told me once when we were alone that Vardy had concocted a brutal plan to deal with the Harold Horwood problem. This had happened while Horwood was writing those scathing, vicious articles, "spitting out his poison," for some six years in the 1950s in the local newspapers. Vardy's plan was to have Horwood assassinated.

When I laughed and said that Vardy couldn't possibly have been serious, Joey replied that he'd been exceedingly serious. Vardy knew some people who could arrange with ease for an expert hit man from the states to fly in here and have Horwood killed in a way that looked like an accident, and then fly out again completely undetected. It had gone beyond a mere concept into the planning stage by the time Vardy pitched the inspired idea to him. Joey sombrely told me that he'd had to force himself reluctantly to veto the execution of Vardy's very tempting murder proposal. When I said that Vardy's plan reminded me that communist leader Joseph Stalin had a similar solution for every problem, to wit, "No man, no problem," my socialist premier looked positively envious.

JOEY'S TABLE TALK now often went back to before his Confederation battle, to his socialist period in New York. Sometimes he referred to Eugene Debs, and seemed surprised when no one seemed to know who the hell he was talking about. He felt his surprise at our ignorance was warranted because Debs had probably been the best-known union leader and socialist politician in the United States. It showed, he said, the transitory nature of one's life's contributions, because Debs was a founding member of the famous Wobblies. (Who the hell were the Wobblies? the eyes of us listeners asked each other.) They were the Industrial Workers of the World, Joey explained, unhelpfully. Anyway, Debs ran for the US presidency as the candidate for the Socialist Party in half a dozen elections from 1900 to 1920—his last election from prison where he was incarcerated under the espionage laws. His sentence was commuted by the American president in 1921, Joey said, and it was after that, when Joey spent time in New York, that he met Debs and became even more enamoured of socialism. All of which led to this paradox in my mind regarding Smallwood:

When he was in New York, he told me, he shared a bedroom for a long time with a black man they called "the negro Debs." Joey spent many days and nights with him and made anti–Ku Klux Klan speeches at great risk to his own life and limb, especially as a white man. He was so against racial inequality that physical peril to himself was entirely irrelevant, he told us. Yet, fifty years after the racial camaraderie he described, and racial tolerance had become much more secure, Ed

Roberts and I were in London on business with Joey, when we saw a white woman and black man walking by arm in arm, nuzzling and kissing. Joey said he hated to see that. I asked him what was wrong with it—surely it was their own business. Joey got annoyed with me and replied that it might well be their own business but he still didn't like to see it—that was what was wrong with it. And then he recounted how broken-hearted many of the family and friends of the right Honourable Sir Stafford Cripps, the great British labour minister, had been when his daughter Peggy got engaged, in the early 1950s, to a black Ghanaian student leader. The very idea was so appalling to everyone, and would have been to leading socialist Cripps, that his wife kept the news of the engagement from him because he was ill, and so the marriage didn't take place until after his death. Even then there was much negative media comment and public consternation. "Evidently," said Joey, "I'm not the only one who doesn't like to see that." I stated that a lot had changed in people's thinking over the past twenty years since Cripps, but Joey dismissed the subject: he didn't think people's innermost feelings on such liaisons had changed very much over the years.

THOUGH HE WAS small in size, I found stories of Joey's physical courage easy to believe. Not only had he been under the constant threat of physical attack during his speech-making in favour of unions and socialism, and against the Ku Klux Klan, in New York in his early twenties, but later in St. John's he showed no fear, either. Les Curtis, who often characterized many of Joey's other stories as "romancing," confirmed to me that Joey, while trying to defend Prime Minister Sir Richard Squires—Curtis's law partner—against rabid opponents at a political event in the Majestic Theatre in 1932, had been thrown bodily, and not very gently, out of the building, but would have gone back for more, had he not been stopped by friends.

Then the very next day, Curtis said, Joey was with Squires and his wife in the Colonial Building when one of Peter Cashin's murderous mobs came for Squires, wrecking everything in sight. Joey helped hide Squires and his wife in the Speaker's room off the House of Assembly, and then helped plan and execute their narrow escape from the building in disguise, with life and limb barely intact.

I actually saw something of Joey's mettle myself nearly forty years later, during these last months before the 1971 election. I was coming into Joey's office for a meeting one morning when a big man there, a disgruntled Liberal supporter whom Joey had just told he could do nothing for, refused to leave and started blustering and threatening him. To be frank, I was unnerved by the man's out-of-control appearance and great size. The hands on him, which he had now raised and rolled into fists, looked like a couple of huge hams.

Joey was pushing seventy years old, but he came out from behind his desk with a speed and agility that a gymnast would have envied and moved aggressively toward the man. At the vision of this tiny, snarling wolverine coming at him, the man stepped back until he was plastered up against the wall. There Joey glared up at the large face hovering nearly a foot above his own and dressed down the big oaf with choice abuse for a full minute for daring to emit such threats. At any moment I feared the man was going to encircle the premier's head with one hand and crush it like an eggshell. But instead he only muttered, "Sorry, Mr. Premier," and skulked out of the office like a chastened schoolboy.

Regrettably, such clear-cut examples of Joey's courage, boldness, and his old chutzpah were starting by now to become rarities.

CHAPTER NINE

Joey's Brilliant Strategists

LEADING UP TO the election of 1971, a number of untoward events occurred that seemed purposely designed to defeat our government. Smallwood added to their negative impact on us wherever he could. One involved the Newfoundland Constabulary, the police force which Queen Elizabeth would designate "Royal" in 1979 for their centuries of admirable service and the respect in which they were held by the public. Unfortunately, Joey himself showed that the respect he himself demanded from the police, he would not return to them.

The Constabulary in 1971 had the lowest pay of any police force in Canada, and possessed no grievance procedure or any right to bargain. They had formed a Police Brotherhood in 1969 to press for improvements. Early in 1970 an officer was caught spying on some rank-and-file members, prompting them to write a letter to the chief of police requesting that the officer be transferred. The chief responded by suspending the letter-writers for a month for breach of discipline. Thereupon, some other members of the force announced that they would go on strike (which was against the law) if the suspended members were not reinstated without penalty. Joey now jumped in on his own and announced that the Constabulary would have to be disbanded if discipline could not be maintained. In response, Constabulary members walked off the job.

During their job action the issue of their right to bear sidearms came up. Joey responded with something like, "Carry sidearms? I wouldn't let them carry pop guns." And the political savaging of the premier intensified. Finally, he had to cave in and the members got their jobs back without penalty. I believe the chief of police was forced to resign over the issue.

Joey blamed Alex Hickman, now in the Opposition, for the crisis. When Hickman had been minister of Justice leading up to the fall of 1969, Joey claimed, he'd received a report that recommended an improvement in benefits for the Constabulary, but the minister had sat on the report for many months, without bringing it to the attention of the premier or the cabinet. Whatever truth that accusation may have contained, Joey's attempt to shift the blame for the police emergency off his own shoulders didn't seem to cut much ice with the police or the public, and the popularity of the premier and our party continued to plummet.

ANOTHER EXAMPLE OF where Smallwood had lost his touch in dealing with unfolding events occurred in 1970, when Richard Cashin travelled around the province, founding and organizing the Fish, Food and Allied Workers union. Joey seemed vaguely uncomfortable with its existence from the start. His pessimistic attitude toward fishermen self-help may have stemmed from his own failure to organize fishermen into some kind of a union in Bonavista in the 1930s. He'd spent several years there with his family vainly trying to emulate his hero Coaker in shaping fishermen into an organizational juggernaut. But instead he reached the point where he couldn't even pay his own rent or feed his family. And for his pains, some Commission of Government members labelled him a Bolshevik. As a result of that fiasco, he seemed to think that fishermen, plant workers, and fish merchants were incapable of cooperating, either as a whole or within their own groups, in their own best interests, despite a fishery continually plagued by fish failures, and gluts, and market collapses.

I remember saying to him once that a historian had written about the secret to Switzerland's success: the Swiss were so independent as individuals that they never co-operated—unless grave circumstances forced them to. But fortunately, grave circumstances frequently forced them to. Joey responded that individuals in the Newfoundland fishery wouldn't co-operate, no matter what grave or disastrous circumstances confronted them.

He sometimes told stories around the cabinet table of fish merchants and exporters sitting down and making a deal together on the price at which they would sell their product abroad. But then each of them would walk out of the meeting oozing camaraderie, only to make his own separate, secret deal with a buyer at a cheaper price, thus undercutting the industry as a whole. There was something inherently cutthroat in the nature of the fishing industry, he thought, that kept people from pulling in the same direction. Consequently, fish merchants were doomed to quick profits one year and bankruptcy the next. And fishermen were doomed to perpetual poverty.

Several times he recounted his demoralizing memories of eating meals with fishermen's families during his unionizing days, which consisted too often of a slice of bread fried in pork fat accompanied only by black tea unembellished with milk or sugar. He wondered aloud why anyone would stay at that.

After I joined his cabinet, I discovered that there was some sort of a tame fishermen's organization in existence supported by the government. But in 1971 this was now superseded in the lives of many fishermen by a genuine independent union of fishermen and plant workers spearheaded by Cashin, and a strike by this Fish, Food and Allied Workers union took place in Burgeo—yet another disruption of the peace in Joey's forced election year.

He expressed to us in cabinet his opinion that the union was in an inherent conflict of interest, trying to represent fishermen who supplied the fish to the plants, while at the same time representing workers in those fish plants. I even heard him give it a taint of biblical proportions: Cain versus Abel; Cain the cultivator and Abel the shepherd—interests so different that one killed the other—same with the fishery.

When the first strike of the then legally unrecognized union took place, many of us pooh-poohed the old minister of Justice, Les Curtis, when he wondered if the police should be sent in. And we'd laugh dismissively, if somewhat nervously, when he'd stud his speculations with such gems as, "The police won't arrest anyone who's not guilty," or "We should give lawbreakers the cold steel." But Joey stayed strangely silent, and I for one had flickers of memory of the IWA strike.

It took a lot of effort and persuasion by some of us in the cabinet to allow a process to start to recognize the union. We wanted to have the union legitimized by legislation, and some steps were taken in that direction before the 1971 election. We managed to get a bill passed in the House of Assembly that year called the Fishing Industry Collective Bargaining Act, which gave inshore fishermen the right to bargain for the price of fish. I believe this was the last piece of legislation passed by the House during the twenty-three years of Joey's government, and I believe that, because of the efforts of Cashin's FFAW, the Government of Newfoundland and Labrador became the first in Canada to give fishermen the right by legislation to collectively negotiate the price of their fish. But our progressive action was too little too late to have much effect on the declining popularity of our government.

MEANWHILE, THE NEWFOUNDLAND Teachers' Association (NTA) was also becoming militant as they tried to negotiate a decent contract with our government on behalf of the teachers. The parties got nowhere and the teachers voted to give their executive a strike mandate. Then some of their executive and bargaining committee met with the spending watchdog committee of cabinet, the Treasury Board, of which I was a member.

I suggested to their negotiators at the meeting that since this was their very first strike that they were contemplating, they should make sure they didn't go off half-cocked and that they consult expert advisers, especially since, at the time, they didn't even have the legal right to go on strike. One of their leaders looked at me, amazed at my condescension, and reacted with appropriate scorn. The first teachers' strike in Newfoundland's history took place in this forced election year, and the teachers contributed mightily to our decline in the polls. Years later I ran into that NTA leader from our pre-strike meeting, and he asked me if the strike, plus the drubbing the teachers gave the Liberal Party in the election, was "expert" enough for me. We had a great laugh.

Meanwhile, as if the animosity of the teachers wasn't bad enough in and of itself leading up to the election, an article appeared in Smallwood's official government publication, *The Newfoundland Bulletin*, that enflamed them even more. Joey had started the publication of this propaganda journal in, I believe, 1968, and continued it right up to the dying days of his administration at the end of 1971.

The article in question was written during the teachers' strike by Minister Bill Keough, who was best known for his evocative line during the Confederation battle: "the last forgotten fisherman off the bill of Cape St. George." His article for the *Bulletin* didn't quite aspire to that literary level. In it he referred to the members of the Newfoundland Teachers' Association as "the NTA turds." Predictably, this intensified the rancour of the NTA's standoff with the government, and the association also used the comment to condemn and officially censure Fred Rowe, the minister of Education at the time. Some fifteen years would pass before the Newfoundland and Labrador Teachers' Association, under, I believe, Roger Grimes as president, rescinded that censure. And in 1985 as well they would award Dad an honorary life membership in the organization. I was at the ceremony where this took place and saw the emotion and gratification in a man who, then well into his seventies, had devoted much of his life to education as teacher, principal, minister of Education, and writer of half a dozen histories on education and culture in our province. But that was far into the future; back in 1971 we were cringing under the fallout from our assorted blunders.

ALSO IN THE watershed year of 1971, to increase our siege mentality, some student leaders at Memorial University proclaimed the provincial government and the university administration their mortal enemies. They marched in their hundreds on Confederation Building calling Joey a fascist and targeting Ed Roberts and myself for defeat. Their reasoning, if I recall it correctly, was that Ed and I were not over thirty, and therefore we were traitors to our own generation.

They also gave Lord Stephen Taylor, the president of the university, a trying time by sitting in at his offices and besieging his official residence on Mount Scio Road. Joey had appointed Lord Taylor as president of Memorial University around 1966. Mose Morgan had been interim president for a year or so, and it must have been a terrible humiliation for him when he was passed over in favour of the lord. I believe Joey considered Mose to be an out-and-out Tory. He would be appointed president later by the Tory government of Frank Moores. (And Mose would show his generous broad-mindedness years into the future by helping to lead a fundraiser to complete Smallwood's *Encyclopedia of Newfoundland and Labrador*.) Meanwhile, Taylor, who'd been a medium-level labour politician back home in the United Kingdom, had built a reputation in Canada as a conciliator in the Saskatchewan medicare debate in 1962. That, and perhaps membership in the British Labour Party, might have been what attracted Joey to him. My own relationship with Taylor was rather rollercoasterish.

One summer weekend in 1971, I spent a Sunday afternoon with him and his wife, Charity (her sisters were named Faith and Hope), at a mutual friend's summer place getting more or less sloshed on Pimm's

Number One and spritzers, and having a grand old time. Then a few weeks later he appeared before the Treasury Board looking for more money for the university at a time when the government was heading for bankruptcy. During the course of our downward-spiralling "discussion," I reacted to his patronizing attitude by referring to one of his earlier jobs in England: "Lord Taylor," I said, "you're not British Undersecretary of State for the Colonies now." He looked at me rather keenly and said, "Now see here, you young fucker . . ." Despite that powerful argument, the good lord didn't get his extra money, because there was none. And the students' metaphorical feces continued to bombard the government fan.

DURING THE SUMMER of 1971, there was talk in some quarters of the Liberal Party that perhaps Joey should bow out gracefully in favour of a new leader. There had long been speculation that the reason John Crosbie had not yet gone with the PC Party was that he was hoping Smallwood would croak, or get sick, or feel that he was too old at seventy to carry on for another term as premier. John was eager to get a call from a grateful party to come and save them, like the summons Charles de Gaulle received from the panicky French during the Algerian war. The problem with John's scenario was that Joey, as he entered his eighth decade of life, was sinfully healthy and energetic and still ruthlessly ambitious.

Except for when he had to have an operation for a detached retina back in November of 1967, from which he recovered with amazing quickness, I never knew Joey to miss a function because of illness. I don't know if he was ever ill—he never seemed to be—or whether he simply did not let illness interfere with his life. I cannot recall that Joey ever complained of so much as a common cold.

He did have some chronic hoarseness in his late sixties which persisted until some around him feared it might be throat cancer. When he got wind of that, he ridiculed the concerns, and when we laughed at the mockery, he made a further entertainment of it. "Gentlemen, why are you laughing?" he would croak hoarsely. "Cancer of the throat is no joke." When we prevailed upon him to see his doctor and get referred to a specialist, it turned out that he had no family doctor. Someone had to supply him with a name. It had been that long since he'd consulted a general practitioner for any reason. Maybe part of the reason he stayed so healthy was his hatred of hospitals. He could hardly bear to go near one to visit a family member or friend who was sick, he told me. And, as it turned out, he considered having gone to the doctor this time a waste of an hour: he didn't have throat cancer.

He recounted to us how much he admired the actions of the great historian Will Durant at a lecture he'd attended during the 1920s in New York. Durant was the main speaker at the event but was obviously sick and nauseous. Even while he was making his speech, he excused himself several times to go off the stage to vomit. From the audience, Smallwood said, you could hear him out in the wings retching. Then he would come back and resume his speech where he'd left off until the next wave of nausea caused him to exit temporarily again. All these years later, he was still in awe of the man's moxie.

A speech therapist once told me that she had listened to Joey's voice on the radio, on television, and in person making a speech, and she had concluded that he had a well-nigh perfect voice for reception by the human ear, at least as far as its sound, if not the content, was concerned, and that its tone and pitch were excellently adapted to long, forceful speech-making without damage to his vocal cords.

JOEY MIGHT HAVE been physically healthy, but toward the end of his reign some of us developed doubts about his psychological well-being. He got seriously paranoid over the possibility that enemies were planting electronic bugs and listening devices in our ministerial offices and on our home telephones. One morning, several of us were summoned to his office where we found the CEO of the Newfoundland

Telephone Company cooling his heels. When we were assembled, the premier announced that it had been reliably reported to him that there were Tory spies at the telephone company listening in on all our phone conversations.

The flabbergasted CEO could protest and deny all he liked, but Joey ordered the office and home phones of some cabinet ministers—Ed Roberts, John Nolan, and I were included—outfitted with electronic scrambling devices designed to render our telephonic conversations unintelligible to the spies listening in. I can remember putting my scrambler to good use only once. After a particularly trying all-day cabinet meeting "chaired" by the premier, I telephoned John Nolan late at night at home. I hereby divulge, heedless of the Official Secrets Act, our entire, coded, confidential discussion:

John: "Hello?"
Me: "Scramble."
John: "Roger, scrambled."
Me: "Fuck, fuck."
John: "Copy that: fuck."
Me: "Unscramble."
John: "Roger, unscramble."

We flicked back to "normal" mode and hung up.

IN THE SUMMER of 1971, Joey talked some extraordinary people into running for the dispirited Liberal Party. One was Rupert Bartlett, the nephew of Captain Bob Bartlett, and an esteemed lawyer—a partner of Senator Eric Cook—and an altogether delightful man. Whenever I used to visit his office on some legal matter on behalf of a client, we'd have such great gabs we found it hard to get any work done. When I asked him what he was doing running, especially in this election, since he always struck me as a solid rock of common sense, he told me Joey had tried to bribe him with a district court judgeship, which wasn't even Joey's gift to make. That appointment was purely federal, and Joey's federal clout these days seemed weak. His running at this point was such a preposterous notion that it appealed to Rupert's sense of humour, and he needed a good laugh around now in his career. He got it.

One of the first things Joey did was drag Rupert and me off to New York for a bizarre photography session. I have no idea now where we went in Manhattan, but it was a huge studio filled with fake plants, fake trees, fake boulders, fake bookcases with fake books, and fake Italian villages in fake Mediterranean seascapes. There we were put in front of cameras which produced these weird 3D pictures of each of us. I still have some, and while their novelty might have been helpful in the coming campaign, they look awfully ridiculous now. Joey also had small mirrors made with 3D lettering on the back saying, "Would the lady on the other side [i.e. in the mirror] please vote for Joey?" Rupert won his seat in that election against then-PC candidate George Baker, although his political career wouldn't last long. And he did indeed get appointed two or three years later as a district court judge.

BEFORE THE 1971 election, Joey told us that he was only interested in putting the Liberal Party back in power on a solid footing, and then he would resign as premier and as Liberal leader and as a Member of the House of Assembly. He would get out and remain out of politics forever, and one of the men on his long roster of next premiers could take over.

Richard Cashin used to joke that he was Smallwood's original "next premier," Joey having announced it as a done deal when Richard ran federally for the Liberals in the 1962 election. And there were many other names on Joey's next premier list. Here are a few of the people whom I heard Joey describe publicly or privately as the indisputable next premier, just as soon as he stepped down in a little while: Don Jamieson, Fred Rowe, John Crosbie, Alex Hickman, Ed Roberts, Bill Rowe, John

Nolan, Bill Callahan, Steve Neary, Tom Burgess, Andrew Crosbie. Want some more? Just before the 1971 election, he enticed Mayor Bill Adams of St. John's and Mayor Noel Murphy of Corner Brook into running as Liberals, with the assurance to Adams that he would name him premier right after the election, and to Murphy that he'd be appointed next lieutenant-governor. Or maybe it was the other way around. Stories varied. As it turned out, the party's political reverses spared them the trouble of flipping a coin for the spoils. And wasn't old Les Curtis supposed to become "interim premier" at some critical point while the party waited for the dust to settle?

Ironically, the person who actually would become the next premier had also been proclaimed as such by Joey at a gathering I was at in central Newfoundland during the early 1960s. But it was not to happen in the way Joey had foretold.

The 1971 fall election was one very zany affair. In the first place, Smallwood appointed Andrew Crosbie, John's brother, to manage the Liberal election campaign, even though Andrew had headed up John's leadership campaign in 1969. Procuring Andrew for the job was a brilliant coup for Joey, he thought, and certainly an embarrassment for John. Many in the Crosbie family and among John's supporters considered Andrew's move a breach of clan solidarity, not to say a treacherous stab in the back of his big brother.

Andrew explained himself by saying that he had always been and still was a Liberal, whereas brother John had joined the PCs that summer, and many of his Liberal supporters for his Liberal leadership, including Brian Peckford, were now running or working for the Tories that fall. Just because John was a turncoat from the Liberal Party, Andrew told us, that didn't mean everyone had to follow him like sheep. However, some Liberals thought Andrew had become Liberal campaign manager in a double capacity, both of them undesirable—one, to spy for the Tories, and two, to make sure Joey and the Liberals lost the election.

Andrew would tell me later that he'd had a big secret meeting with

Al Vardy in Montreal that summer of 1971 before the election, arranged by Smallwood, where Vardy asked him on Joey's behalf to consider taking over as premier at once. Then, on Andrew's return to St. John's, Joey offered to take him to the lieutenant-governor "right this minute" to be sworn in then and there as premier. When Andrew declined that opportunity, Joey told him that as soon as the election was won, and the Liberals were safely back in power, he would resign, turn the premiership over to Andrew, and support him in the formality of becoming leader of the party. Andrew said that what impressed him most was how sincere and convincing Joey looked and sounded.

Meanwhile, Andrew, as campaign manager, convened a strategy meeting so secret and remote that a bunch of us plotters had to be flown in by air. It took place on Kaegudeck Lake, Andrew's hunting and fishing resort in the middle of the Newfoundland wilderness. We were supposed to be there to plan the line of attack for the upcoming election. Present were Smallwood, John Nolan, Ed Roberts, Andrew Crosbie, Andrew's devoted friend Barron Macdonald, and myself. Andrew never went anywhere without Barron. I found him to be a great fellow, a pillar of strength in helping Andrew cope, among other things, with his alcoholism.

The only strategy at Kaegudeck Lake that stands out in my memory was Andrew's suggestion that Joey lie low for the duration of the campaign because he was the lightning rod for all criticism against the Liberal Government. The measure of Joey's loss of nerve and our demoralization, not to say idiocy, was that Joey agreed with the notion and none of the rest of us argued strenuously against it. And this was even after Joey had proved for the thousandth time how effective and persuasive a speaker he still was.

Just a year or so before our strategy meeting, he'd flown to Happy Valley-Goose Bay to explain to an unruly and disappointed crowd that their promised wood chip mill, designed to feed the new pulp mill under construction at Stephenville, would not now be built in the Lake

Melville area, but was going to Stephenville instead. We fully expected the premier to be lynched, and a lesser bullshit artist would have been. But, after his three-hour speech, the crowded hall gave him a standing ovation. This was the guy whom we brilliant strategists, hiding away in the wilderness, decided should be buried under a bushel for the duration of the campaign.

THAT INSPIRED DECISION gave John Crosbie the ingredients to cover up his embarrassment and chagrin at brother Andrew having become his political enemy during the election. John began spouting a variation on this piece of doggerel at every turn: "Where oh where has Joey gone, where or where can he be? He was the boss for twenty-three years, but now it's Andrew CrosbIE." Silly though it was, it was highly effective because it zeroed in on Joey's perceived liability to the Liberal Party in a way that, as usual with John, had everyone laughing.

My most vivid memory of that famous strategy trip of ours in the wilderness of Kaegudeck was being on the lake in a small outboard motorboat, rocking in the waves, as someone took potshots with a powerful rifle at a moose on shore. It required several shots before the moose, who was looking out at us short-sightedly and sniffing the breeze curiously the whole while, was finally brought down. That moose hunt was about as exciting as creeping up on a cud-chewing cow in a field and smacking it on the arse with a two-by-four. I have remembered that incident from our trip so well because the poor stunned moose reminded me of us, and I wondered afterwards who was the stupider—that pitifully dim-witted animal, or we, the super strategists.

BY OCTOBER OF 1971, the House of Assembly and the Smallwood government had persisted for the full legal length of the term, and perhaps beyond, until finally he had no choice but to call an election. A month over five years had elapsed from the last election in September of 1966, and the Tories raised public doubts over whether Joey still lawfully held office. The premier responded that the legal term was five years from when the House of Assembly first met after the last election, so there was no question of his legitimacy as premier, but this subtlety was lost on most people and bored the rest stiff. Many people thought, buttressed in their thinking by Frank Moores and John Crosbie, that Smallwood had pushed the election call beyond the five years because he was scared to death and he knew he was going to be defeated.

In addition to losing his normal political chutzpah as the election approached, the Tories alleged that Joey had also lost his touch. He didn't even know how to cover up his own shitty tracks anymore: he had appointed John Mahoney as minister of Justice to replace the retired minister Les Curtis, but Mahoney was a member of the same law firm as Curtis. This allowed John Crosbie to claim that Curtis, who was now acting for Shaheen and Doyle in private practice, was therefore negotiating with a minister of Justice who was also his own law partner. It did leave a sickening taste in many people's mouths, including some of us among Joey's own colleagues.

The Tories also claimed that, leading into the election, Joey had been abandoned by most of his senior colleagues. Indeed, Joey's impressive cabinet from the 1966 election was almost entirely gutted. Gone were stalwarts like Dr. Jim McGrath, Phil Lewis, Beaton Abbott, Max Lane, Les Curtis, Alain Frecker, Eric Jones, Aiden Maloney, Charlie Granger, Bill Keough, and Val Earle, as well as the then-young Turks, Clyde Wells, Alex Hickman, and John Crosbie. The only old-timers remaining, apart from Joey himself, were Jim Chalker and Fred Rowe.

But Joey had not lost his touch as badly as the Tories hoped. He added to his cabinet some surprising and impressive election candidates: former top Tory organizer and Tory leadership candidate Hubert Kitchen; Gus Oldford, a former provincial court judge; George Warren, a former top deputy minister in the provincial government; top Labrador businessman Mel Woodward; as mentioned, a former Tory leader, and now Corner Brook mayor, Dr. Noel Murphy; and St. John's mayor

Bill Adams. Some among the media were astonished. One well-known and politically shrewd TV journalist said to me: "The mayors of our two largest cities running for Joey! Christ, that doesn't sound like a premier who's on the ropes."

Of the two, I liked Noel Murphy more. Years later he and I would talk on the air when he'd call VOCM *Open Line*, especially after his Corner Brook radio station CFCB joined in on the show. We also spent a season or two together as Peter Gzowski's Newfoundland and Labrador correspondents on *Morningside*. Noel had a touch of an English accent left over from his early days in school there. When he called up my open-line show one time and said he was calling from an aircraft flying between Newfoundland and England, I said, "Oh *that* explains the mid-Atlantic accent." He had the good grace to laugh.

Back to the lead-up to the 1971 election: Crosbie and the official PC Opposition kept us busy in the House. For months, they had often acted in concert, but Crosbie had resisted formally joining the Tories. This was the continuing proof to Smallwood that the PCs were going nowhere, as otherwise Crosbie would have jumped in bed with them. Some of us thought it strange that Joey condemned Crosbie's bad judgment in everything else, but considered his judgment good when it happened to coincide with his own wishful thinking.

In fact, we knew that "Frankie and Johnnie" had been negotiating concerted action in the next election, possibly dividing up the districts in which each faction would run one candidate so as not to fragment the votes opposing the Liberals. There was even talk leaked of a possible deal with Moores for a coalition government between the Crosbie forces and the PC Party. We were not surprised when that moronic notion was scuppered in disbelief by the old Tories in charge of the party machinery. But while it lasted, the perceived split in the Opposition did give comfort to Joey.

Finally, the Opposition factions got their act together. We heard that Frank had assured Crosbie that he could run the show as de facto premier when the Tories got elected and that when Frank was finished as actual premier in a few years he would pass the job over to John. With that, Crosbie reluctantly let go of his pipe dream that the Liberal Party would anoint him leader and premier. He joined the Tory Party.

That Moores was serious about organizing his party and getting it ready for the election was hard to miss. He had retained George McLean of McLean Public Relations, who weighed over 300 pounds and was much in evidence about the province. We heard that one of their big strategies was to convince the party and its supporters that getting elected was all just a matter of numbers . . . one, two, three: If you could count you could get elected to the government; for example, if the PC candidates had picked up only thirty votes per polling booth during the 1966 landslide election for the Liberals, the PCs would have won the government. Yes, Joey commented to us, and if your aunt had balls she'd be your uncle.

Moores scorned in return the Liberals' economic development projects. He took the adjective off Smallwood's "Happy Province" licence plates and proclaimed that Newfoundlanders were a happy people who should not be herded into massive manufacturing plants to push buttons. To which Joey replied, no, but it was okay with Mr. Moores for Newfoundlanders to stand up to their ankles in fish guts and gurry all day in one of his fish plants to make big bucks for Frank and his money-grubbing family. I don't recall if Joey ever said that publicly, or just privately to us, but if he didn't, he should have. Sadly, though, he wasn't as certain and timely in his demolition of enemies now as he was in the old days, and missed a lot of opportunities like that.

Moores must have figured that Steve Neary had been deputized by Joey to get under Moores's skin because he called him Joey's flunky and master of gutter politics and hatchetman. But anyone would have had to be naive to think Steve needed anyone's encouragement or go-ahead to tear strips off a political opponent's hide. It was just that, with Smallwood lying so low, Steve was more conspicuous.

What really undermined Joey's stature and credibility was when Frank announced he was going to run personally against Smallwood in his own district of Humber West, and Joey hightailed it out of there to run somewhere else, settling finally on Placentia East. "Frank chased old Joey out of Humber West like a rat caught in the pantry," one Tory scoffed to me. In better days, it was Joey who'd hunted down PC leaders to defeat personally. Now he himself was the prey. We Liberals found it hard to credibly deny that our leader was scared to death.

TO ANNOUNCE THE election of 1971, Smallwood at long last held a news conference in the cabinet room to proclaim that he'd called it for October 28. We all sat there listening to his statement, and it was hopeless—the worst I'd ever seen or heard him make. Inexplicably, his main point seemed to be that his campaign would be as "clean as a hound's tooth." He kept saying it—or at least that's the way I remember the announcement—as if he had to change everyone's belief that, on the contrary, his campaign was going to be as dirty as a sheep's arse. And our campaign slogan was equally clueless in its arrogance: "Of course I'm voting Liberal." It must have been concocted by the same advertising genius who dreamed up Trudeau's slogan, which would nearly lose him his federal election the next year: "The land is strong."

In fairness to Joey, though, those of us who had strategized at Kaegudeck had all agreed with our lame campaign slogan. I seem to recall a comic book being presented as part of the campaign material, as well. And there was a film featuring Joey and his accomplishments called *The End of the Beginning*. It would not be long before the Tories had turned that around to the more believable jibe, "the beginning of the end." John Nolan reminded some of us that the day Joey had chosen for the election was the feast of St. Jude, the patron saint of lost causes.

The charismatic Frank Moores, who'd been given more than a year by Joey after becoming leader of the PC Party to prepare and become well-known, came across as a breath of fresh air. His big grinning TV face, big voice that sounded like highly popular singer Dick Nolan's, and his stand-up comic routine with a limitless supply of one-liners, many people found hard to resist. He had expanded his campaign slogan from "It won't be long now," that had been so useful in his federal election of 1968, to "Ladies and gentlemen, the time has come." Nothing else needed to be said. People would grin knowingly and give the thumbs up.

Even the fact that he was being sued for divorce by his long-suffering wife and mother of his many children, on top of Steve Neary's very plausible allegations that he habitually went skinny-dipping, and more, in mixed company, didn't reduce his attractiveness to a lot of the electorate. Indeed, every hint of scandal seemed to add to it. I recall a friend of mine I came across in Gander, who was a big PC supporter, saying to me, "Frank Moores? Jeez, Frank would screw a pile of rocks if he thought there was a snake under it." It was said in mock reproof, but he couldn't keep the grin and the good-ole-boy smug admiration off his face.

OUR OWN CAMPAIGN seemed to be heading nowhere fast. Leading up to the election, before going into hiding, Joey had gotten off a few good lines in spite of himself. When Frank Moores challenged him to an election or a debate, Joey had replied that Moores might drop dead if he accepted either challenge, and Moores was too much of an asset to the Liberal Party to risk losing him. But after the election was called, it seemed to be all Frank Moores all the time. Only when Joey came belatedly out of the hole into which he'd been poked and started to campaign vigorously in person, accompanied by the best feature of the campaign, his theme song, "All Around the Circle," did we start to come up in the polls. Late in the campaign, his appearances on media and on talk shows were successful. By election day, the tide was starting to turn. By then it was too late.

*

I SPENT MOST of the election in my own district, sensing a paradigm shift—as the new vogue term went—in the political thinking of the province. I couldn't watch a great deal of television, but what I did see convinced me that Moores had made himself a master of the medium, delivering his lines as effortlessly as a comedian in the Catskills. I remember his description of us in Joey's cabinet: The Liberal ministers were like Hush Puppies, he said. You buy them, lace up the tongue, and find them comfortable to walk on. A lot of it was pretty thin stuff like that, but effective, a measure of what easy targets we'd become for ridicule.

Moores beat all over the province accompanied by his girlfriend, Janis Johnson. Dodie—his wife—and the kids stayed home. The word was around everywhere that his marriage was on the rocks because he was a two-timing, unfaithful husband, but no one seemed to care. A lot of people were just too eager for a change to heed anything except getting rid of Joey. I could deduce from media reports that we'd more or less had it when a Liberal rally in Corner Brook was overshadowed and effaced in size and enthusiasm by Frank's PC rally.

Clyde Wells had been out of active politics, practising law in Corner Brook, for a year, but he reportedly made a radio commercial supporting the Tories. And Steve Neary told me that Wells was actively helping Tom Farrell, the PC candidate in Wells's old district of Humber East, to get elected. One cute Tory trick was an announcement that they were gathering affidavits signed by voters who had witnessed corruption and abuse by Liberal candidates. I never heard afterwards that they got any, but the propaganda impact beforehand was effective in adding to our negative image.

Scores of letters appeared in the newspapers, especially the *Evening Telegram* in St. John's, supporting the Tories and attacking the Liberals. This was before letters to the editor had to bear the name of the writers, but the *Telegram* assured the public that all the anonymous letters they published were legitimately sent by identifiable individuals and were not staged or fabricated by the Tory organization.

Frank was seen at rallies surrounded by worshipful supporters, many of whom he was calling by their first names. The word put out by the Tories was that he knew thousands and thousands of people personally from his travels throughout the province. A PC organizer told me later that the party's tactic was to arrange to place a local person next to Frank in his entourage who knew everyone in the community and who could whisper names of approaching people to him. One or two of the reporters covering his campaign sounded to me like the executive members of the Frank Duff Moores Booster Club. Meanwhile, the Liberal Party seemed to be operating an underground movement, with Joey playing the role of the closeted leader of a covert campaign, until much too late in the day.

CHAPTER TEN

The "Smooth" Transition to Frank

I WAS IN Baie Verte on election night, October 28, 1971, watching the returns with friends. Besides the plummeting fortunes of the Liberal Party as the counts came in, the fact that Joey was missing in action played on our minds. It turned out that he was driving around in his car all night avoiding media, and humans in general, as he listened to the devastating results on his car radio.

The turnout of voters was huge, nearly ninety per cent, probably the highest in history, with some districts reporting returns of over one hundred per cent of the voters list. This would become a big joke both in Newfoundland and on the mainland—names of voters must have been taken off headstones, or people must have voted multiple times under different names. In truth, it only indicated that there had been no revised voters list for years, and that the huge interest on election day required thousands of voters, including the droves of young people attracted to the polls, to be sworn in.

The PC Party reaped fifty-two per cent of the votes cast, compared to the Liberals' forty-four per cent, a clear moral victory as well as a political one for the Tories. The Liberals had dropped from thirty-nine seats in the last election to twenty now, and Joey suffered the loss of a half-dozen or more of his cabinet ministers.

The Tories had risen from the three members they'd elected last time to twenty-one. The popular vote should have produced a runaway majority government for Frank Moores. Only the previous gerrymandering of districts to weight them overwhelmingly in favour of the rural voter, where most of Joey's strength still lay, had kept the Liberal Party from dropping to a dozen or fewer seats.

Former Liberal Tom Burgess, now leader of the New Labrador Party, got elected in Labrador West. Because his seat could be used to either tie the election or put the Tories clearly in power, he proclaimed himself the "real premier," or in the alternative, "the kingmaker." One of my more irreverent colleagues said to me, "Tom is kingmaker now, is he? I guess he got tired of being the princess-maker."

I'd gotten to know Tom a little when he was elected in 1966 as a Liberal. I was surprised that, unlike everyone else I knew who'd come over here from the UK or Ireland as an adult, he did not seem to retain more than a vestige, if that, of his native accent. His pronunciations sounded like neutral Canadian. I thought to myself that this was a guy who really worked at fitting in. Which was, of course, exactly what any determined adventurer—or con man—would do.

One evening, I'd driven up Kingsbridge Road in the middle of a sudden blizzard in the winter of 1967, heading eagerly for the house of my fiancée, Penny, who had cooked up a scoff of Lobster Newburg for us. En route I'd spotted a lone straggler trudging along the road in the storm and I'd stopped to pick the unfortunate up. It turned out to be Tom Burgess, MHA, and he had on ordinary dress shoes and no gloves and, at most, a skimpy jacket, without an outer coat.

I told him I knew our winters had nothing on Labrador West but his attire tonight was ridiculous. He said with a laugh that he'd received an urgent call to visit a "friend" who had a room at the Newfoundland

Hotel. We stopped at Penny's house, where Tom came in to dry off, and after a hasty, muted-in-tone phone call, he joined us in the meal. Penny's parents were out of town. Together, Tom and I succeeded in considerably damaging the bottle of Rémy Martin cognac I'd brought, before Tom left with enthusiasm, considering the weather, for the nearby hotel.

When my future father-in-law got back a day or two later, he wondered what had happened to his rubber overshoes that he had left in the porch. He needed them in the snow and he couldn't find them anywhere. For years afterwards, he would fix his steely eye on mine and ponder aloud the fate of his favourite overshoes, suspecting with uncanny insight that I was somehow the culprit. It was a wonder he ever gave me his consent to marry his daughter. Even years later, following this 1971 election, I never mustered the courage to tell him that the man who had now become our great "kingmaker" had made off with his overshoes back then so as not to miss his urgent rendezvous at the Newfoundland Hotel.

After the election, Tom Burgess was on a dangerous political high, crowing everywhere that he was holding the balance of power in the province. It was in effect a tie election because no one, including Tom himself, had any idea what he was going to do or what party, if any, he was going to side with. Though relishing his own description of himself in the media as "the real premier," he was absolutely clueless in his balance-of-power role.

There ensued a bidding war from both sides for Tom's loyalties. Some realists on either side threw up their arms in despair: it was hopeless; you couldn't buy Tom Burgess, you could only rent him by the hour, like a room in a sleazy hotel. Smallwood himself would ultimately broadcast his own painful conclusion: "Newfoundlanders should get down on their knees and pray that Mr. Burgess does not hold their fate in his hands."

One of the rationales Joey gave for not winning the 1971 election, when he finally spoke publicly, was that he'd been the only premier since Confederation, and, therefore, people had no one to compare him with except God Almighty: even the very best premier would suffer, he said, by comparison with divine perfection. It was nice that he quoted me, even without attribution, but I noticed that he'd left out the main point I'd made to him in Hong Kong (i.e. when voters got the opportunity to compare him with another mere mortal, he would really shine). Whoops—I was slightly off there.

A couple of weeks after the election, when the media belatedly reported what appeared to have been blatant insider trading of securities by Frank Moores, Joey waited in vain for it to benefit him. The news stories narrated that a couple of months ago, in August of 1971, just a day before the Toronto brokerage firm Malone Lynch had gone insolvent and was suspended from trading, Moores had transferred out of that company a quarter of a million dollars' worth of securities. The principal of the firm, Terry Malone, was one of Moores's best friends from their school days together, and there were serious allegations that Moores had saved a fortune by acting on insider information, while other investors had lost their shirts. Amazingly, the scandal had no apparent effect on Moores's political ascendancy or Joey's descent. No consequences, criminal, civil, or political, resulted against Moores, and he sailed blithely on. One naughty woman said to me that Frank should be called K-Y Jelly because he was able to slip and slither smoothly in and out of anything. I think it was the first time I'd ever heard of the product. But it seemed to suit.

Meanwhile, Joey obstinately refused to give up the premiership to Moores until every question arising from the election was finally resolved, and the House of Assembly had met to see which administration, if any, would have the support of a majority of MHAs. At the same time, according to the reports we received, Moores was resorting to every manoeuvre and expedient to try and seize the government.

He badgered the lieutenant-governor orally and in writing to do the right thing (i.e. make him premier). He contacted the federal minister of Justice, John Turner, to intervene or, at least, to meet with him on the issue, neither of which Turner would even contemplate. He tried to park his car in the premier's parking place at Confederation Building, only to be rebuffed in the attempt by a zealous and irate Joeyite—this was the laughable battle of the limos, Frank's Cadillac El Dorado versus Joey's Chrysler Imperial. And he continued the more depressing battle of the payoffs, hoping to win over the heart or, to exaggerate wildly, the mind of Tom Burgess, who had set himself up in a suite at the Holiday Inn, coincidentally near John C. Doyle's.

When fellow Newfoundlander Senator Eugene Forsey, a nationally recognized constitutional expert who never disguised his hatred of Joey, nevertheless pronounced that the lieutenant-governor was acting entirely in accordance with the Canadian constitution in not forcing Smallwood's resignation in favour of Moores, Frank fled the country. He and Janis Johnson and Tom Farrell and his wife took off for the Caribbean, leaving John Crosbie and others to deal with what one prominent Tory described to me as this "fiasco, farce, and fuckery." It was certainly all of that. And the battle raged on in Frank's absence.

Many observers said that Andrew Crosbie was some cute: he had cleverly engineered this virtual tie election. He had cooked it up so that he didn't lose for Joey but he didn't beat his brother, John, either. The evil genius had deliberately concocted this mesmerizing struggle for supremacy.

Joey, despite trailing in the popular vote, still clung to power because some seven Tories had been elected by less than a hundred votes in their districts. A change of just three or four hundred votes overall, he claimed, would have given him a clear majority in the House of Assembly. A general election was not a popularity contest or a beauty pageant, he lectured. It was not the total number of votes for a party that counted, but the number of seats: therefore, he had a solemn duty to wait until the official count was conducted and the recounts had taken place and the true result of the election was crystal clear. The proper exercise of democracy and the rule of law, the premier intoned, required nothing less.

For their part, the Tories screeched that Smallwood's actions were anti-democratic and a violation of the rule of law and nothing short of the actions of a Third World tinpot dictator. John Crosbie threatened to issue a call for civil disobedience throughout the province. I remember the dismay of some of his strongest supporters at that thought, especially those who could well recall the mob scenes and riots of the 1930s. Hearing Crosbie's threat, Joey reminded us in cabinet of our solemn oaths as ministers, sworn on the very Bible itself, to defend against "intestine insurrections." One of my colleagues whispered to me, "Don't tell me he's got the shits now, on top of everything else."

The recounts in six close districts confirmed the election-night results, so that was no help to us. But it was discovered that the returning officer in Sally's Cove in the district of St. Barbe South had inadvertently burned the ballots. Joey ordered that matter to the Supreme Court, claiming that the election there was null and void and that a new by-election had to be held. I can still see lawyer Nat Noel, a former MHA and thorough gentleman, trudging away from Joey's office carrying his instructions. He did not look optimistic. And the judge did turn the Liberals down, deciding that an election result could not be determined by the improper actions of a returning officer. On the judicial recount, the PC candidate was confirmed as the member by a handful of votes. And that should have been the end of the wrangling, with the PCs forming the government and Frank Moores becoming premier.

Meanwhile, however, an incredible amount of toing and froing between parties by several elected members was taking place, including Tom Burgess, Hugh Shea, and Alex Dunphy. Tom Burgess, especially, was allegedly involved in swanky hotel meetings, knocking back expensive single malt scotches, trips to the tropics, private jets, bribe offers, all mostly orchestrated—allegedly—by John C. Doyle. These machinations kept Joey in as premier beyond Christmas of 1971.

Premier Smallwood started off using camaraderie during all this to try to make Ed Roberts and me pull in the same direction as himself—"We three make a pretty good team," he insisted at the beginning. But he was soon calling us the "Bobbsey Twins" because we stuck together in resisting his own efforts to benefit Shaheen and Doyle. And he did do his damnedest to try to divide us and turn us against each other. John C. Doyle, a crook? Joey would demand incredulously when that possibility was suggested. Ridiculous, he'd say. The man inadvertently sent fifty unregistered shares through the mail. It had been a minor matter, to which his lawyer advised him to plead guilty and get a slap on the wrist. Instead, the vindictive American justice system sentenced him to three months in an American jail. Have you ever spent time in an American jail? Ask Al Vardy what that was like. No wonder Doyle jumped bail.

In addition to contending with the Tories for Tom Burgess's fleeting affections, Joey reported to us that he'd received signals from two newly elected Tories that they wanted to join the Liberal caucus. I, for one, found it hard not to laugh out loud when I heard that. You mean to say there was actually *one* politician in the province, let alone two, who wanted to climb out of the lifeboat and back onto the deck of the *Titanic*?

I didn't know of any on our side who believed that there was anyone that stupid, even among the Tories. But we were wrong. Evidently, Progressive Conservative MHAs Hugh Shea and Alex Dunphy were preparing to do precisely that—Shea because he wanted a cabinet position that Moores would not promise him, and Dunphy because he was on a drunken binge.

John Crosbie telephoned me at home one night. I listened to his accurate description of Smallwood's ghastly activities and to his threats to bring charges against everyone in the Liberal Party for something or other regarding Dunphy. Among the allegations was that one Father Ron Kelly, the parish priest over Dunphy's way and the son of long-time big Liberal Hubert Kelly, had gotten alcoholic Dunphy on the booze over Christmas and enticed him to go Liberal. Apparently it became a close-run thing, Dunphy's defection being barely prevented by threats, undercover operations, and physical restraints by his family and colleagues. I told Crosbie the truth: I didn't know squat about any of that. (Incidentally, this was the same Father Kelly, I'd be later told, who would be charged with sexually abusing boys, and leave the priesthood to become a real estate tycoon.)

That would not be the only time during these days that John Crosbie contacted me. He called again to implore me to end the political stalemate by making Smallwood "come to his senses." I told him he should know from personal experience that what he was asking was impossible, though probably still easier than him trying to make his own leader, Frank, come to *his* senses.

Here's a hint at the magnitude of Crosbie's task vis-à-vis Moores: Frank had a well-earned name for copulating with anything with a discernible pulse all during the election, and afterwards he did nothing to tone down the notoriety; he exuded a devil-may-care attitude to the allegations against him of insider trading; there was a media field day on reports that his wife, Dodie, the mother of his seven children, was petitioning for divorce in Supreme Court against him for adultery and mental cruelty; reports abounded that Frank was meeting down south with the great Satan, John C. Doyle; and while all this turmoil raged at home, the PC leader himself was "hove off" on a beach in the Caribbean drinking rum punch by the gallon and enjoying an adulterous affair. The word we got, and what spurred Joey's hopes, was that a growing number of elected Tory members, perhaps even a majority, wanted Moores to resign. Crosbie was said to be leading a bloodless coup to topple Frank's leadership. For the first time in years I heard from Joey no criticism of John Crosbie's ruthless ambitions.

In the middle of all this, Joey appointed me acting minister of Justice and acting minister of Economic Development. If that was meant to keep me in line with his own political, legal, and economic finagling, he was mistaken. One afternoon, Joey asked me to come up to his office. A man was there I didn't know, chatting with Al Vardy, my "deputy minister." Just before, at lunch that day, during a discussion about what might be going on with Tom Burgess and others, Vardy had made the point that the safest of all illegal transactions was the cash bribe. Both the giver and the taker would incriminate themselves if they ratted, so there was a big incentive against doing that, and if it was done properly, cash could not be traced. At worst it was one person's word against another. Vardy's points seemed to be academic and in general at the time, although one of us listening had joked, "You're not talking from experience, are you, Al?" To which he'd replied, "My God, no."

That afternoon in the premier's office, Smallwood and Vardy introduced me to the stranger. He was from the mainland, and he was interested in setting up some sort of enterprise with government approval and help. Would I talk to the man on general principles here now, Joey asked, so that when the matter came to cabinet in proper form, I, as minister, would already be up to scratch on it? It struck me as a bizarre way to approach it, especially since our government didn't appear to have a long life expectancy, but after a hesitation I said, okay, no harm in listening. I expected the man to make pitch to all three of us, but the premier said he'd already listened to him, so I could just go outside the door into the cabinet room and talk there. Meanwhile, he would sign letters and documents on his desk.

Outside, the man started his proposal and was not far into it when he said that, of course, there was $20,000 up front for me. I looked at him incredulously, wondering if I'd heard right. He was grinning at me like a hyena. It now became all too clear that I had heard right. This was the first time in scores of deals involving government action or approval, big or small, whether involving John Shaheen or John Doyle or their minions or the owner of a Bull's Eye shop, that I'd ever been offered anything that even looked like a bribe. I turned my back on the guy, walked past Vardy into Joey's office, and said to the premier: "Whatever that deal is, I'm not interested in having anything to do with it, and I'm not interested in having any further dealings on anything with that fellow." Joey said there must have been some misunderstanding. I said yes, there must have been. Joey said we'd talk later. But the deal was never brought up later, and I never laid eyes on the guy again.

There may have been one later bribe attempt, but my memory of it is as hazy now as my understanding of it was then. Ed Roberts and I experienced, separately and confidentially, the same vague approach by John C. Doyle regarding some benefit in the works for each of us. It may have been a hint of largesse in the event of a leadership race. Whatever it was, we mentioned it to Steve Neary for his opinion before deciding how to confront the premier with it. But Steve took the bull by the horns and went to Smallwood with it immediately. Soon after, he told me that Joey had gone off the head in denial that any bribe, inducement, or kickback could possibly have been intended by Doyle. There the matter died and nothing went any further. But I do remember it as an additional incentive to Ed and myself to bring the Smallwood government to an end as soon as possible, while endeavouring to salvage some dignity and future life for our Liberal Party as a viable political institution.

On the matter of bribes, years later I would ask Andrew Crosbie if he had ever, to his own direct knowledge, become aware of the commission by Joey Smallwood of a personally crooked or corrupt act. Andrew replied that he had observed something like that only once: leading up to the election, he was coming through the door into Smallwood's office unnoticed one day after hours when he saw the premier trying to stuff a wad of folded money down into the shirt pocket of a leading St. John's journalist. The journalist seemed to be resisting the move and batted Joey's hand away, whereupon Joey tried again, only to have the journalist remove the wad and force it back into Joey's hand. Joey then put the bills into his own jacket pocket. Andrew said he never knew if the journalist's coyness regarding the money had resulted from his having spotted Andrew coming in or if it was genuine rejection of a bribe attempt. The journalist left immediately, and Andrew and Joey discussed their election business. The matter never came up. I remarked to Andrew that if it was the bribe attempt that it looked like, it was awfully amateurish. Andrew grinned back and said, yes, it was almost as if Joey wasn't used to doing it.

AS PART OF Joey's continued attempt to play Ed Roberts and me off against each other, I could count on a telephone call or a meeting at least every couple of days in which the only purpose seemed to be to make one or more of the following statements:

"I just finished speaking with Roberts on this and his comments were not very penetrating compared to yours. Don't be misled by him, Bill. Now don't, I'm telling you. You're way ahead of him."

"I told Ed earlier—didn't I, Al?—that, no, Bill Rowe is not a dumdum."

"I just finished speaking to Ed and he could offer nothing by way of real analysis of the situation, as you just did. I was grossly mistaken about his reputed brilliance, and unfortunately it was I who earlier caused his intelligence to be so greatly overrated."

"The tremendous contrast between Ed's political skills and yours have become very apparent to me, Bill. It is the huge disparity that exists between a natural political leader"—here Joey's forefinger pointed at me—"and a competent but unimaginative deputy minister." Here he threw his thumb over his shoulder in the general direction of the absent Ed.

"To think that his father wasted tens of thousands of dollars sending him to a school for sow's ears [i.e. private school], hoping to turn him into a silk purse. It must have been heartbreaking for him to see all that money down the drain."

"I would rate Ed's cunning self-interest as equal to that of Alfred B. Morine, and, of course, Morine has gone down as the evil genius without parallel in our history."

"Did you know, Bill, that when I mentioned to Ed that I wanted you to run in the 1966 election, he thought it was an extremely bad idea? Yes, way back then. His jealousy and animosity didn't start yesterday; it has been breeding and festering and swelling for more than five years."

I could only imagine what Joey was saying about me whenever I or we stood in his way. But whatever he said or did, it didn't work. Ed and I had long ago initiated an informal pact to withstand together anything Joey tried to do that we didn't like the look of or the sound of, until this ordeal ended.

IT WAS MORE than a week into the new year, 1972, before Frank Moores wended his way, slow and snail-like, back to St. John's. Perhaps the thought of having to see John Crosbie's face made him drag his feet. We received word that John was insisting on getting together with Frank immediately on his arrival, very late at night, "as soon as he gets off that effing plane." At their meeting, near fisticuffs ensued, with John demanding his resignation and Frank drunkenly refusing, at least for the time being. Everything was going to be all right, Frank assured him—John would soon see.

Whoever first said that Frank Moores was "as lucky as a shithouse rat" was onto something. Within days, the Supreme Court came down with that decision on the disputed election in St. Barbe South. Smallwood raged that the decision had nothing to do with the law. It was caused, he claimed, by "Unsavory" John Carter. There were two John Carters involved in public affairs in Newfoundland. One was the Tory politician John Carter, who owned a savory farm on Mount Scio—hence "Savory John Carter." The other was a leading reporter with the *Evening Telegram*—hence dubbed "Unsavory John Carter" to distinguish him from the first one. It was Unsavory John who, Joey ranted, buggered up the Liberals' chances in St. Barbe South.

Unsavory John had earlier written in his paper that Judge Arthur Mifflin had resigned years before as a Liberal member at Joey's request to allow Max Lane to run in the by-election. In return, Joey would see to it that Mifflin was appointed to the Supreme Court. Mifflin went furious and beside himself, naturally, at Unsavory John's insinuation of improper misconduct.

Now Mifflin overcame a serious illness at this time, it was said, by strength of will alone in order to make sure he heard the case on that judicial recount in St. Barbe South. He would make it blindingly obvious to all that he was not—understand? *not*—under Joey's influence. His proof: the Supreme Court decision confirmed the election of Frank's PC candidate there.

Then Frank's wife, Dodie, went public with a statement that, contrary to vile rumours, she was not divorcing her devoted husband. And Moores declared that his leadership was not in fact being challenged, and there were no contradictions on the point from Crosbie or anyone else within the party. And Tom Burgess confirmed by statement and letter his undying loyalty to Moores and the PC Party. And one of our Liberal MHAs resigned out of the blue to go back to his job as magistrate.

It all made Steve Neary shake his head during a conversation we had at the time: no one gave a shag, he said, about Frank's boozing or fornication or naked orgies, or inside trading, or fancy trips in the Mediterranean on a yacht he suddenly and mysteriously owned, or adultery, or divorce, or abandonment of wife and half a dozen children, or illegally inducing a disenchanted Liberal MHA to resign by offering him his job back as provincial court judge. I agreed and asked a question neither of us could be bothered to even try to answer: How badly did people want us out of the government, in the name of God, if they were prepared to tolerate all that and more from their prospective new premier?

Then, something happened around this time that brought Ed Roberts and me right to the end of our tethers. Before Christmas in 1971, cabinet had passed an order-in-council guaranteeing a loan of $30 million to Doyle's Canadian Javelin to keep the linerboard mill project from collapsing utterly. But there was a huge safeguard in the order, at cabinet's insistence. It required the minister of Economic Development to negotiate a backup agreement and security for the guarantee, which then had to receive the prior approval of cabinet before anything else could proceed.

Instead of that legal procedure being followed, as Ed Roberts and I would learn later, John C. Doyle came into possession of the unauthorized guarantee, which he then used to borrow the money without any agreement about the disposal of the funds. Our suspicions that something untoward was afoot were first aroused when Joey was leaving for his Christmas vacation. He regularly spent his Christmas breaks in Florida, and this Christmas, despite the ongoing political crisis, was no exception.

At lunch the day he left, during a wide-ranging conversation on the necessity of teamwork and solidarity in politics, Joey quoted to us a British prime minister's advice to his cabinet: "It doesn't matter what lie we tell, gentlemen, just as long as we all tell the same lie." Ed and I looked at each other. That sounded ominous. Then, on leaving the dining room to get ready to go down south, Joey gazed at me feelingly, shook my hand fervently, and issued a rousing declaration: "Be bold." As he skedaddled away, I wondered to myself, what the hell was that all about?

I soon found out. Guests were arriving at my house for a Christmas party, when I took a call from Deputy Minister of Finance Dirk Peper. He'd been notified by his contacts of what looked like funny business overseas. John C. Doyle was in Europe raising $30 million prematurely on the strength of an unauthorized government guarantee. We had to immediately track down and secure the money, which Doyle now appeared to be in the process of moving to an offshore bank in the Caribbean.

Dirk Peper, Ed Roberts, and I, together with other civil service stalwarts, spent much of the Christmas period in Dirk's office in Confederation Building chasing down the loot. We contacted Joey and said we would be resigning and announcing why unless the $30 million that

Doyle had raised on the unsanctioned government guarantee was put under government control at once. Joey claimed he didn't know what we were talking about.

At length, after finding out what London hotel Doyle was in, and ascertaining from hotel security that he was in his room but was refusing to respond to knocks on the door or answer his telephone, we had the hotel security slip telexes under his door stating that we were alerting Interpol. We also reached his lawyers in Montreal and St. John's, with whom we had some tense conversations in the nature of ultimatums. At last, we succeeded in having the millions deposited in a reputable bank under the control of trustees including our deputy minister of Finance and lawyers. We issued each other a grim Merry Christmas, and went home to belated or missed family festivities.

BY NOW, RUMOURS were floating throughout Confederation Building and around the province, fanned by the PC Party, that there was a threat of a revolt in Joey's own caucus. I'm not aware of any general revolt, if one had been brewing. What was happening was that, because Ed Roberts and I had been taking the premier on constantly regarding the Shaheen refinery and the John Doyle paper mill, our actions were well-known in the system. We were totally fed up with Joey's attempts to prolong the life of the government with him at the helm, and we certainly didn't hide from top officials that we were not striving fanatically or officiously to keep our government in power. At various meetings with high officials over the period, I certainly made my feelings and intentions clear.

Interestingly, one of those officials, who was mid-level at the time but would go on to greater things in the bureaucracy and in private industry, told someone whom I approached for support during my own run at the party leadership five or six years later that I'd been prepared to give up after the 1971 election. The implication appeared to be that I hadn't acted strongly enough to keep the Liberal Government in power.

Obviously, he had forgotten how out of control things were with Joey and how dispiriting, and stupid, it was to try to cling onto power by your fingernails when another party and leader had the support of a majority of the voters. John Crosbie, who would become the top minister and deputy premier in the new Moores government, would find out all about what had been going on, and he didn't forget. He told me privately and stated publicly how aware he became of what Roberts and I had been through, and what we'd done to stabilize government activities, especially to keep Shaheen, Doyle, and Joey under control as the political crisis unfolded in those latter days.

THROUGHOUT ALL THE shenanigans on both sides, Joey kept the Liberal Party leadership issue alive and well. At one point, when the St. Barbe South election was still in doubt, and Joey expected it to be overturned in our favour by the court, he invited FFAW president Richard Cashin to lunch and explored with him the possibility of his running in a St. Barbe South by-election, and becoming leader of the party and premier. I doubt that Richard was ever tempted by Joey's wacky initiative, but it might have changed the direction of politics in the province if it had come to pass. It was rendered academic, anyway, when the judges upheld the election of the Tory candidate in St. Barbe South.

When a Liberal leadership convention was called for early February, I had yet another hallucinatory experience with Joey. He asked me to come and see him privately. There he urged me to run for leader with his support. He would arrange, he said, to have $100,000 put into my campaign. I managed not to roar with laughter. This $100,000 was starting to get a bit worn out from overuse. The word I'd received from a confidant of Tom Burgess was that Joey was prepared to instruct his backers to finance Tom's campaign in the same amount if he would come over to the Liberals and run for leader. I left Smallwood and immediately encouraged Ed Roberts to run for the Liberal leadership, and publicly supported his candidacy.

John Crosbie called me up at home out of the blue the same night and asked me why I wasn't running for the leadership myself. Didn't I have the guts? He didn't think Ed had the royal jelly for successful leadership. I asked sarcastically how on earth John would know anything about that—someone running for leader who lacked the essential qualities of leadership. He did laugh, but it was rather thin.

I also asked him how come he was still trying to divide the Liberal Party. I thought he had moved on from that and was now trying to cause a split in the Tory Party. Didn't he have his hands full with his brand new palace coup, trying to oust his current leader, Frank Moores? John rather spritely moved on to his real reason for calling: "What in the name of fuck is Joey up to?" I replied that I was hoping John could tell me. And, while he was at it, give me a hint what Frankie was up to, as well. Except for a few chuckles at all the absurdities confronting us, our conversation ended no further ahead than when it started.

At last, with all his escape routes barred off, Joey announced the inevitable: he'd be resigning as premier on January 18, 1972, and advising the lieutenant-governor to offer Frank Moores the opportunity to form a government. On that day, which was my young son Dorian's fourth birthday, John Harnum, Joey's hand-picked lieutenant-governor, passed the government of the province over to Frank Moores. Joey took off for Clearwater, Florida. I went home and enjoyed my son's birthday party. After the past few months in Newfoundland politics, I was pleasantly surprised at how mature and well-behaved I found the preschool celebrants there.

CHAPTER ELEVEN

Frankie, the Chairman of the Board

UPON BEING SWORN in as premier, one of Frank Moores's first public duties was to proclaim that he had found the intercom system in the premier's office where Joey could secretly listen in on his ministers in their own offices. I recall that the point made an excellent public impression: Frank was replacing a dictator as premier who was now revealed to have been more paranoid and tyrannical—and laughable—than anyone had ever thought.

Moores also made much of having himself sworn in, not just as premier, but also as minister of Fisheries. At last, he would be bringing attention from the very top of the government to this vital area so neglected by Smallwood, he claimed. As the most powerful person in the land, with vast previous experience in the fishing industry, he was now personally taking charge of straightening out the perennially troubled fishery. It turned out to be a brilliant con that lasted less than three months, just long enough to get through the next election.

*

COMPARED TO THE leadership contest in the Liberal Party between Smallwood and Crosbie in 1969, there wasn't much to this one in February of 1972, either in the lead-up to it or at the convention itself. Tom Burgess, in a breathtaking display of egotism, had decided to run for leader as well. Just days before, a couple of weeks after the PC Party had taken over the government, the Liberal Party had received a consolation prize—some of us called it the booby prize: Tom Burgess and Hughie Shea formally joined us. At the convention, Roberts beat Burgess easily, 564 to eighty-two.

But a lot of people, myself included, were surprised that Tom got so many votes. Smallwood played no open part that I was aware of, but supporters of Burgess told me that Joey had undertaken to deliver the leadership to him. Why that would be so at this stage, I couldn't fathom—perhaps simple dislike of Roberts—but if true, it may have explained why Burgess looked so shocked when he lost. He'd actually believed that Joey could still deliver.

AFTER THE CONVENTION, following the previous months of political stress and chaos, Ed Roberts and I took a few winter days of a working holiday down south. We visited with Andrew Crosbie and Barron Macdonald at Andrew's villa on Lyford Cay in the Bahamas. A private gated community founded by the great Canadian buccaneer E. P. Taylor, Lyford Cay was home to the world's wealthy and celebrated. Ten years before our visit, we were told, US president John F. Kennedy stayed at E. P. Taylor's place to hold talks with British Prime Minister Harold Macmillan on solving the problems of the world. Our own talks were out of that league but probably equally futile—we were plotting the imminent comeback of the Newfoundland and Labrador Liberal Party.

One day, soon after we got back to Newfoundland, I ran into lawyer Nathaniel Noel, former Liberal MHA, and later to be a Supreme Court judge. In the House and in his practice of law, I'd always found him to be a fount of common sense and of no-nonsense, penetrating insights. What he said to me today, therefore, after I'd told him of our bullish political outlook, unnerved me a little: the Liberal Party had a long ways to go down yet, he believed, and would be out of power for nearly as long as Smallwood had been in.

I argued against his analysis, but even at the time I had the feeling that it was pure bravado on my part. We had to remember, Noel added, that the Tories had the whole power of the state in their hands now to undermine Joey's legacy and besmirch his reputation, and the Liberal Party was going to be tainted by association for a long time, especially if they laid charges against him. Noel wondered when Smallwood was coming back to Newfoundland to face the music, by the way. Not soon, I thought: if Bully Boy Crosbie and Witch-Hunt Willy Marshall were up here jangling the keys to the dungeon every time my name was mentioned, I'd probably stay down south for a while, too.

Late in February 1972, rumours abounded over what a couple of our more timorous colleagues called "an election scare." But Frank couldn't call an election, we told them. The new premier had summoned the House of Assembly together for the beginning of March, and before anything else could happen, he had to find out if he had the support of the House.

Because of defections from the Tories since Joey had resigned, Frank did not now have as many members in the House as the Liberals, let alone a majority. Therefore, if he were to advise the lieutenant-governor to dissolve the House and have an election, the Queen's representative would have to say no. When the House would come to meet, Moores's government was bound to be defeated, and Ed Roberts, with more MHAs supporting him, would no doubt be asked to try to form a government.

Then, a short time before the House was to reconvene, Ed Roberts got wind of an attempt by Moores or his minions to corrupt by bribery one of our MHAs, Bill Saunders, the member for Bay de Verde district.

The report, which I believe originated with Smallwood from Florida, was that Saunders had been paid cash to stay away from the House when it opened. If true, that would deprive us of the one-seat advantage the Liberals had over the PC caucus, and put government and Opposition in a tie position.

Ed Roberts and I drove over to Bill Saunders's hometown of Carbonear—the same as Frank's—to meet with him and try to find out what was going on. In person, Bill Saunders displayed shock at the very suggestion that he was resigning or even that he would not be in his seat when the House opened. He tearfully denied any inducement attempts along those lines, and bawled his eyes out swearing up and down that he was loyal to the Liberal Party and to Ed as leader. Ed and I left him, full of misgivings—the man had clearly been deranged by something traumatic. What we didn't know while we listened to Bill's vows of undying loyalty was that Frank Moores had Bill Saunders's resignation in his pocket.

When the House opened soon afterwards, Saunders was not in his seat. And it stayed empty all through the afternoon sitting. Lieutenant-Governor Harnum read the Throne Speech, which contained so many PC Government promises that it set the record as the longest Throne Speech ever delivered in Newfoundland's history. Later the same day, Frank went to see Lieutenant-Governor Harnum to advise the dissolution of the House and try to get Harnum to issue a writ for a general election.

Already pretty pleased with himself over engineering the bribing of MHA Saunders, Frank would boast later how well he also sucked in and pulled the wool over the eyes of Lieutenant-Governor Harnum. He would brag that he cajoled and fast-talked an assurance out of the Queen's representative that, in the hypothetical event of a tie or equal support for both parties in the House, he would grant the erstwhile premier, Moores, the right to call an election in order to break the logjam. Having secured that giant concession, without full disclosure, from the naive lieutenant-governor, Frank only then whipped out of his pocket Bill Saunders's resignation from the House. Each party now had equal support, thus meeting the lieutenant-governor's threshold requirement, and a writ was issued for the calling of an election.

Speculation was rampant later over exactly how big the bribe had been. It was well-known that if Saunders had sat in the House for just that one afternoon, he would have received his sessional indemnity of $10,000 and his pension benefits would have been greatly enhanced. Knowledgeable outside guesswork and inside information trickling our way concurred on this: Saunders had been paid at least $100,000 in 1972 to resign, an amount worth over half a million in today's dollars. How the criminal bribe was actually brought about was another question.

One school of thought credited a big Tory family member of Saunders by marriage with steering the transaction to a successful conclusion. Others believed the deed combined the adaptable political loyalty and business genius of Andrew Crosbie. After all, hadn't he been brother John's top 1969 leadership campaign backer, then Joey's 1971 election campaign manager, and now wasn't he rumoured to be back as Frankie and Johnnie's 1972 close adviser and confidant? Certainly John Crosbie himself denied nothing and, although he was always sparing in his praise of Frank Moores on every other matter, he did believe that Frank deserved his and everyone else's praise and congratulations for being so good at that sort of thing—removing by any means, buying off or other underhanded method, a legitimately elected member who stood in the way of their assuming power.

Frank was always cute and coy in his response to the allegation of bribery. He wouldn't be surprised, he grinned, if money had changed hands, but he certainly had no knowledge of it. Oh my goodness, no, he'd insist, an Oscar-winning look of hurt at the very thought appearing on his face—sure that would have put him in the same cesspool with John C. Doyle.

*

A CYNIC IN the gallery of the House of Assembly would have been amused to look down at the government members of Frank Moores after the election of March 1972. Many had won their seats largely as a result of allegations of corruption against the "previous administration" of Joe Smallwood. And now they had self-congratulatory looks of holier-than-thou righteousness on their mugs. But sometimes the mask would slip to show Cheshire cat grins of pleasure at how clever they'd been. Because they knew, unless moronically stupid, that the opening for their government to become ensconced there had resulted from a criminal act.

Niccolò Machiavelli would have been delighted to observe that, more than 400 years after composing his political insights for the loathsome Borgias, the glorious end still justified the shitty means. You had to hand it to Frank Moores—he was a genius at it. Ed Roberts and the rest of us, including Joey Smallwood himself, were like children in traffic when it came to a manipulator of Frank's stature.

Years later, when I mentioned on the air the buying off of MHA Bill Saunders, I received a sad and plaintive letter from one of Saunders's family members, heartbroken at such terrible allegations. They were all absolutely untrue, she claimed: Bill Saunders would never have been a party to anything evil like that.

THE ELECTION RESULTS of March 24, 1972, were not surprising. Besides everything else he had going for him, a big picture appeared in all the papers of Frank being kissed by Dodie, his darling wife, happily reunited in love for the election. Right afterwards, though, she would waste no time divorcing him. But perhaps the most devastating single blow administered to the Liberals by the Tories had happened in the district of Humber West.

Ed Roberts had told me many times that Clyde Wells, now apparently supporting the Liberal Party, was in charge of making sure that the west coast districts had Liberal candidates. When nomination day arrived, however, Frank Moores was allowed to go in Humber West by acclamation, completely unopposed. When I heard that, I told myself that our credibility as a party had been so sabotaged, I'd be surprised if we won any seats at all. In the event, individual Liberal candidates managed by trench warfare in their districts to pull a handful of seats out of the fire. The PCs won in thirty-three districts, and the great Liberal Party was reduced to a rump of nine members. Only four of us possessed any experience in government: Earl Winsor, Steve Neary, Ed Roberts, and myself.

WHEN THE HOUSE of Assembly opened after the March election, the Moores government was so accusatory and vengeful concerning "the previous administration" that the leader of the Opposition, Ed Roberts, and the caucus decided we needed to launch a spirited and accurate defence of our own individual roles. Ed asked me to give our story in the House of Assembly regarding our dealings with Shaheen and Doyle in the last days of Joey's government. I did so with no punches pulled, especially about the machinations of John C. Doyle.

I was gratified to receive publicly and privately the thanks of my colleagues, especially Neary and Winsor, who, along with Roberts and myself, had been coming under a barrage of criticisms and accusations. Earl Winsor described how demoralized our caucus was in the face of the Tory onslaught, but that our morale and backbone had been revived by the facts I was able to state in the House. The upshot from Joey's point of view, though, as he stewed and festered down in Florida under reports of our "disloyalty," was that he formed a visceral animosity toward me, as well as Ed Roberts.

It would be nearly ten years before Smallwood spoke an amicable word to me again. Perhaps the worst of it from Joey's standpoint was that, after John Crosbie had had an opportunity to look into the actions of the last weeks of the Liberal Government, he conceded publicly that Roberts and I had stood up to Smallwood's excesses. Joey took that statement as proof, in his perverse moral scheme, of our disloyalty, where his concept of loyalty was a one-way street which led only to him, never back from him.

THE MOORES GOVERNMENT commissioned Fabian O'Dea, former lieutenant-governor, affluent lawyer, and big Tory, to investigate Smallwood. According to O'Dea's report, seven liquor stores owned by a company with three shareholders had been leased by the government or its agency at high rent for twenty years. Joey was alleged to be a one-third owner of the buildings, with Al Vardy as one of his partners. Joey claimed complete ignorance of the deal.

O'Dea's report also stated that Joey and two other individuals had put up their shares in the liquor store company as collateral to borrow a million and a half dollars to buy shares in Brinco at the same time that Joey's government was negotiating with Brinco about the Upper Churchill. Some saw this conflict of interest as the explanation for Joey's turning down a proposal from Premier Lesage and his then-Energy minister, René Lévesque, that the governments of Newfoundland and Quebec develop the Upper Churchill jointly themselves or in combination with the Government of Canada. It was Joey's conflict of interest, the allegation went, that led to the fiasco of the Upper Churchill contract between Brinco and Hydro Quebec, which left Newfoundland and Labrador with virtually nothing, and Quebec with nearly everything, when energy prices later escalated.

LESS THAN A year after Smallwood's resignation as premier, the media reported that early one morning, just over a week before Christmas in 1972, eight RCMP officers surrounded his house at Roaches Line and took possession of all his documents. I recall that earlier there were reports that some PC Party henchmen had looted some papers of Joey's from some premises or office of his, and I accused long-time party stalwart Harvey Cole, an assistant to John Crosbie, of the deed. Crosbie told me that the gaunt-looking Harvey hadn't done it; I must have seen "some other cadaver," he laughed. And Harvey himself bawled out the next time he saw me at a public function, "Hello, you shit." Crosbie offered no defence, however, to my public statement that he himself was acting like someone "unhinged" in his vendetta against Joey. It was my final attempt to get across to Smallwood and the public that he was not being abandoned by all his old colleagues. It didn't work with Smallwood.

At the time of the RCMP raid, Joey was in the middle of writing his memoirs, which came out in 1973. No charges were ever laid against him, but the police kept his personal papers for five years, impeding his research. Meanwhile, Frank Moores and his cohorts spread the rumour around that Joey—who claimed he had travelled to London to study documents for his memoirs—had actually visited Switzerland. They alleged that he was seen entering a bank there, where he was reputed to own a numbered bank account. A member of our Liberal caucus told us that a well-known PC woman had recounted to him that she had actually witnessed with her own eyes Joey going into a bank in Geneva. I don't recall any of that being substantiated.

Another Tory supporter I chatted with at a social event, a businessman, told me that he didn't know if Joey was as uninterested in money as he claimed to be, but he knew from personal experience that Joey loved to travel by private jet, whether John C. Doyle's, or Lundrigan's, or CFLCo's, or the aircraft of one of the banks. He'd heard of many a multi-million dollar deal that was consummated with Joey as a result of a ride to New York on a Lear Jet. You could have your way with Joey, he claimed, if you gave him a ride on a private jet. It reminded him, he said, of the stories after the war of Allied soldiers obtaining sex from Italian or French prostitutes in exchange for a pack of American cigarettes or a pair of nylon stockings.

Meanwhile, Crosbie announced that over half a million dollars of shares in Javelin, Doyle's company, had been transferred to a company owned by Al Vardy as fully paid when not one cent had ever been paid for them. An American lawyer was quoted in the media as saying, during one of Doyle's run-ins with the US Justice Department, that Canadian Javelin was the most mysterious company known to mankind.

FRANK MOORES HAD one unmistakable gift: he kept his eye on the big picture and, by dumb luck or devious design, his timing was always virtually perfect. While those around him were publicly preoccupied with nailing Joey, and privately anxious about Frank's own scandalous behaviour, tut-tutting over his drinking, screwing, fishing, and hunting all the time, and never working, Frank's eye and mind had been on one thing only: by hook or by crook, by election or bribery or fast talk, get a majority in the House of Assembly so that he could then heave off as premier and enjoy. He didn't want to be a working CEO. He wanted to be chairman of the board like Frank Sinatra, with all the perks thereunto pertaining, including—his admirers and detractors would say in equal numbers—just as much nookie as his namesake.

John Crosbie and the other ministers could do the work if they felt like it, and, if they took it into their heads to make reforms in liquor licensing, or the rules of the House of Assembly, or tendering for public works, or conflict of interest legislation, or the analysis of project proposals, they should feel free to fill their boots.

But, as John Crosbie was to say to me behind the curtain in the House one day after he'd been in government for a few months, the problem was that outside of a few do-good politicians ranting and roaring about all that reform stuff, "no one else gives a sweet shit about any of it." The public cared more, he thought, about how he had ended Joey's mother's allowance of twenty bucks a year in his first budget, and Steve Neary's characterization of Crosbie as the biggest backstabber of mothers in the entire universe. And they cared, not that government projects and deals were being looked at prudently now with an eye to their cost-benefit, but that, compared to the good old days of Joey, bugger-all seemed to be happening in the field of "industrial development."

THE ROT DID seem to set in early and fast in the public's perception of the Moores government. In May 1972, just a few weeks after the March election, Frank passed the Fisheries portfolio over to someone else, which allowed us to immediately begin the process of undermining his credibility. He had pretended to take on the Department of Fisheries himself, with great fanfare before the election, we said, and it had all been just a big show, just part of Frankie Baby's glitzy deception and flashy snow jobs.

The man seemed to have no shame. In spite of his condemnation of Joey's deal-making with Shaheen and Doyle, it wasn't long before it became known that Moores and Shaheen were themselves getting extremely cozy, with the possibility of another cooked-up joint project in the works. And in 1973, just a year or so after his majority election, won mostly by denouncing the likes of Shaheen, Frank Moores was accepting the dubious honour of having Shaheen name an oil tanker after him—the *Frank D. Moores*—which was christened in fine style by two of Frank's daughters. Then, far from toning down his raunchy lifestyle, Frank made it a badge of honour by taking over for himself the *Altuna*, the vessel that Al Vardy had used on Conception Bay, and rechristening it the *Rowdyman*.

It was also obvious to us that Frank wanted no struggles or clashes or even hard decisions in his life. When it came to labour negotiations, he avoided all confrontation. In a province that John Crosbie had described as heading over the brink of bankruptcy under Smallwood, public servants, under the easygoing negotiations of Moores, received unheard-of increases in pay and benefits.

The argument Frank used was that the raises were only a reasonable catch-up, but many others, including his own colleagues, thought he was all too willing to give away the farm. Whether in the House or outside, he could never be bothered to respond to pointed criticism, personal or political. And the spectacle we saw every night in the House was starting to become general knowledge outside: booze in the PC caucus room was flowing exceedingly freely and some government members were even propping themselves up half-sloshed in their places to speak.

In Labrador South district, where Liberal Joe Harvey had won by one vote over New Labrador Party candidate Mike Martin in the March 1972 election, the Supreme Court overturned the result, and a by-election was slated for the end of August 1972. I spent a fair amount of that campaign travelling with Joe, by float plane and boat where there were no roads. A man in one of the busy summer fishing communities said to me, "You could be sat down in a big law office in St. John's making money—what the hell are you doing out here beating around in a trap skiff?" "Especially with me," added the genial Joe Harvey with a laugh. I wasn't sure the fisherman quite believed me when I told him the truth: that this was extremely enjoyable and there was nothing I'd rather be doing.

Joe was a great travelling companion and personally popular, but I was getting the decided feeling that there was an undercurrent in the electorate of "a plague on both your houses" when it came to Liberals and PCs. Mike Martin was well-liked and admired and he managed to win this time, by over 150 votes. Tellingly, Frank Moores's government candidate hardly got a look-in.

THE COME BY CHANCE refinery had its official opening in October 1973. In honour of the occasion, John Shaheen chartered the *Queen Elizabeth 2* cruise ship to ferry guests by the hundreds from New York to Come By Chance and return. Shaheen Natural Resources Company Inc. sent registered letters to people all over the world, enclosing first-class, round-trip plane tickets and stating that hotel accommodations had been reserved for the recipient for several days at the Waldorf Hotel in New York. The Cunard tickets for the *QE2* would be sent at a later date.

Meanwhile, as others received invitations, I didn't get one. And I was delighted at the neglect. I'd had a bellyful of Shaheen and the refinery—enough to last several lifetimes. Then a business friend called and, in the course of conversation, determined that, while he'd been invited himself, I'd been left off the guest list. He couldn't believe his ears. He kept saying that in the last years of Smallwood, I'd been instrumental with Ed Roberts in helping to keep the monstrosity on the straight and narrow legally, and from going under, to the financial detriment of the province. Either Shaheen was still smarting from the legal hoops we'd made him jump through, or Joey's vindictiveness was behind the snub. We'd see about all that, my friend said. I told him to forget it—I wanted nothing to do with it.

But soon I did receive an invitation. I was never sure if it was because my friend ignored my instructions and told Shaheen to wise up, or if it was because so many important people turned the initial invitations down. I suspected the latter, and that I was mustered from the B-list to help fill empty staterooms. Whatever—with invitation in hand it was difficult to resist having a little gawk at what might be going on aboard the ship.

On the flight to New York, I found myself seated next to John Crosbie, in first class, no less. As the plane waited to taxi out for takeoff, he complained about the slowness in getting a drink on Air Canada. "If this were an airline in the States," he said, "we'd have a drink by now." No wonder, when he later became a top federal minister, he would push so hard for free trade with the US.

Upon boarding the *QE2* in Manhattan, I heard the stentorian tones of federal minister Don Jamieson. Walking up the gangplank onto the deck of the flashy cruise ship, he said with disdain in his pipe-organ voice, "Christ, this thing looks like a floating Holiday Inn." I would note, however, that he didn't allow the kitschy surroundings he scorned to spoil his appetite for a fair share and more of the free food and booze on offer.

On the ship, as I had suspected, there was a paucity of big names. I spotted only two "celebrities." One was the bestselling author James Michener, who was supposed to be travelling incognito but who was easy to recognize by anyone who'd seen his picture on the dust jacket of one of his forty books. The other was William Buckley, Jr., the pre-eminent American conservative writer. A stately six-foot-tall woman accompanied him, dressed in what looked like a huge green teepee. She must have been his Canadian wife from British Columbia, heiress Patricia Taylor Buckley. I would be interested a couple of years later to read that she'd been named to the International Best-Dressed Hall of Fame. Obviously, with that admirable frame of hers, she could get away with any sort of a rig-out. Meanwhile, my esteem for her couldn't help but go way up when someone on board told me what she'd said to Ted Kennedy a little while after he'd drowned Mary Jo Kopechne in the Chappaquiddick incident. He had been visiting the Buckleys at their place outside Gstaad, Switzerland, and had asked if he could borrow her car to nip into town with a female guest. "Certainly not, Ted," she'd replied. "There are three bridges between here and Gstaad." It made you proud she was a fellow Canadian.

Meanwhile, the casino and bars were maggoty with us small-time Newfoundland politicians and business types. Every now and then, though, I'd run into familiar American faces, members of President Nixon's old law firm, Nixon Mudge, who still represented Shaheen. They were mainly interested in discussing the latest development each day in Nixon's trajectory toward disaster in the Watergate scandal.

Sometimes in a bar at night, someone would point out this or that man tossing back the free drinks, identified as some Arabian oil sheik said to be worth ten billion dollars. He's a very frugal man, though, someone might say—his loss limit per night at the tables is $100,000.

When the ship cruised up Placentia Bay to Come By Chance, and tied up at the long federal wharf, passengers had to brave the incredibly bad weather to join the degenerate party hosted by Premier Moores on shore. A giant orgy of gluttony and inebriation was being held in a canvas marquee—a big tent full of food and booze for thousands flapping in the wind—that turned into a food-and-drink riot similar to those seen in a Third World country during a famine. There were reports of gourmet-vandals in their hundreds making off with hams, sides of roast beef, and bottles of costly scotch and vintage wine. The word was around that the new Mrs. Moores, Janis Johnson, was making her first official appearance at the event. We were lucky she was there at all, the gossip ran, because Frank had already grown tired of her before their recent wedding. If it hadn't been for his formidable mother putting her foot down, Frank had intended to leave her, jilted at the altar.

Years later, after they had parted, Frank's buddy Prime Minister Mulroney would soften the pain by elevating her, at Frank's behest, into the Canadian senate. Local talk had it, at the time of the appointment, that she had been appointed from Newfoundland. When I ran into a prominent federal Tory at the time, I asked him how someone living in Manitoba was being appointed to represent Newfoundland in the senate. He replied, "She might not strictly be a Newfoundlander herself, but she was bonked by a Newfoundlander, and that's close enough for Mulroney."

JUST A YEAR after the election of March 1972, Roy Cheeseman, the minister of Fisheries and PC member for Hermitage district, could take no more. I saw written on his face, day after day in the House, his distaste for his colleagues' antics and the constant criticism from us across the floor, and he resigned as MHA to go back, he said, to his private business. A by-election, the first real electoral test for the Moores government, was called for late November of 1973.

Former St. John's city engineer and enthusiastic Liberal organizer Dunc Sharpe travelled with me around Hermitage district beforehand to scout things out. We determined that the district could be won by a good Liberal candidate. Roger Simmons jumped into that role, and I think Bert Meade ran for the Tories. Both sides pulled out all the stops. My brother Fred, the member for St. Barbe North, became our campaign manager, and he moved into a motel in the district for the duration. Leader Ed Roberts and most of the rest of our caucus campaigned throughout the district by land and sea.

The worst uneasiness I experienced during the campaign was caused by my sleeping arrangements one night. During our tour of settlements along the coast in a small fishing vessel, a storm sprang up, and Ed Roberts and I had to put into a community unexpectedly for the night. The only available sleeping accommodation remaining in the boarding house turned out to be one double bed, which had to serve for the two of us. Ed had recently gotten married, and, that night, as we climbed into opposite sides of the bed, which sagged ominously in the middle, I cautioned the newlywed against conjuring up any false matrimonial fantasies in his sleep: "And Ed, please regard my back, not as any form of invitation, but as an absolutely firm rejection." Upon waking in the morning, we were pleased to realize that our night had passed without drama.

The next evening, we arrived after heavy seas at future MHA Jack Winsor's community and were welcomed into his house. The weather had been so stormy en route that Ed and I had become extremely relaxed on Gravol by the time the boat reached the wharf. In Jack's living room, oblivious of our Gravol overdose, he gave us each a generous glass of his finest scotch, which we downed with alacrity. Then we both phoned home to relieve our anxious spouses. I'm not sure we succeeded.

Jack told us the next morning that, judging by what he'd overheard us saying on the phone, neither of us had made one pick of sense to our mystified wives, each of whom was no doubt wondering who that babbling idiot was on the line, harassing her with incomprehensible protestations of undying love.

Meanwhile, for most of the PC campaign, Moores and his colleagues took to the skies. People in the district marvelled that there were so many helicopters flitting about all day, the place looked like a TV report of a Vietnam war zone. The only difference, people said, was that the big brass on board these choppers all had handsome cheques to hand out.

During a couple of nights, campaigners for both parties were installed in rooms at Camp Boggy, the living quarters of the main campsite of the Newfoundland and Labrador Hydro operation at the Head of Bay d'Espoir. A young female reporter from St. John's was also present to report on the election campaign to her media outlet. One night, four or five of us, including her, were chatting over a drink in one of our rooms about the day's activities when we heard a commotion outside the window. Dunc Sharpe pulled the curtain aside and peered out. "Lord Jesus," he exclaimed, "it's Frank. He's right outside there taking a piss." That intelligence enticed some of our group, the ones with strong stomachs and overdeveloped curiosity, to the window.

Sure enough, a few feet away, facing our window, was the urinating premier of the province. He was swaying and twisting, and as we took in the sight, he fell forward on his knees on the piss-sodden grass, and commented, "Fuck." But it did not interrupt the stream. One observer in our room—I don't think it was the female—said, "I thought Frank was supposed to be well-hung. Christ, that's pathetic."

Then out of the dark from the side, Tom Farrell came weaving over to Moores. He caught a good glimpse of the gawking, smirking faces, noses to the window, as he helped his buddy up, and the two of them exhausted their lexicon of obscenities on us, while staggering back to wherever they had surfaced.

The next day, as we campaigned, the news all over the Head of Bay d'Espoir was how, and with whom, Frank had passed the rest of the night before. People we met shook their heads as they related that a local young lady, a fish plant worker off the cutting line, had shared Frank's room with him until dawn.

Before the campaign was over, the paving machines arrived to lay some asphalt, but, as chance would have it, while that was going on, an early snowfall occurred. The constant question we heard from livyers was, how stunned did Frank and the Tory government think they were down here, trying to buy their votes by paving roads in the middle of a snowstorm? All things considered, I wasn't totally surprised when the Liberal candidate, Roger Simmons, won the by-election by 600 votes over the poor, benighted PC candidate.

A COUPLE OF months after that, John C. Doyle of Javelin was arrested and charged with fraud and breach of trust. The RCMP flew him from Montreal to St. John's. Al Vardy was also charged with receiving kickbacks, but he had already taken off for Florida, where a comic opera of manoeuvrings on and off aircraft ensued, as police tried, vainly, to bring him back. Doyle himself would later jump bail and hightail it for Panama, alleging that there was no way he would receive justice in Newfoundland with the scales tipped against him so badly by Moores, Crosbie, and Marshall.

After the O'Dea Royal Commission findings against Smallwood regarding the liquor store leases came down, a lot of people inside and outside of the Tory caucus and cabinet were pressuring Moores to bring charges against the former premier as well. Celebrated Canadian criminal lawyer John J. Robinette was asked to look at the material, and the word around town was that he gave the opinion that there was sufficient evidence to charge Joey with crimes. Some zealous Tory insiders leaked with disgust the observation that Moores vetoed the idea of prosecuting Smallwood with a "joke": he didn't want to set a precedent of charging former premiers because it might come back later to bite him in the ass.

Moores as premier had very quickly telegraphed to the world that he wanted no hassles or stress. He hated question period altogether and was seldom in the House, leaving everything to the top ministers, especially John Crosbie, flanked by Bill Doody and Bill Marshall. Doody was sharp and amusing, even keeping his cool when Steve Neary would frequently goad him by contrasting his job now as a bigwig running the province with his past days serving customers in Duff's supermarket with his arm in the pickle barrel up to the elbow. As for Bill Marshall, Moores had put him in charge of reviewing the contracts and deals from Joey's day. Gliding around his side of the House like an avenging phantom, dour-faced and mostly ignored even by his own colleagues, he looked every bit the part we accused him of playing: Witch-Hunt Willy.

We dubbed the government the Crosbie-Moores administration. Crosbie was the day-to-day battler par excellence, but Moores hardly ever replied to our direct criticisms against himself, with the result that the Opposition got away with murder. Neary was especially effective in getting his goat. The most we could fear from Moores, even when he was present, was some one-liner like when he called the cronies of "the previous Smallwood administration," Lundrigan, Shaheen, and Doyle, "the LSD Boys."

It wasn't long, though, as noted, before Moores himself was being seduced by John Shaheen's charms. President Richard Nixon, Shaheen's former lawyer, may have been wrong on many things, but he'd surely been dead-on when he called Shaheen the greatest salesman in the world. Small potatoes like Premier Moores were soon in the palm of his hand. Eyebrows shot up when Frank and his righteous-seeming colleague, Minister of Justice Alex Hickman, became Shaheen's guests on a trip to Cape Kennedy to gawk at a moon shot. And Shaheen, in Crosbie's absence from the province, talked Moores into backing a second oil refinery. This sent Crosbie around the bend with fury when he got back. But perhaps in fairness to Moores, part of the deal was said to let the province off the hook for $135 million on the first refinery.

We would laugh our heads off in the Opposition whenever Crosbie told the House of the good relations—the excellent rapport—he enjoyed with his premier. We knew from loose talk on the other side, combined with our own eyes, that Crosbie couldn't stand the disorder of Frank's political and personal life while he himself was saddled with the unappreciated burden of straightening out Smallwood's schemes and the province's near-bankruptcy, and at the same time having to be allied too closely for personal comfort to self-appointed hatchetman Bill Marshall in going after the former premier of the province.

We could see that it drove Crosbie and some of his colleagues bananas that Moores was such a soft touch. Frank was absolutely obliging. Some politically incorrect person on his own side said that it was a good thing Frank was not born a female or he'd be pregnant every year of his life—the guy simply could not say no. He okayed a whopping forty per cent raise for teachers to bring them up, he said, to Maritime standards. But his colleagues all knew and whispered that he had simply caved in and took the path of least resistance. He allowed so many fish plants to be licensed and boats to be built with government backing—anyone who asked, evidently—that it seriously contributed, together with the mismanagement of the feds, to the later disastrous collapse of the northern cod fishery.

He talked a good line: when Crosbie revealed the calamitous shortcomings for this province of the Upper Churchill deal between Brinco and Hydro Quebec, especially with regard to equalization payments, Frank made a big show of ranting that Ottawa under the federal Liberal Government was to blame and that he would force a transmission line across Quebec. But when it came to serious action on the project, like his government deciding to expropriate the Upper Churchill development from Brinco, the word from Confederation Building was that he became waffling and spineless in his negotiations with Brinco's hard-nosed top brass on the takeover. And we saw and heard clearly how poisoned with him Crosbie and other ministers were with his wavering and dithering.

Ed Roberts and I knew personally, though, how uncompromising and ruthless Brinco and the banks could be. He and I were actually flown to Montreal by the Bank of Montreal in their private jet one night for consultations, as the Official Opposition, with their top officials, including the CEO. They hammered home the catastrophic mistake they alleged the government was making in taking over the asset. Their arguments were self-serving, of course, but that didn't necessarily make them wrong. Frank, as the person ultimately responsible for the millions of provincial tax dollars involved, vacillated. We learned he was actually cowed by their firm position and their arguments, but he was equally cowed by John Crosbie's strong takeover position. He would say later that he had concluded the takeover was a mistake, but while it was happening he would neither stand up to Crosbie's stance nor, having caved in to Crosbie, galvanize himself into sturdily negotiating the very best deal for the province. One of his colleagues across the House said to me at the time, "On the Brinco takeover, Frank was the exact opposite of what he was like in bed. He was soft, limp, and useless."

What Frank was good at was the big dramatic public gesture, with apparently no thought or concern over whether it would be perceived later as hollow posturing. Before one of the elections in the 1970s, he would have Newfoundland and Labrador Hydro set off some dynamite—"a couple of firecrackers," we called the spectacle—on either side of the Strait of Belle Isle. The exercise was supposed to be the initial move to construct a tunnel across from Labrador to Newfoundland to convey the power from the Lower Churchill. After the election, the "construction" stopped and was never heard of again. The empty busywork cost millions of taxpayers' dollars, but it served its purpose of bringing in a few gullible votes at the time.

In between the big dramatic gestures, according to his colleagues and news reports, Frank divided most of his time between hunting, fishing, stocking up his wine cellar, fornicating, dining out, and lying back on a southern beach. He liked angling for salmon on our rivers so much that some opined he was starting to resemble one. Many times we in the Opposition would ask about his vacant seat in the House: "Where's Frank? Gone upstream to spawn?" We never heard any denials from the other side.

*

IN THE MIDDLE of one summer afternoon, I was just returning to Confederation Building from an outside meeting when I met Frank walking down over the front entrance steps by himself. Jacket off, tie skewed, top two or three buttons of his white dress shirt open, he was heading for his parked car. The look of him reminded me of how the great satirical British magazine *Private Eye* described their own politicians whenever they were spied drunk: "tired and emotional."

Frank came toward me. This could be good, I thought: after all those scurrilous attacks we in the Opposition had been making on him in the House, and now just the two of us out here all by ourselves.

"Good afternoon, Premier," I ventured.

"I'm some fucking tired," the premier replied. He left out "emotional," but *Private Eye* wouldn't have. He swung his jacket up, intending to rest it over his shoulder, but missed and draped it around his head. Unwrapping it from his face, he gave me a twisted but affable grin. "Christly cabinet meetings," he went on.

"Uh huh," said I. Some cabinet meeting. This must have been around the time that Brian Peckford was appointed to the cabinet as minister, because, for something else to say, I remember remarking, "Breaking in the new guy, were you?"

Frank replied, "Yeah, he was my parliamentary assistant since the last election, and Jesus, I'm only now finding out he's a complete socialist—no, an out-and-out total fucking commie. Worse than Crosbie." He laughed and made his way over to his parked car. I stood there deciding how I was going to stop him from getting behind the wheel. Luckily, I saw his driver barging out the door of the building and flying down over the steps. Resuming my walk up the steps, I turned to look at Frank's departing car. He waved and gave me a big Newfoundland wink. What a nice fellow, I thought, at least until he had you where he wanted you. Which I would find out about.

*

MEANWHILE, SMALLWOOD WAS temporarily off the political scene, lying low, composing his memoirs. He had often quoted Winston Churchill's observation that history would treat him well because he intended to write it himself. Joey set out to do that, and to put everyone in their rightful place, sort of a pyramid with himself at the pinnacle and his enemies buried at the base. I was amused to see, when his book, *I Chose Canada,* came out in 1973, that I had a unique place in its pages. There was no mention of me whatsoever anywhere. I do believe that every single one of Joey's other colleagues was at least named. Yet, in spite of all the time he and I had spent together, my name does not appear, not even in the index. To Joey I had become a non-person.

I was okay with that, but out of pure curiosity, I asked Bill Smallwood about it later, and he replied that his father never got over what he considered my betrayal of him in my speech to the House of Assembly in 1972 about the activities of Ed Roberts and myself during his last days as premier. I said to Bill that I had to tell the truth—I couldn't let the likes of John the Big Sook Crosbie and Witch-Hunt Willy Marshall and Fornicating Frank Moores get away with their twaddle and tripe. Bill said yes, he understood, but "you know the truth didn't make any difference to Dad if he didn't come out of it looking good." He went on to say that his dad had earlier come to consider me like a son, his true political heir, and was only waiting until I was ready so that he could pass the torch. So he was really broken-hearted when I "stabbed him in the back." I asked Bill to tell his dad I said this: the two biggest groups of people in Newfoundland were, number one, his "political heirs"; and, number two, those who, in the interests of truth and self-defence, were forced to "stab him in the back." And often, they were the same people.

CHAPTER TWELVE

Joey, the Comeback Kid

IN 1974, UNDER the Liberal Party constitution, there had to be a leadership review that year. The party called a convention for the fall to reaffirm or kick out Ed Roberts. Ed had lots of support in the party, especially among those, including myself, who believed he deserved a fair crack at an election, something he had not had two years before, in the debacle of March 1972. But there were others who thought we needed a change. There were only eight of us in the Opposition under Ed and we seemed to be going precisely nowhere. The Tories under Frank Moores had rapidly lost much of their popularity, but many Liberals grumbled and carped that Ed didn't have the charisma and energy to pick up the pieces and rebuild our party to the point of success. Oppositions don't win elections, governments lose elections, some of us would say in defence of Ed. To which someone on our side would invariably reply, yes, but Christ, we've got to present some kind of an alternative for the government to lose to.

There was pressure on me, some of it from inside the caucus itself, to throw my hat into the leadership race. Steve Neary, who in the eyes of some was already de facto leader with his constant fusillade of outspoken attacks on the Tories, was contemplating entering the contest. But many people were ambivalent about the possibility of Steve as leader. Once, when half a dozen of us Liberal supporters were chatting about the leadership, someone said, "Neary certainly has a good gut instinct for going for the jugular." Someone else responded, "Did you say 'gut instinct'? You meant 'gutter instinct.'"

I liked Steve, though, and admired many of his qualities. We spent a lot of time together talking politics, even to the point of arranging monthly poker games among friends to chat things over. But that "gut" and "gutter" exchange between two strong Liberals did encapsulate the divided view on Steve's potential as leader.

Ed Roberts asked to meet me in private. He confirmed that he was going to run again for the leadership himself, and he was wondering what I was going to do. The only one he was worried about entering the race, he said a little disingenuously as he tried to feel me out, was me. Now, I admired Ed's intelligence and knowledge and dedication, and he and I had really been through the wars together, first with Smallwood in his latter days and then in trying to mend the party's tatters during our first two years of Opposition. In the course of all that, we had actually become good friends.

But the big issues with me by then were my young family and the fact that I'd had more than a bellyful of petty politics, and needed a breather to take stock. This political distaste was exacerbated by reports from reliable sources, astonishing but all too believable, that Joey, well in his seventies, was going to enter the leadership fray again. Whenever his age had come up in years gone by, he used to "joke" about Gladstone having been re-elected British prime minister, and Konrad Adenauer chancellor of Germany, when both were well into their eighties. And now the cannibalistic machinations about to go on once more inside the Liberal Party in its position of pathetic impotence looked like they might destroy all hope of future success. I experienced a profound empathy with Sir Robert Bond's statement more than half a century before:

"I have had a surfeit of Newfoundland politics lately, and I turn from the dirty business with contempt and loathing."

I told Ed what I had decided: I'd be retiring from politics, temporarily or permanently, late that summer and travelling to France with my young family for an academic year of study and writing. Then, after that sabbatical away from Newfoundland, I intended to come back again and settle earnestly into the practice of law.

I resigned my seat, rented our house, and travelled to France with my wife and two small children. We set down in the town of Grasse, just up from the Mediterranean, in the Alpes-Maritimes department of France. Grasse was the perfume capital of the world, and the surrounding countryside was covered with hundreds of species of beautiful flowers. It was a positive change from provincial politics back home. Penny and I did courses of study in French and our two children went to a little one-room elementary school down the road. In between it all, I wrote the first draft of my first novel that was to become *Clapp's Rock*.

Meanwhile, in the Liberal leadership race back in Newfoundland toward the end of October 1974, Roberts was challenged by Roger Simmons and Steve Neary, and, yes, Joey Smallwood. Ominously, it took two ballots for Ed to finally beat Joey by just over a hundred votes. Reading all about it in the *Evening Telegram* I subscribed to from home, I was happy to be on the other side of the Atlantic Ocean.

WHEN I GOT back to Newfoundland the following summer, I learned that the old warhorse had been greatly encouraged by his showing at the leadership convention. In just two years, he had bounced back from the Tory attempts to thoroughly discredit him, and was now busily forming his own Liberal Reform Party. A fall election was in the air, and the word around was that Moores or his backers were helping to fund their recent enemy, Smallwood, to establish his new spoiler party and divide the Liberal vote. The PC premier knew he would need all the help he could buy or rent.

What truly spurred Smallwood to run candidates under the banner of his Liberal Reform Party was a matter of debate. Some blamed or credited a letter to him from Prime Minister Pierre Elliott Trudeau in November 1974, just after Joey had lost at the leadership convention to Roberts. Why Trudeau wrote it is difficult to fathom. But, in the letter, PET said he was not writing to offer sympathy at the outcome, because he knew Joey had no time to listen to sympathy when there was a future full of challenges. Trudeau attributed his own leadership success back in 1968 to Joey's support, and he praised him for the historic difference he had made to province and country. Then he predicted, now that the convention was over, that Joey was not ready to retreat into retirement and that he still had much to contribute to Newfoundland and to Canada. Trudeau concluded that he would be watching with great interest and continuing fascination. Steve Neary told me during the lead-up to the 1975 election that, if Joey needed any encouragement to get back at it, that letter certainly did the trick. Others maintained that the simple answer could be found in a psychiatric handbook: Smallwood was a loony old megalomaniac incited by a Machiavellian psychopath, Moores.

Frank called the provincial election for September, and it began as a rather lacklustre affair. The Liberals under Roberts seemed to be fairly well prepared and plodded along, but then the word started going around that Joey, who wasn't expected by the pundits to do much with it, was attracting larger crowds to rallies than Moores himself, let alone the Liberals. Some individual candidates also provided some interest and colour.

Steve Neary, whose old district of Bell Island had been transformed by redistribution into Harbour Main-Bell Island, sought the Liberal nomination on the other side of Newfoundland in Lapoile district. When he lost his nomination bid there, he claimed that the party (i.e. leader Ed Roberts) had defeated him with dirty tricks because he'd challenged Ed in last year's leadership convention. This dissension didn't help the Liberals' cause. Steve ran as an Independent Liberal and ended up winning handily, with the official Liberal candidate coming in third.

In St. George's district, the much-admired Liberal candidate Hazel

McIsaac defeated the PC incumbent Alex Dunphy and became the first woman elected to the House since Confederation—the first one elected in her own right in the history of Newfoundland, really, because the very first woman ever elected was the wife of the prime minister.

Media magnate Geoff Stirling became a candidate for Smallwood's Liberal Reform Party and took on Premier Frank Moores himself in Humber West, drawing great attention to himself and the splinter party by doing so. Moores won handily in the district, but Stirling came in second, ahead of the Liberal.

Unquestionably, after less than four years in power, Frank had worn his welcome pretty thin with the Newfoundland electorate at large. But informed opinions differed on whether the presence of Joey's party increased substantially the chances of Moores and his PCs stealing electoral victory from Roberts and the Liberals. I think it did. I wasn't a candidate myself, but I helped some Liberal candidates to campaign and saw how close they came to beating Tory heavyweights.

For example, PC Alex Hickman barely eked out a win in Grand Bank district by just over a hundred votes against an untried Liberal newcomer. And that was after Joey's Liberal Reform candidate had drained away over 1,000 Liberal votes. Giant-killer John Crosbie was only a little over 400 votes from defeat in the Tory stronghold of St. John's West.

Moores had given himself and his party a big boost the year before by bringing in legislation to increase the number of seats in the House from forty-two to fifty-one, and placing the new seats in mostly urban Tory strongholds, which had been desperately under-represented under Smallwood. But that had probably not been enough to secure victory for Moores. His popularity had plummeted as his disrepute for using his high office to engage in his playboy activities rose. This negative sentiment in the land had been exacerbated by the resignation as minister early in 1975 of sober-sided Witch-Hunt Willy Marshall in complete exasperation, as everyone knew, at dilettante Moores's antics. Moreover, the PC administration was largely regarded as a do-nothing government. All the reforms and rooting out of evil by Crosbie and Marshall cut no ice with the electorate. Voters were good and sick of hearing everything bad, including the Tories' perceived inactivity and all their cutbacks, blamed on the "previous administration," that is to say, Joey Smallwood.

It was a good bet, though, that even if Joey's new party did help nudge Moores and the Tories over the top in this 1975 election, that was not Joey's motivation for forming it. He didn't do it to keep Moores in power. He formed it to try to keep both Roberts and Moores *out* of power. In his self-confidence—some said, his foolish arrogance—he actually thought he could win the election. This was despite the fact that he could not even muster a full slate of fifty-one candidates. He did field enough, twenty-eight, to delude himself and, he hoped, the public, that he could form a majority government and elect a Speaker—if they all won. At the very least, he figured he would end up with the balance of power in either a PC or Liberal plurality situation and therefore be able to dictate his terms in forming a government. I'm sure he didn't see himself as a second Tom Burgess, but he accepted the Tory help and money on the same basis. Smallwood and Moores were like two con men trying to out-manipulate each other. Except that Frankie turned out to be a way better rogue than Joey.

Even though the Liberal vote was split down the middle by Joey's party in twenty-eight districts, five Tory cabinet ministers still went down to defeat, and the party as a whole only managed to elect thirty out of fifty-one members, down by three from the last election despite the addition of some nine Tory-heavy seats. The popular vote plummeted from the sixty per cent the Tories had enjoyed in the previous election to below fifty per cent now. The Liberals—with Neary who later rejoined—won seventeen seats, and Joey's Liberal Reform four.

Friends of Frank were saying that when he got back home to his wine cellar, and the full nightmarish enormity of having to face twenty-one energized members of the Opposition in the House dawned on him, he finished off three bottles of vintage burgundy by himself that night.

Tories whispered behind their hands, "It won't be long now," meaning it wouldn't be long before Frank took off like a scalded cat.

Friends of John Crosbie told me that he saw the writing on the wall after that election. It was bad enough that he had received no appreciation for his hard work of reforms and cuts, largely seen as mere housekeeping and bean counting and do-nothing and just blaming Joey, while Moores worked hard at only one thing—enjoying life to the hilt. But what Crosbie minded more, and made no bones about publicly or privately, was the fact that Frank, who was intelligent and talented, had thrown it all away because of his need to be liked by everyone—to the point where he was a mere baby with candy in the hands of the hard-nosed or manipulating executives he was forced to deal with. After one more year, Crosbie would be gone.

At the dinner for Liberal candidates and workers after the election, Ed Roberts got up and thanked people by name for their support. I had been invited by the party and heard him say with a disbelieving air that he'd been told Bill Rowe had done some campaigning in the election. Surprised and hurt to be damned with such faint praise by the leader in the room full of Liberals, I determined then and there that, if I ever ran again, it would not be under my former friend Ed Roberts's leadership. I'd run for the leadership myself first.

Joey, who'd been personally elected in Twillingate district, hung on in the House for only a year and a half before delivering his final speech there in June 1977, and, as some scoffers said, resigning for the "really, really, really last time!" When the Speaker of the House asked if all members would give their consent to suspend the rules to allow television and radio coverage of the historic Mr. Smallwood's farewell, everyone in all parties agreed, except for PC John Carter of St. John's North, who responded: "No, Mr. Speaker." And so, lacking unanimity, the province was deprived of the opportunity of seeing and hearing Joey's concluding appearance and words in active politics.

*

JOEY USED TO tell us all the time that he'd only lost one election in his entire life, and that had been in a Bonavista district during the depression in 1932, when the party of Sir Richard Squires he was running for was practically wiped off the political map. But, in truth, he'd lost half a dozen times.

The first loss, for practical purposes, if not technically, was when he was all geared up to run in Corner Brook in the 1928 election for Squires, only to have his great mentor and leader grab his seat out from under him and run there himself. Joey ended up not running in a district in which he'd invested so much time and effort that he would have won it handily. And next he lost indirectly leading up to the 1971 election, when his man in Labrador South was defeated in the Liberal Party nomination by maverick Joe Harvey, which was a harbinger of how much his control was slipping even in what used to be the most Smallwoodian of districts. And he lost as Liberal premier to Frank Moores's Tories in 1971, with a popular vote well below his opponent and one seat less. Then he lost to Ed Roberts in the Liberal Party leadership race of 1974. And his last loss was when his Reform Liberal Party came in a distant third to both Moores and Roberts in 1975. As Steve Neary and I agreed after that election, what constituted Joey's wins and losses was largely in his eye as the beholder.

AFTER HE HAD left politics altogether, and before he really got going on his encyclopedia, Smallwood popped out a couple of volumes of what I used to describe as "non-books" to my father, which was unfair of me, but I used to say it anyway just to hear him chuckle. I actually went to Joey's launch of two of them for old times' sake, one on Dr. William Carson, which had been compiled by Joey forty years earlier and was resurrected now, and another called *The Face of Newfoundland*, consisting of snaps of scenery and mug shots of some Newfoundlanders.

When I walked in at the designated hour at one launch, there was no one at all there but the author. I was entirely alone with him. Now, the fact that I was apparently the only person on the planet who had bothered to come to Smallwood's book launch didn't seem to impress him very much. He more or less scowled at me, and it was very painful trying to carry on a conversation. Judging by his demeanour and some cryptic comments, he still harboured a grudge for my publicly telling the truth about the last year of his government. After one long awkward silence, I said goodbye and walked sedately out, restraining myself from making a mad dash for the door. On the way, I met Joey's second visitor coming into the empty room. It was Elmer Harris, the man he used to keep standing out in the rain, sleet, wind, or snow for fifteen minutes every morning at VOCM. A true Christian gentleman if there ever was one. Elmer looked around at the dearth of people and we silently shook our heads at each other in pity. It was a credit to us both that we didn't bawl at each other, "Are we nuts?"

MATTERS WENT FROM bad to worse, politically, for Frank Moores, as he entered the last half of the 1970s. The only happy considerations for him were that one thorn in his side had already been removed, and another was about to go. Bill Marshall had been edged out of cabinet by an ultimatum issued by Moores, though contrived, we were told, by Janis during their pillow talk: "Tell him to shit or get off the fucking pot." Either Marshall was to become a full departmental cabinet minister instead of one without portfolio practising law, or get out of the government. The interesting thing was that Marshall's resignation caused hardly a ripple in caucus or government. Though he perceived himself as the conscience of the government, he was so ill-loved even among his own crowd that many, including Moores, were delighted to see him depart. And then, the next year, the understandably discontent John Crosbie found the exit, too.

In the spring of 1976, a little over six months after Crosbie's re-election, the Come By Chance refinery closed. Less than three years had passed since Moores and Shaheen had held the biggest party in Canadian history to open the refinery, and it now became the biggest bankruptcy in Canadian history. Over $500,000,000 went down a sinkhole, injuring heretofore thriving companies everywhere, and toppling the gigantic Ataka Corporation in faraway Japan. Cunard, the owners of the *QE2*, had not been paid a cent for Shaheen's extravagant opening cruise, and the word was that they were coming after the Newfoundland government for the millions still owed. Little wonder that John Crosbie would bail out of the House of Assembly that fall to run in the federal by-election in St. John's West.

Moores pretended publicly that he was of two minds on John's decision. On the one hand, he professed to be sorry to see his most talented and intelligent minister go. On the other hand, he thought John would be a great asset for the province in Ottawa. In fact, privately, he couldn't wait to see Crosbie's arse disappear out the Confederation Building door. It was with crocodile tears that he "reluctantly encouraged" the goddamned nuisance to run for the House of Commons "in John's own best interests."

A lot of people could not believe that Crosbie was again demonstrating what had become his trademark—a colossal lack of good timing regarding his leadership aspirations. I recall Steve Neary asking me rhetorically at the time, "What is wrong with the Big Sook that he commits hara-kiri every chance he gets?" From what I could gather, Crosbie thought, evidently, that the hedonistic, self-indulgent, money-loving Frank Moores was going to stick around suffering the worsening slings and arrows of petty provincial politics for many years to come. In fact, if only Crosbie had stuck around himself for a couple more years, he would easily have become what he'd expended so much money and grief on before to no avail—the Premier of Newfoundland and Labrador. In retrospect, it was excellent for this province that he went federal: he would become the best minister in Ottawa that we ever had.

Meanwhile, Brian Peckford seemed to have taken the place of Crosbie and Marshall in cabinet as the fly in Frank's ointment. I was absent from the House for a couple of years and so didn't see what was going on first-hand, but I would hear that Peckford was inordinately independent and active as a minister, both behind the walls and out in the public chamber. He was cocky and self-assured, having increased in 1975 his margin of victory in Green Bay substantially over the previous election. In 1972, he'd won by a slender margin one of the historically most Liberal districts in the province. In the 1975 election, the gap between himself and his closest opponent became, I believe, the widest in his party for a rural district. Hence, with leading lights like Leo Barry out of the House and cabinet after that election, and John Crosbie soon out by resignation, the talent was severely diminished, and Peckford had a freer hand to act. But I would hear that he was being forced to act, or was himself choosing to act, from outside Frank's charmed circle—the inner group of Bill Doody, John Lundrigan, Joe Rousseau, and especially the premier's best buddy, Tom Farrell.

A COUPLE OF regrettable incidents took place in my experience with Dr. Farrell in 1975 and 1976 which are distasteful to narrate, but necessary, because they would form part of my perception of the man when he would come to be involved in a more serious, life-threatening incident later.

The first time I met and got to know Tom Farrell a little was at a poker game in the mid-1970s. Before that, I'd only known him by reputation and seen him in operation in the House of Assembly over a few months. He and Frank had appeared inseparable there, and members of the Opposition would joke openly with PC members that the two buddies must have shared the same bottle of liquor during night sessions, since there was seldom a time when both of them did not look and sound well-oiled.

In 1975, when I was practising law and out of politics, I got invited by Craig Dobbin to a poker game at his house on a street in Kent's Pond. Tom Farrell happened to be there as one of the seven participants. The evening started out on a humorous note. Someone wondered jokingly how, when Moores and Farrell travelled everywhere together on government business, they were able to squeeze any business in between their boozing and screwing. Farrell replied that the boozing he could take his full share of the credit for, but as for the screwing, he could share none of the glory for that whatsoever, except vicariously, and he attributed the misunderstanding to the fact that Frank did enough extracurricular fornicating for the both of them.

The evening did not proceed on such a droll note. Farrell got drunk and abusive to everyone there, and since I had an eye irritation which was adding to my unhappiness, I used it as an excuse to leave early. One of the men who stayed at the poker game told me the next day that Farrell had wanted to fight with someone and picked up a table lamp and threw it at the wall. He was not, my friend said, what you'd call a jovial drunk. It was a far cry, it seemed, from the good times that Farrell was reportedly having all the time "drinking 'er up" with Frank Moores, home and abroad. (Bizarrely, at an inquiry a few years later into arson charges against Farrell, a witness would testify that on the night of the fire, Farrell, in violent anger, threw a potted plant at the far wall of his apartment.)

My father and mother had an apartment at Elizabeth Towers in St. John's during the time that Farrell was also a tenant there, and whenever I visited them I would be bombarded with grumbling, some of it semi-amused, some of it irate, from other tenants I encountered, about the parties and rackets and the drunkenness from Farrell's flat. Indeed, during the very early 1970s, I had to discourage tenants at the Towers from gossiping to me about how Frank and Tom supposedly shared an apartment there, but how Frank spent his nights in Janis's apartment in the building, while his sainted wife, Dodie, was abandoned in a house down the road with all the children and the heartbreak.

Some months after that poker game at Dobbin's, I saw Minister Tom Farrell on another best-forgotten occasion. It was early afternoon, just after lunch, and I was in my car waiting for the light to change at the Portugal Cove Road-Prince Philip Drive intersection so that I could turn left and proceed to Confederation Building on some legal business. Suddenly, and alarmingly, I noticed Farrell all by himself starting to cross Portugal Cove Road on foot from the Holiday Inn side toward the island between the lanes of traffic. He was swaying and staggering as he went, and raising an unsteady hand to stop the traffic bearing down on him. Very fortunately for him he did make it across, but only because the cars, which would otherwise have run him over, braked hard to let him pass. At the island he grabbed hold of a signpost for support, but he spun around the post and ended up on his back on the ground, where he remained motionless. I was thinking that I'd better pull my car over on Prince Philip and go back to help, when thankfully I saw that some people closer to him were already out of their car and approaching him. I didn't hear on the news that evening that he was hospitalized, as I half-expected. Instead there was some departmental announcement in his name as minister as if everything was normal.

I recall saying to myself at the time: well, why wouldn't an ambitious straight shooter like Brian Peckford want to make himself free and independent of that kind of crap? And he did. One case in point: at the federal Progressive Conservative leadership convention a few months later, early in 1976, there were eleven candidates. Premier Frank Moores supported Brian Mulroney, and John Crosbie went for Flora MacDonald. But Brian Peckford, in an act of autonomy that showed uncanny foresight, supported the unknown Joe Clark, who came up the middle between the better-known candidates and got himself elected on the fourth ballot. Three years after that, it would be a huge feather in Peckford's own political hat, and a pivotal event in Newfoundland and Labrador politics, when his choice became prime minister of Canada.

CHAPTER THIRTEEN

Frank on the Skids

MEANWHILE, IN THE fall of 1977, the Liberal Party of Newfoundland and Labrador held yet another leadership convention. The usual suspects were in the running—incumbent Ed Roberts, and MHAs Steve Neary and Roger Simmons, plus Hugh Shea, and, this time around, me. Since the 1975 election, members of the House had been expressing discontent, to me privately, and sometimes even publicly, over the leadership of Ed Roberts. Several of them, including Steve Neary, urged me to run for the leadership, with an assurance of support when the time was ripe. Months before the convention I threw my hat in and beat around the province trying to attract supporters. At first my campaign appeared to flourish. Nearly all sitting Liberal MHAs travelled around their districts with me, many indicating to constituents their tacit support. The omens were good.

Then something happened. Joey Smallwood talked Steve Neary into running for the leadership with the promise of his considerable help in attracting supporters, organizing, and gaining access to money. Steve told me that he could not pass up this best opportunity of his life.

The whole atmosphere changed; Steve's entry utterly polarized the race. The campaigns of the candidates now began to resemble a civil war. There was no registered membership requirement in the party anymore because the concept of being a "card-carrying Liberal" had fallen into disrepute in the Smallwood-Crosbie sign-up competition during their 1969 Liberal brawl. This meant that whoever could now bus or drag in the most bodies with discernible brainwave activity from the general public, many of whom would have been startled to hear they were Liberals, got his slates of delegates elected at the meetings. Neary's forces were alarmingly good at executing that manoeuvre.

For several St. John's district meetings, the entire fleet of cars of a taxi company was employed to round up "Liberals," including the emptying of bars and bringing the habitués to the gatherings, to vote for the slate of names thrust in front of their noses. When a few voters of Chinese ethnic origin turned up at one meeting, I heard a leading female organizer for Ed Roberts's campaign let out a roar of panic: "Mother of God, Neary's after getting the Chinks out." But supporters of the other candidates didn't have to be racist for Neary's successes in electing delegates to frighten them witless.

Most Liberal members of the House, while appreciating Steve's talents in eviscerating Tory ministers, regarded him as a brash, impetuous, impulsive loose cannon. Some also resented the fact that he'd gotten elected in the 1975 election as an Independent, defeating the official Liberal candidate, and they figured he had only rejoined the Liberal Party afterwards to have this new crack at the leadership. Moreover, he was considered to be Joey's stand-in. One or more of Smallwood's former Liberal Reform MHAs were organizing for Steve. The upshot of it all was that the leadership race now became, in the minds of many Liberal MHAs, a "stop Neary" exercise. They decided that to achieve it they had to swallow any earlier misgivings and support and work for incumbent leader Ed Roberts. The result was that candidates Roger Simmons and I were lucky we weren't squeezed out of existence altogether.

Ostensibly, Smallwood was off the political scene and innocently working on the first volume of his encyclopedia of Newfoundland and Labrador. He operated out of a house on a pathway off Portugal Cove Road, memorialized since as Smallwood's Lane. My campaign advisers were saying, "You've got to talk to Joey, you've got to go see Joey. He's behind Steve Neary, and you probably won't get him on side, but at least he won't be able to say you ignored him." I didn't want to meet with him, certainly not to play the role of suitor to him, but political desperation can make you crazy, so I called him and asked for a date. To my surprise, he agreed, though in a voice devoid of enthusiasm.

Except for those lonely book launches, this would be the first time I'd seen Smallwood in four or five years. Off I went on the big night carrying with me the mandatory bottle of plonk. He opened his door, eyed me glumly, observed my offering of wine with greater enthusiasm, seized it without comment, and put it in his fridge. That was the last I saw of it—or any other refreshment for the entire night. He himself was already drinking something transparent from a tulip-shaped glass, which he would replenish several times without missing a beat in his speech rhythms.

He sat me down and talked at me. And he talked at me. For three solid hours, pacing the room in his bedroom slippers, he talked at me. To save my life, I couldn't swear that I emitted a single word after, "Good evening, sir." And to save my life, I would not have been able to conjure up in memory the next morning one single topic of his monologue. I felt my brain contracting that night into the size of a peanut. The only thought I could muster was that my sins must be extremely numerous and exceedingly grave if this was my punishment for them. Of course, I deserved everything I got. Quite rightly, the canny old fart was taking full advantage of my insincere ulterior motive for going to see him in the first place, and he mercilessly turned me into an enslaved audience of one.

I do remember one further thought: What in the name of Christ was I doing here? Didn't the compassionate electorate of Newfoundland defeat our government specifically to save me from ever having to suffer this torture again? Finally, he sat down and seemed to go somewhat semi-comatose. I jumped up, said, "Heavens, look at the time," muttered good night, and dashed for the door. A glance back at Joey's face confirmed my good sense: he was struggling to stand up and, judging by the movement of his lips as I closed the door behind me, entering his "conversational" second wind. I hopped in my car and laid rubber. I recall nothing of my drive home except this repeated mental note to self: tell my advisers that I will happily throw victory in the leadership contest away, or myself over a cliff, before doing that again.

I was pretty sure I never brought Smallwood on side that night. That was verified the next time I saw him, in the dining room at Hotel Gander. Some sort of a Liberal function was going on leading up to the leadership convention. He was sitting at a table when candidate Steve Neary strode in to sit down with him. Joey jumped up from his chair and bawled out, "Stand up for Steve Neary." And he started clapping. The dining room was crowded, but the only other person to stand was the man at his table—I think it was his driver—and no one else clapped. Steve sat down at Joey's table with a semi-amused, semi-exasperated grin, and affected nonchalance at Joey's flopped attempt to cheerlead a spirited recognition of his presence.

THE CONVENTION TOOK place in October 1977, at the Arts and Culture Centre in St. John's. Most members of the Liberal caucus, and many district executives and ex-officio delegates, were sporting Ed Roberts paraphernalia. Nearly every malcontent in the party or otherwise alienated Liberal was hollering Neary's name. Roger Simmons and I, judging by the quantity of our posters, banners, and badges being waved or worn, were decidedly also-rans. The civil war polarization taking place between Roberts and Neary was reflected in the results of the first ballot. Ed Roberts was well ahead of the rest of us, though substantially below a majority. Steve Neary was in a healthy number-two position, and I was third with less than half Ed's number. Roger Simmons was behind me in fourth place, and Hugh Shea in last place had to drop off the ballot.

On the second ballot, Roberts was the only contender to gain votes. The rest of us, Neary, Rowe, and Simmons, still in second, third, and fourth position respectively, all dropped a few votes. Ed hadn't achieved the necessary fifty per cent plus one, but he was fewer than fifty votes away. Any sensible person would have to predict he'd go over the top on the next ballot. But then a bizarre phenomenon began to take place.

Roger Simmons, being in last place on the second ballot, was forced off the third, and his hundred votes became free and untethered. During the voting on the third ballot, Steve Neary asked for a private discussion with me. He wanted to bargain: if I were to go ahead of him on this third ballot and he had to drop out, he said, he would direct his delegates to vote for me on the fourth ballot against Roberts—provided that I agreed equally I would direct my delegates to vote for Neary, if he went ahead of me on this ballot.

I said, no, I couldn't agree to it; if I was forced to drop after this third ballot, which at the time appeared highly likely, my delegates would vote as they wished. There was no way they would follow any instructions from me to vote for Steve. When I told my advisers what I'd told Neary, they said I was nuts. Tell him yes, they said. But the truth was that, although I liked Steve more as a comrade and simply as a person, I would rather that Roberts regain the leadership for the overall good of the party, and I was sure that most of my supporters felt the same way; I couldn't lie about that to Steve. Some of my advisers said to my face that I was so simple-minded they doubted if I should even be in politics at all.

On that third ballot, Roberts dropped a handful of votes. So did Neary. Apparently, none of Simmons's votes went to either of them.

Some of his delegates didn't vote at all, but nearly eighty of his hundred came to me. As a result, I had now slipped ahead of Neary by the skin of my teeth—just a dozen votes—and he instead of me had to drop off the next and deciding ballot.

This last ballot contained just the names of Roberts and Rowe. When the results were announced, Ed had gained only a few votes. Despite our lack of agreement, Steve Neary told me that he had asked his delegates to vote for me, and apparently nearly all of them did come my way. I was as incredulous at the outcome as most other observers: I had won the leadership, with a little over sixty votes more than Roberts.

There was no actual conspiracy among Neary, Simmons, and me, as alleged by some commentators, to knock off Roberts. ("The day of the jackals," one columnist described the convention.) It was in fact every man for himself. But evidently both Neary and Simmons, individually and separately, so disliked Roberts, or so badly lacked confidence in him, that the voting became a matter of Anyone But Roberts. As a result, there was great bitterness after the balloting among many in the Roberts faction. A substantial number of his delegates and supporters stomped out of the convention. The bouquet of flowers the party had bought in anticipation for presentation to the wife of the newly elected leader, whom the executive had assumed was going to be Ed Roberts's wife, was left behind—a pathetic sight lying derelict and abandoned amidst the paper cups and fast-food containers on a table.

I WOULD BE facing Frank Moores across the House as leader of a caucus where every member but my brother Fred had supported another candidate. Deep divisions remained between factions. I asked Steve Neary to become Opposition House leader, which increased the disgruntlement of some. Steve had received the next-highest number of votes to Roberts, but as former leader, Ed didn't want the inferior job. He commenced a notable law practice while retaining his seat in the House, and would go on to distinguished public service to the province.

At our first caucus meeting, MHA Freeman White, a stalwart supporter of Roberts in the leadership, broke the tension. Referring to the fact that Ed had been ahead on the first three ballots—all but the last decisive one—he joked, "Hey, three out of four ain't bad." Most laughed, but not everyone. It was not yet a guffaw of camaraderie.

Wisely, and characteristically, Frank Moores moved fast to take advantage of the turmoil and discontent from the Liberal leadership convention. Telling his caucus he was going to liquidate me as leader before I knew what hit me, he called a by-election for December 8 in Smallwood's recently vacated Twillingate district, and challenged me to run in it.

I took him up on it, and met with the district Liberal executive. I recognized them—the last time I'd seen them, they were all delegates sporting badges of support for Ed Roberts. When they issued the call for nominations for a Liberal candidate, a well-known figure in the district met me to say he was going to run for the nomination. Liberals in the district advised me he'd been a big supporter of John Crosbie way back in the 1969 leadership battle, and was now being put up to run against me for the Liberal nomination by Frank Moores, with the secret financial backing of the Tories. Frank's idea, they said, was to emphasize a lack of solid support for me in the district as new Liberal leader, and try to finish me off at the nomination level.

I had then, and have now, no idea if any of that was true, though it certainly bore all the earmarks of Frank's handiwork. And I didn't care—I simply made it clear that I was going for it against any and all obstacles. In the end, the man did not run for the nomination. I believe it was because the inveterate Liberals there warned him they intended to make certain that he was totally wiped out at any nomination meeting. That result would have shown the exact opposite of what the Tories wanted to demonstrate, and the district Liberal executive told me that their PC friends in the district had heard that Frank had yanked him out.

The Liberal Party I took over did not have one red cent. And its credit was so bad that it could not even get a loan. Knowing what we'd be up against with the entire government as my opponent in the by-election, I personally borrowed $50,000 from a bank, with payment guaranteed by a kind businessman who had not even been a Liberal Party backer in the last election but who was now behind us.

My campaign was managed by two MHAs—my brother Fred and Freeman White of adjoining Lewisporte district—both of whom combined great election management experience and media savvy. Working with the local executive, those two were terrific. And it was a good thing they were, because Frank pulled out all the stops and poured on the heavy artillery. He and cabinet ministers galore spent most of the campaign period in the district. Every time we turned around, Public Works minister Tom Farrell or the premier was handing out yet another cheque to this town council or that local committee for every kind of public works imaginable, large or small. At one point, I was told, they were giving money to wharf committees in every community—work that came under federal jurisdiction, and was not even provincial.

We spread the word that they were trying to buy the election with the people's own money, and it rang true, especially since the belief everywhere was that nothing had been spent on the district ever since the PCs had come to power over five years before. Just as in the Hermitage by-election, helicopters flitted in and out of the district, accentuating the contrast between government attention now and the complete lack thereof previously. Frank, for a clever and cunning man, seemed to have learned nothing from the earlier by-election fiasco in Hermitage district, except maybe these lessons: at least he didn't pave any roads in the snow this time, and he seemed to stay away from the female cutting line in the fish plant.

The management of our campaign on the ground was superb. All I did as candidate was knock on doors all day and evening in the icy

November-December wind and rain, and gab. Our organizing team put together a couple of "monster rallies," one on New World Island and the other in Twillingate, and each of them attracted hundreds of people. One actually had more than 1,000 in attendance, out-drawing the Tories' rally by at least two to one. More than half of all the people who would vote on election day attended our rallies. The media work the team did was excellent. And nearly every morning and every evening, they'd interrupt my door-knocking to have me call the radio talk shows. A day or two before voting day, Freeman and Fred arranged for me to be on a Grand Falls call-in show as sole guest, with the show's regular host, for the entire two-hour program. They had engineered a magnificent pre–election day coup.

One positive feature of the PC campaign was their candidate, Jerry Canning, of Too Good Arm. When it had come out that he would be running for the Tories, St. John's mayor Bill Adams telephoned me. Bill had been briefly the member for the district after the 1971 election and he told me that he knew Canning to be very well-respected, intelligent, and hard-working—the most formidable opponent the PCs could have chosen. I appreciated Bill's information, and it galvanized our campaign into even more action. In the end, we managed to win the by-election by just over 500 votes.

The morning after polling day, I was in the dining room of a local motel having breakfast with Penny when Dr. Tom Farrell came in by himself. He looked my way once and then sat on the other side of the room. I figured he must be angry at me for the way we had portrayed him, accurately, as Frank's "chief money bag," the major dispenser of government cheques during the campaign. Nevertheless, I decided to get up and go over for an amicable good morning.

The closer I got to him, the worse he looked. It was not warm there, but his face looked like it was covered with a slick secretion of sweat. I stuck out my hand and said, "Congratulations on a hard-fought battle." He looked out the window away from me and said, "Yeah, well, fuck off." I attributed the reaction, not to the nastiness of a bad loser—after all, he and Frank revelled in their reputation as fun guys—but to a hangover that hurt as much as it looked.

THE VICTORY IN the Twillingate by-election was a huge morale booster for our caucus. During the next year or so thereafter, the Liberal Party rode high. And Moores went into steady decline in popularity and effectiveness, beset by one setback after another. Already there'd been allegations of fraud and bribes, including an earlier accusation from Ed Roberts that Moores had been given a television set by a company doing business with the government, which led to a judicial inquiry. Moores was not personally implicated, but the company owner was convicted of fraud in other government dealings.

The auditor general reports, investigations by the Public Accounts Committee of the House, and testimony at a public inquiry were scathing about government violations of public tendering and uncontrolled spending on favoured contractors, while at the same time ministers were obliged to announce that there was no government money for many essentials.

We probed Frank on his conflict of interest statement, filed in January of 1978, which showed him with upwards of 400 acres of land in the Harbour Grace-Bristol's Hope area, and over thirty acres in Outer Cove, and ten acres on the Gander River. How had he come into these huge areas of prime real estate? And why weren't any corporate shares or other financial interests listed on his statement, especially since he'd managed to whip all those hundreds of thousands of dollars of investments out of his school friend's brokerage firm mere hours before it went bankrupt?

Frank Moores had previously been touted by his party and himself as *the* great authority on the fisheries, but now he was being widely blamed for abuses and lack of control in a fishing gear replacement program. The joke going around was that Frank had only created the program because, if one of his women ever got mad and cut his cock off, the operation to transplant another one back on would be covered by the gear replacement program. A stupid joke? Yes. But you'd be surprised at how easy it is to make people laugh at politicians.

Moores did make heroic efforts to defend our seal hunt and render it more acceptable in the eyes of the world. Among the other tactics of himself and the industry, I recall the organizing of a blessing of the sealing fleet in St. John's harbour in the spring of 1978. A huge crowd of seal hunt supporters assembled down on the harbourfront, and I was there myself sporting an early sealskin parka to show my solidarity. After the ceremony was over, someone with one of the vessels invited me on board for some refreshment down in the saloon. I followed him down and, as I approached the room, I heard Frank Moores's unmistakable baritone reciting poetry. I was pretty sure it wasn't Shakespeare or Tennyson, but I couldn't be absolutely certain because I only heard this snippet before I entered: "Down from the hills came Piss Pot Pete, with fifteen pounds of swinging meat . . ."

I said hello to the three or four buddies holding their Sunday-afternoon glasses of scotch, but I didn't really feel welcome enough to linger and join in the literary performance.

THE PROVINCIAL BUDGET in 1978 was a public relations disaster. The slash-and-burn budget speech by Finance minister Alex Hickman with its tax increases and service cuts ended with "Vive le terre-neuve libre." If that was supposed to sound dramatic or even just funny, it only came across as silly. Someone fluent in French said to me, "*Le* Terre-Neuve libre—Christ, he couldn't even get the gender right." John Lundrigan, one of Moores's very best friends inside the government and out, felt obliged to resign from cabinet because the budget made no provision for the promised hospital extension in his district.

In this last year of his reign, Moores could no longer control—even as loosely as he'd done in the past—his cabinet colleagues. When he invited recently elected separatist premier René Lévesque to St. John's to announce a deal they had cooked up in a closet to harness the Lower Churchill and several Quebec rivers that had headwaters in Labrador, we in the Opposition heard from government insiders that Energy minister Brian Peckford "went completely ape-shit." He threatened to resign and conspired to lead a revolt to topple Moores. In retrospect, following failure after failure over the years regarding the Lower Churchill River, both political and legal, some have argued that it didn't look like that bad a deal. At the time, though, everyone I talked to thought Frank was ready to sell out the province for thirty pieces of silver. The reaction was so hostile that Frank sent René back home empty-handed and dropped their intended big announcement in the garbage can.

Meanwhile, during budget discussions in committee in the House of Assembly, we spotted the fact that we members of the Opposition outnumbered the government numbers in the House thirteen to eleven, and Opposition House leader Steve Neary moved that the salary of Ed Maynard, the minister of the department then being debated, be reduced to one dollar. It passed. Frank, to his embarrassment and chagrin, had to appoint Maynard to the sinecure of president of the Council at a full minister's salary, while he remained minister of his regular department at the salary of one dollar a year.

During the same time, the word downtown in St. John's was that Frank was contemplating a proposal by Shaheen's Ultramar to buy the $600 million, bankrupt Come By Chance refinery as a storage facility for around $12 million. We heard that the United Kingdom's Export Credit Guarantee Department rejected Shaheen's proposal, and Frank was therefore forced ultimately to follow suit. But while the talk about his proposed sellout lasted, it did untold discredit to Frank's reputation.

Meanwhile, the students at Memorial University had become agitated. It was déjà vu from the early 1970s, except that this time the protesting scholars wanted to eviscerate our PC opponents in the government instead of us. Over 2,000 students at Memorial marched on Confederation Building to demonstrate against the budget cutbacks in education. Both Frank as premier and I, as Opposition leader, met them on the front steps. Frank tried to mollify them with statements of how ready he was to sit down and talk to their representatives about raising the quality of education, but he spoke in vain. I didn't have to say anything except reiterate wholeheartedly the question on the students' placards: "When is the next election, Mr. Moores?" It received the most applause for the fewest words of my political career.

Frank possessed physical courage, though, no mistake. I observed a display of it during one student demonstration. After some official dinner in the university dining room involving MHAs on both sides of the House, we all left through the front door to the outside. Frank was a short distance ahead of me. Below the steps, lining the walk to the street where his car was waiting, hundreds of students were also waiting. They were yelling and waving placards on sticks, directed at Frank and his government. To realize you were personally on the receiving end of that uproar of deafening chanting and the seething spectacle of discontent had to be frightening. From the top of the steps, it was easy to see that for Frank to run such a gauntlet was to knowingly risk a blinding clout or other harmful blows from placards wielded as weapons. Just one out-of-control lout could deliver serious injury. If there was a police presence, it had not yet formed a guard to surround him and escort him out. I saw Frank pause and take a deep breath. No doubt he was wondering what to do—keep moving ahead, linger where he was, or retreat. He plunged down the steps by himself—perhaps there was a courageous aide or two in tow—and strolled along the walk while students on both sides screeched into his face until he reached his car. His action might only have been an example of courage as defined by a cynic: courage is the fear of being thought a coward. But I felt it was a display, in unsettling circumstances, of considerable nerve and mettle.

*

THE SESSIONS OF the House of Assembly in the winter and spring of 1978 became enormously rough-and-tumble. Already, the previous year could only have been described as Frank's *annus horribilis*: The linerboard mill closed; hospital workers went on strike for months; there were abuses reported at a home for physically and mentally challenged children. The list seemed endless. And there were continuing allegations of payoffs and secret lists related to government construction, with the auditor general issuing accusations of legal violations relating to the building of the Health Sciences Centre. Frank's sea of troubles was growing ever more tumultuous.

When I came back into the House early in 1978, I noticed that Premier Moores was seldom there, and when he was, he couldn't seem to be bothered to defend himself. He hardly ever answered our attacks on him inside or outside the House. I remember only feeble attempts by him to retaliate. When someone in the Opposition said the government's position on a policy was up and down like a yo-yo, Frank jumped out of his seat and bellowed at us across the House, "Yes, Mr. Speaker, and all the yo-yos are over there." It was not his greatest moment of devastating wit, but even that stood out as one of his few attempts to emerge from what looked like demoralization or listless indifference.

Most of our attacks on Moores were based on information leaked by concerned public servants, and centred on favours done and contracts awarded by the government without tender. We got wind of information that two or three years before, ministers John Crosbie and Bill Marshall had been outraged when Minister of Public Works Tom Farrell indicated to them that he and Frank had entered into a deal with Craig Dobbin to construct a large extension, basically a whole new office building, in the Confederation Building complex, and that the arrangement had not been tendered as required by law. I raised the matter in the House of Assembly.

Frank stood in his place and stated that there was absolutely no such deal with Craig Dobbin to build any such office building, as I was scurrilously alleging. I then revealed in the House a copy of a letter, given to me by a concerned official, which had been signed by Moores as premier and Farrell as minister of Public Works, containing that very deal with Dobbin. Initially flabbergasted in his seat that we had the letter proving he had just uttered a brazen-faced lie to the House, Frank recovered his audacity quickly and claimed that the letter was only a directive and not a legal contract with the government. He tried to maintain that posture even after I revealed that Dobbin had used the letter to obtain millions of dollars of bank financing and had already spent nearly half a million dollars on design work for the new building.

We in the Opposition caused an absolute uproar in the House of Assembly on that scandal. A long, rancorous debate took place that went on all day and all night with Craig Dobbin in the gallery. During the debate, Dobbin and Moores left the House together for a short time. We found out that Moores had asked Dobbin down to his office, where the premier tried to cajole Dobbin into writing a letter saying he had never believed he had a binding legal contract with the government to put up the new building. Friends of Dobbin told me he was absolutely disgusted with Moores for trying to save his own ass by asking Dobbin to do something that would indicate he had earlier committed a fraud on his banks. He called Frank a coward to his face, and said he didn't have the balls to take on his opponents either in the cabinet or in the bureaucracy or in the Opposition.

To add to the drama, a number of us in the Opposition contrived to get ourselves kicked out of the House by the Speaker for our accusations of government crookedness, thereby bringing even greater public attention to the failings of Frank and his Tory government. A few of our members stayed in and filibustered. Tom Rideout, then a Liberal MHA, distinguished himself by speaking for many hours on end without letup, greatly augmenting public awareness of what the fuss was all about.

This all boosted our popular ratings. A scientific political poll commissioned, I believe, by the CBC, showed that the Liberal Party and leadership enjoyed, during this period, the support of over sixty-five per cent of the voters. Support for Moores and the Tories hovered below twenty-five per cent.

The contempt felt by many in the public over Frank's government and the flexibility of some of his "born-again PC supporters" in the business community was often demonstrated by letters to the editor. Here's an excerpt from a copy somebody sent me in the late 1970s:

> "Dear Sir: Haw, haw, haw. You've got to admit it. That Frankie Moores really knows how to make people laugh. The other day he appointed Andrew Crosbie to head up a Development Council to give advice to the government. What are Mr. Crosbie's credentials for giving economic advice to the government? He built Atlantic Place which turned out to be one of the worst commercial disasters in the annals of Water Street. A few days before naming Andrew . . ., Frankie had to remove this financial albatross from around Andrew's neck by renting 80,000 square feet of office space for the government in Atlantic Place at rates much higher than the lowest tender received by the government. Andrew Crosbie, chief economic adviser to Frank Moores, had to be bailed out by Frankie's government, snatching Atlantic Place from the brink of total collapse. Haw, haw, haw. The problem is, it only hurts when I laugh. Signed, Observer."

THE ONLY CIVILIZED exchange between Moores and myself during this period concerned Joey Smallwood. I sent a letter to Frank stating that the Honourable J. R. Smallwood, as a former premier, should have full secretarial, clerical, and research assistance, plus adequate office accommodation, to carry out, in dignity and comfort, research and writing relating to his tenure in office. Part of the impetus for me to write the letter was that, when Joey resigned from the House of Assembly, he took one of the Opposition secretaries with him to help in his work. In other words, secretarial help for Joey in retirement was being paid for out of the Opposition's meagre funds instead of by the government.

It took Moores nearly four months, but he did reply. He said that, in response to my letter, he had written Mr. Smallwood suggesting that the government would like to institute the payment of a small grant to him to look after his secretarial costs. Someone close to Moores told me he had an ulterior motive. When he retired, she said, which "won't be long now," he would like to avail himself of the precedent that former premiers got money for their office expense.

THE WORD WE were hearing from across the House in the winter of 1978 was that Moores was in fact close to resigning. Indeed, he told delegates at a PC Party convention that this might be the last time he'd be speaking to them as leader. But party organizers stirred up the delegates into making sure, for the good of the party, that when he went out, he'd go out, not in ignominy, but in some style, and the convention endorsed him overwhelmingly. Thereupon, Frank said he'd be taking the party into the next election. Those at the top, however, knew, and relished the knowledge, that he had already decided to tough it out for only a few more months, and to get a new leader elected to replace him in 1979.

Meanwhile, one day in April of 1978, and adding to Frank's misery, someone in the Opposition—I believe it was our Opposition House leader, Steve Neary—revealed in the House of Assembly that Industrial Development minister Tom Farrell had spent a vacation at a resort hotel in Panama, all paid for by the former great Satan, John C. Doyle. Farrell responded that he didn't know who had paid his bill at the time of his sojourn, and stated: "I must have been sucked in."

Steve Neary also tabled information in the House that alleged Farrell had been corrupt while he was minister of Public Works and accused him of bribery and the covering up of illegal activity, specifically with a company called Pelcon, which Neary accused of fleecing the Newfoundland government out of some $7 million. This followed months of documented allegations of corruption provided by Steve that Farrell and others had received kickbacks in return for hospital construction contracts. Added to it were our accusations that the Moores government was making under-the-table deals with contractors, that Moores misled the House and lied to MHAs on the issue, and that Moores had sabotaged the public accounts committee after the auditor general was critical of spending practices. Then, late in April of 1978, came the night of the fire in Dr. Farrell's apartment at Elizabeth Towers.

CHAPTER FOURTEEN

Frank's Department of "Justice"

THE BLAZE STARTED in Farrell's fifth-floor apartment, causing severe damage and practically destroying his suite of rooms. Other apartments in Elizabeth Towers sustained substantial smoke damage. All of the more than 150 people living in the building, many of them elderly, had to be evacuated to save them from injury or death. According to the fire commissioner, several people only narrowly escaped. A large number of tenants were forced to relocate to alternative accommodation. Two tenants had to be rushed to hospital and treated for smoke inhalation. My own aging parents were three floors above Farrell's and were seriously alarmed by the fire and its aftermath, as well as gravely affected by it. To say that I and the rest of my family were seriously perturbed by such a threat to lives there would have been an understatement.

The day after the fire, the minister of Justice in the House of Assembly ordered a full police investigation into the allegations of illegal activity made against Farrell. On top of the suspicions about the cause of the fire, allegations had been made that Tom Farrell had created a preferred list of contractors for work with the government. Premier

Moores asked Supreme Court judge John Mahoney to conduct a public inquiry into the spending practices of the Department of Public Works from 1974 to 1977. At the inquiry, a witness testified that Farrell had remarked in his presence about the alleged illegal activity, "Don't worry about it, the civil servants will take the fall." Early in August of 1978, some three months after the Elizabeth Towers fire, as a result of accusations of corruption, Farrell resigned from cabinet to await the results of the Mahoney Inquiry.

Meanwhile, a police investigation was supposed to be going on into the cause of the Elizabeth Towers fire, but for several months after the fire, despite demands by the Opposition and the media for the results of the police investigation, absolutely nothing was disclosed. I was advised by a former Crown prosecutor that, usually, after a serious fire, there would be a public statement issued quickly by an authorized person on whether arson was suspected or not. In this case, neither Minister of Justice Alex Hickman nor any other official gave any substantial report on progress being made with the investigation, and month after month went by with no charges being laid regarding this serious fire. The lack of action concerning a suspected grave crime caused media and many in the public, including endangered tenants, to accuse the government of stonewalling and obstructing justice regarding one of their own, Tom Farrell. We in the Opposition were receiving communications from inside sources about what had allegedly occurred.

They included statements that the fire had broken out as Farrell was attempting to burn incriminating documents in his apartment, and that an accelerant had been used for the purpose. Astonishingly, we were told that Farrell's actions had been triggered by information he'd received from Joey Smallwood, of all people, earlier in the night of the fire, after Steve Neary had tabled in the House the information of corruption regarding Farrell and the Pelcon corporation. Joey had phoned Farrell to advise that he was being set up. We were also informed that, just before the fire started, Farrell had met for hours that very same night with the principal of Pelcon, the same company accused of being in a corrupt relationship with him and whose apartment was in Elizabeth Towers. Premier Moores's wife, Janis, was brought into the narrative as well: she had had dinner at a restaurant that same night with the girlfriend of the principal of the allegedly corrupt corporation, who lived with him in the same apartment, and they had been joined by Farrell at their table. And as the months of government stonewalling went by without any news from minister of Justice Hickman on the progress of the arson investigation, reports were even surfacing of a "gay conspiracy" between someone in the administration of justice and someone close to Farrell, who were allegedly in a relationship. That allegation would be mentioned later by at least one newspaper journalist. One of our inside sources at the time connected that "conspiracy" to a cover-up in the Department of Justice three years previously, in 1975, concerning allegations of sexual abuse of boys by Christian Brothers at Mount Cashel Orphanage. In the absence of any official information by Hickman, the reports and accusations grew to the point where they seemed to be so outrageous that we were taking them with a grain of salt. Little did we know.

DURING THIS PERIOD of inaction and non-information on the fire, Hickman announced as well that as minister of Justice he was not taking any action over the failure of his department to move against Premier Moores or ministers who had deliberately broken the Public Tender Act during a by-election. The auditor general's report in March of 1978 had drawn attention to that violation of the law. Minister of Justice Hickman now did the unthinkable: he dragged out the highest non-partisan legal officer of the Crown, his own deputy minister of Justice, to make a statement politically defending the lack of legal action against Moores and the ministers. The public reason he gave was the technicality that more than a year had gone by between the breach of the Public Tender Act in June of 1976 and the auditor general's report in

1978. This episode was described in one newspaper editorial as the low point in the administration of justice in this province.

Suffice it to say that the political atmosphere during the spring and summer of 1978 was permeated through and through with rampant allegations of corruption, obstruction, cover-up, and abuse of justice by the Moores administration. Then, finally, about five months after the Elizabeth Towers fire, the St. John's *Daily News* published a story on the cause of the fire based on information leaked to them by a concerned member of the Royal Newfoundland Constabulary. A few days afterwards, late in September, copies of two police reports came into my possession which entirely substantiated the concerns over the failure to lay charges, and implicated Tom Farrell directly in deliberately setting the fire.

Sergeant Art Pike, one of the police officers involved in the investigation, had told me before I received the reports that, in his professional opinion, there was a cover-up attempt in operation regarding the fire, just as there had been, he insisted, a successful cover-up of the police investigation in 1975 into complaints of sexual and physical abuse of boys at the Mount Cashel orphanage.

The reports on the fire were dated June 7 and July 12, 1978, two to three months before they came into my possession. They concluded, after investigation by provincial fire commissioner John Cardoulis and George Sparke, a special investigator with the Insurance Crime Prevention Bureau, that the fire had been deliberately set. Among other things, the reports confirmed the meeting on the night of the fire between Minister Farrell and John Weston, president of Pelcon, the company implicated by information tabled in the House of Assembly, and to whom the government had agreed to lend millions of dollars, of which hundreds of thousands of dollars had been actually paid. Three senior police officers of long experience agreed that arson was involved and advised that charges be laid against Farrell. One of the reports referred to an earlier case where another person, identified in the report, had recently been convicted of arson in a fire, and stated that the evidence at his trial was less conclusive than the evidence in the Elizabeth Towers fire.

I discussed the matter with advisers, including a senior lawyer, and decided that, in these appalling circumstances, copies of the reports had to be given to experienced publishers and editors of responsible media for their independent judgment on whether they thought any of the contents should be made public. I called them by telephone to tell them what I was about to do and why. It would be entirely their choice, I told them. Some members of the media who received the reports from me chose not to publish anything from the reports. Two of the most senior local media, the *Evening Telegram* and the CBC, decided that in the best interests of the public they had to disclose the information in the reports.

At the end of October, Farrell was charged with arson, and a preliminary inquiry was held. Fire Commissioner John Cardoulis testified that in his expert opinion the fire was deliberately set and that an accelerant was used, and other investigators, including RNC officers, testified to their belief in Farrell's arson.

A few days before Christmas, the presiding magistrate, Joseph LeClair, who'd been appointed by the Moores government in 1972, dismissed the charges against Farrell because, in his opinion, there was a lack of evidence of arson. In his later reasons, he concluded that the fire could have been deliberately set but that it was equally possible to conclude it had originated from other causes. The prosecution was only able to establish that arson was a possibility for the fire that occurred in the apartment. All the evidence was as consistent with innocence as it was with guilt. The magistrate stated that none of the "expert" witnesses who testified were competent to establish the cause of the fire, and it would be dangerous to convict a person solely on the opinion evidence of someone with rather limited knowledge. The police in the province, he said, had no one who could be termed a specialist in fire investigation. He characterized the evidence gathered by Fire Commissioner John Cardoulis as "virtually useless."

That was very strange. And Justice minister T. Alex Hickman himself seemed to have some serious doubts about the magistrate's conclusion on the evidence. When asked by the media afterwards about the competence and expertise of Fire Commissioner Cardoulis, Hickman expressed satisfaction with Cardoulis's work in investigating fires. Still, the case against his colleague Tom Farrell, owing to the dismissal of that expert evidence at the preliminary inquiry, never went to full trial, and no charges were ever laid against anyone else for the fire that risked the lives of 150 people, many of them aging and frail, at Elizabeth Towers.

A senior criminal lawyer said to me, after the dismissal of Farrell's charge of arson, that he saw a huge irony in Magistrate LeClair's decision: the magistrate had called everyone else's expertise into question, and rejected them all as incompetent, but had no problem with his own lack of qualifications or lack of expertise as a lawyer. He had attended law school but was not admitted to the bar at the time of his decision, had no experience in the practice of law, and would not be admitted to the bar in this province as a novice lawyer until some two years after he dismissed the charges on grounds of everyone else's lack of qualifications and expertise.

I said to the same lawyer that, upon reading the transcript of the preliminary inquiry, I thought Clyde Wells's defence of Farrell had been brilliantly effective. The lawyer agreed. "If I were ever charged with murder," he said, "I'd certainly retain Clyde to defend me." And he laughed, "Especially if I was guilty."

AN INTERESTING, NOT to say extraordinary, corroboration of what I'd heard earlier about Smallwood and Farrell came out of the preliminary inquiry in the testimony of Frank Moores's wife, Janis, and John Weston of Pelcon and his girlfriend. Mrs. Moores testified that Mr. Smallwood had telephoned her that night of the fire to say he needed to talk to Dr. Farrell. She was having dinner with the girlfriend of Weston, and Farrell sat at their table at the restaurant. Farrell did talk to Smallwood, and both he and Janis were told by him that Farrell was being set up and that there was a taped telephone conversation involving Farrell. A little later that same night, Mrs. Moores dropped Farrell and Weston's girlfriend off at Elizabeth Towers, and for the rest of the night before the fire started, Farrell had meetings with Weston of the implicated Pelcon, back and forth between their apartments, during which, Weston testified, Farrell threw a potted plant against a far wall. After that, a fire started in Farrell's apartment.

Steve Neary would tell me later that he had mentioned to Joey before the fire his intended public exposé of the corruption of Farrell and other ministers. Then, after Steve had read the transcript of the preliminary inquiry and confronted Smallwood with the testimony, Joey admitted he had called Farrell—for what motive Steve couldn't get out of him at the time—and betrayed Steve's trust. Steve relayed to me Joey's opinion that he was the impetus behind Farrell's panic that led to the starting of the fire and all the later ruinous consequences on several careers. It would be a mark of Steve's broad-mindedness and big-heartedness regarding the old guy that, in spite of Joey's actions, he became in Smallwood's last disabled years one of his most devoted and kindly visitors.

IN THE HOUSE of Assembly, immediately following Magistrate LeClair's decision and the total lack of closure on the apartment fire, I questioned Premier Moores and Minister of Justice Hickman on whether the government was now going to order a full-fledged investigation and inquiry into its cause. Hickman initiated a shock wave when he replied that there would be no further investigation into the fire. Instead, he announced, there would be a Royal Commission of Inquiry into the leak of the police reports. Hickman smirked with enjoyment across at me, and no wonder: I had stated publicly a day or two after I had received copies of these reports that I had them in my possession, and nearly every news medium in St. John's was well aware, of course, that I had made them available to them.

The *Montreal Gazette*, on February 20, 1979, reported on the Opposition's reaction to Hickman's announcement. The newspaper stated that the legislature had gathered for a formality and a three-hour session had gone on for eighteen hours, closing at nine in the morning:

"Opposition Leader William Rowe, a young and fiery speaker, accused the government of trying to cloud the issue by appointing a Royal Commission to investigate the leaking of the police report on last April's fire. 'The cause of the fire is what should be investigated,' he said. 'To do otherwise is to drag a gigantic red herring across all the other matters.'" But unfortunately, by my own stupid handling of the police reports when I had received them, I had already given Frank Moores and Hickman and their colleagues the whip for my back, and no amount of "young and fiery" speech-making could change that.

The way Hickman dug in his heels on not investigating the fire caused immediate outrage in the media. Articles, columns, and letters to the editor described their dismay over the cause of a life-threatening fire being ignored while the government concentrated on who had leaked the police reports. Nearly every major news medium in the province issued editorials stating that the cause of that fire was the important thing to be investigated, not the leak of the police reports. They also demanded an inquiry into whether there was in fact no one in this province who had the skill or ability to investigate fires properly, as contended by Magistrate LeClair. If that was true, the question arose over what should be done about all the people who had been sent to jail for arson over the years based on the evidence given in court by "incompetent" investigators.

An *Evening Telegram* editorial late in February 1979 stated that the most disturbing aspect of the appointment of Hickman's Royal Commission was the fact that, almost a year after the fire at Elizabeth Towers, the commission's terms of reference seemed more concerned with the simple fact of determining who actually leaked the report to the newspapers, radio, and television stations than with the many unanswered questions that surrounded the incident. The first and urgent task of the commission, the newspaper said, should be, "and it's likely most of the public would agree, to commence a new and comprehensive search into the Elizabeth Towers affair which, whatever its cause, put the lives of scores of persons, many of them elderly, into jeopardy."

Ray Guy wrote in his column:

> "Two birds with one stone seems to be the aim. Draw attention away from perhaps the larger skullduggery the smoke from Elizabeth Towers might be hiding and get in a political stab at Opposition Leader Bill Rowe who had a copy of that leaked report on the fire."
>
> "And try to put the fear of God into the nosey press while they're at it.
>
> "There's been every sort of trick and dodge to keep the facts of the matter from coming out."

There were letters to the editor demanding a proper investigation into the cause. One to the *Daily News* from a resident of the building, Art Scammell, the author of the "Squid Jiggin' Ground," and, coincidentally, my uncle by marriage, said he merely wanted to know what started the fire that threatened 150 or more lives. His letter sparked an editorial in which the newspaper stated that the cause of the fire was the most important question still unanswered: "It's not too much to ask, is it?" And yet there was no indication that this vitally important question, said the editorial, will be part of the terms of reference, for the Royal Commission apparently intended only to trace the course of a leak of a police report on the fire. "We say with Mr. Scammell that it should be." And the paper called upon the minister of Justice, Mr. Hickman, whose responsibility it was to see that it would be.

For some unknown reason, Moores and Hickman were strangely unmoved by this universal demand to find out the cause of the fire, and instead they persisted in appointing Judge Lloyd Soper of Corner Brook, Farrell's hometown, to inquire into the release of the police reports. As well, the government appointed lawyer Frederick Woolridge, also a resident of Corner Brook, as counsel to the commission.

I'D HAD ONLY one encounter in my life, a laughably absurd one, with Judge Soper before the appointment of this commission of inquiry. It had occurred years before in Corner Brook, when I had a legal matter before him in his chambers. On my way to the judge's office that mid-morning, I asked the local lawyer, who was accompanying me, what Soper was like, because the other lawyers I'd talked to generally sniggered whenever his name came up, or acted as if they were dismayed by the man. The lawyer with me now cackled, too, and said, "You'll soon see."

When we went in to see him, Judge Soper glowered up from his desk impatiently and demanded what we wanted. As I told him, I remarked to myself that his desk looked really neat and tidy. There appeared to be nothing at all on it. Then I noticed that it was in fact nearly completely covered with something flat. Suddenly I realized that it was a large three-quarters-finished jigsaw puzzle. His impatience with us had clearly stemmed from the fact that we had interrupted him with a legal matter while he was in the process of completing his jigsaw puzzle on the otherwise empty desk in his judge's office. When I ended my presentation and was walking out, having received a rather terse and unsympathetic response, I glanced back. The judge was holding a piece in his hand and already engrossed again with his jigsaw puzzle. Outside the courthouse, the Corner Brook lawyer with me giggled, "I told you."

BEFORE THE COMMISSION hearings, all the major media knew I had caused the police reports to be delivered to them, of course, since I had telephoned their news directors and editors to ask them if they wished to have copies. When I called, I undertook not to divulge where they had obtained them and I undertook never to divulge my own source. Those considerations, plus my desire not to implicate my executive assistant, Brian Tobin, who had physically delivered sealed envelopes to the media on my instructions without being told what was in them, had induced me to make a misguided and senseless denial when asked by reporters of the same media about my role in their distribution. When Judge Soper's hearings began, however, I sent a message to him offering to appear in front of the commission, before the media were called, to volunteer the testimony that I had caused the reports to be delivered to them. Among other things, I wanted to relieve the media of any need to protect me as their source. And at the hearing I fully described my involvement.

When my executive assistant, Brian Tobin, was called as a witness at the inquiry, commission lawyer Woolridge tried to pin him down to admitting that he actually knew what was in the envelopes. At this point in the hearing, Judge Soper jumped in, interrupting Woolridge and disclosing his frame of mind, as he demanded intemperately:

"In other words, Mr. Tobin, in that particular aspect you were conducting your own cover-up with Mr. Rowe, weren't you? Weren't you?"

Tobin: "No, sir. That particular aspect—"

Soper: "Yes, but you knew it was a police investigation?"

Tobin: "I knew the police were asking questions, yes."

Soper: "Was that a police investigation?"

Tobin: "Yes, I assume it was a police investigation."

Soper: "And you were refusing to give information. You didn't make a full disclosure, did you? And you and Mr. Rowe are the people who are talking about cover-ups?"

Tobin: "Pardon?"

Soper: "And Mr. Rowe is the person who has been talking about cover-ups, and you were covering up Mr. Rowe, weren't you?"

Tobin: "No. I answered his question."
Soper: "Well, I understand that. Sorry, Mr. Woolridge."

In his later report, Soper would find in fact that Brian Tobin was unaware of what was in the envelopes he had delivered to the media. Interestingly, a few months afterwards, when Tobin would run in the federal election of 1980 in the west coast riding of Humber-St. George's-St. Barbe, some of his opponents there accused him of slickness and glibness and general slipperiness in escaping from blame, this in spite of the factual finding by their own hometown judge.

I HAD NO intention of disclosing who had provided me with copies of the police reports, but the police officer who had done so in fact revealed himself as the source. It was RNC Sergeant Art Pike and he testified, as he had earlier told me, that he had done so because he feared a cover-up in the Department of Justice over the fire similar to the cover-up of the investigation into the sexual abuses at the Mount Cashel orphanage in 1975 when Alex Hickman had also been minister of Justice. Judge Soper found Pike's reason inadequate, and said he considered Pike's action inexcusable. Instead of the demotion Pike had received, the judge stated he would have fired him. In truth, to my mind Art Pike was the only genuine hero, as will be seen, in this whole sickening travesty.

Probably because Pike had been so severely discredited by Soper, his allegation of a cover-up of the physical and sexual abuse at the Mount Cashel orphanage would not be probed or investigated immediately after the Soper Inquiry. But Pike's allegation did keep alive a tiny spark regarding the abuse of justice by the Department of Justice under Minister Hickman in the Moores government back in 1975. And years later, as we shall see, that spark would burst into an inferno of heartbreaking truth about the decades of brutalization of helpless boys by degenerate men in a position of trust.

Farrell sued the *Evening Telegram* and the CBC for libel and was awarded damages by the Supreme Court, which were substantially reduced by the Court of Appeal. Meanwhile, after long-drawn-out stonewalling against public and media demands that the cause of the Elizabeth Towers fire not be swept under the rug but be investigated by a proper inquiry, Gerry Ottenheimer, the new minister of Justice, had finally appointed another judge, A. S. Legrow, to inquire into who or what had started the near-lethal fire. In December 1981, three and a half years after the conflagration, Judge Legrow would conclude that "by accident or design the flame was applied by Dr. Farrell."

AS FOR SOPER, I would see him years later for the third and last time under more amusing, if startling, circumstances. I was in a hotel in Corner Brook as a member of a panel of arbitrators hearing a serious grievance in one of the hotel's meeting rooms. During a lunch break, we on the panel walked out into the public part of the hotel conversing about the case to ourselves at a normal volume. Suddenly, we heard a strident, reverberating screech, many times louder than anything we were saying: "Stop your goddamned racket!" We flinched in shock and looked over. There he was, Judge Soper, sitting in a chair outside the door to one of the public rooms and, as one of my colleagues put it, "glowering at us dementedly."

This was his way of reminding us that there was a music festival in progress inside the room and that he was acting as its doorman and enforcer of silence. Moving away rather spritely from the unnerving scene, we heard a similar blare from the judge at another hapless group of guests walking unwittingly along. Squelching our incredulous laughter out of respect for His Honour, we agreed that he certainly was a dedicated, if ear-splitting, defender of quiet at music festivals. Years after that, I ran into one of my fellow arbitrators again, when Soper was being named MUN alumnus of the year, in great part for his contribution to the music scene in Corner Brook. We both heartily agreed that he deserved that honour for his raucous, cacophonous defence alone of music-festival silence.

THERE WOULD BE, as mentioned, a gut-wrenching aftermath to the fire and Soper's inquiry. In mid-February of 1989, when I was the host of VOCM *Open Line*, I mentioned on the air one morning a local news story I'd seen a few evenings before on CBC Television's *Here and Now*. Presented by reporter Deanne Fleet, the story had revived allegations of a suspected cover-up by the Department of Justice in the Moores government regarding complaints of sexual and physical abuse at Mount Cashel Orphanage years previously. That morning on *Open Line*, Steve Neary called the show and said that he had heard my mention of the CBC story, and he wondered vehemently why nothing had ever been done about the allegations of abuse and the cover-up by the Department of Justice under Alex Hickman, now a Supreme Court judge.

A listener to *Open Line* that morning heard my remarks and Neary's question, and was appalled by the thought of a cover-up of abuse of vulnerable children at an institution she herself so enthusiastically supported. She immediately called her husband, who also happened to be a Judge of the Supreme Court of Newfoundland and Labrador, to tell him what she had heard on *Open Line*, and he in turn contacted a high official of the Department of Justice to express his dismay over the question and the lack of answers. The next day the Crown prosecutor's office resuscitated their file on the physical and sexual abuse allegations of the children, and the Royal Newfoundland Constabulary was instructed to reopen its aborted 1975 investigation and to ascertain why criminal action had not been taken against the alleged perpetrators.

A month or so after that, the great weekly newspaper of Harry Steele's, the *Sunday Express*, under writer-publisher Michael Harris, started to issue a series of articles on the alleged sexual and physical abuse on many boys by many Christian Brothers and staff at the Mount

Cashel orphanage reaching back some forty years, and on the cover-up by the Department of Justice, and by high church officials. There were fervent public demands for a judicial inquiry. As a result, recently elected PC leader and new premier Tom Rideout appointed a Royal Commission, the Hughes Commission of Inquiry, to get to the bottom of the accusations of obstruction of justice.

When it issued its report in 1992, the Hughes Commission stated that the members and staff of the Christian Brothers who had been investigated by the RNC in 1975 ought to have been criminally charged at the time, but that the Department of Justice had obstructed the police investigation.

Information from the Hughes Inquiry and the reopened police investigation disclosed that, back in 1975, three years after the Moores administration came to power, the RNC had begun to investigate allegations of sexual and physical abuse of residents at Mount Cashel. At least twenty of the boys there had made complaints against at least five Christian Brothers, but the investigation was abruptly halted by the chief of police on orders from the Department of Justice. At least two Brothers in 1975 had actually confessed to sexual abuse of the children, but, instead of receiving criminal justice, they were sent to "treatment centres" outside Newfoundland and then posted at other institutions of the Christian Brothers in Canada, where they could continue their perverted, pathological practices. After that, all further interviews by the police of the boys at Mount Cashel had been stopped by the Department of Justice.

Apart from further complaints of sexual abuse at the orphanage in 1982 and police action against just one Christian Brother, who was convicted and got four months in prison, the whole matter went dormant until resurrected, as indicated above. In 1989, later criminal charges were laid against Brothers and civilians at the orphanage in connection with the obstructed 1975 investigation and for sexual abuse dating from the 1950s and 1960s.

In 1990, Mount Cashel was locked up, and suddenly the authorities could not send in the wrecking balls quickly enough to demolish, and render invisible, the cesspit of evil brutalization they had tolerated and turned a blind eye to for decades.

Back at the Soper Inquiry in 1979 into the leaking of the police reports on the Farrell fire, Judge Soper would write that what Sergeant Art Pike had done was inexcusable and his reason—fear of another cover-up like the Mount Cashel cover-up in 1975—was unacceptable. And perhaps back then, that might have seemed reasonable to many. But in retrospect, the ray of light Art Pike shone in 1979 on the corruption and obstruction of justice that had taken place regarding Mount Cashel Orphanage in 1975 stayed alive. I remember how it continued to cause talk and questions and whispers of concern for a decade afterwards. And I know that Pike's public allegation was greatly responsible for starting the building pressure that finally, years later, blew the top off that official cover-up of unspeakable evil. Inexcusable? Unacceptable? Perhaps so to Soper and the legal establishment at the time. But I believe that Art Pike's revelation merits the erecting of a monument to his memory.

CHAPTER FIFTEEN

Frank's Retreat

FRANK MOORES WAS cute enough to get out of politics when the time was right. In 1978 and 1979, we in the Opposition had done to Frank as premier what Smallwood used to do with Opposition leaders. Joey kept scuttling the ineffective ones until, finally, he got one who could scuttle him. And ironically enough, it was the same Frank Moores whom we had now scuttled in turn, and who was about to abandon ship in favour of a new leader.

Early in 1979, Moores commandeered television and radio time across the province to announce a PC leadership convention for the spring of that year, at which time he'd be retiring as premier. His statement was full of the usual platitudes of retiring politicians—proud accomplishments, time with family, and such—but he also emitted a few strangely defensive statements. He was not leaving, he insisted, because he was afraid to face an election. He had tried in his public life to make a contribution, and, while skeptics might find it hard to believe, his motives had been none other than to serve his province and his country to the best of his ability. Being premier was no easy job, he said, and contrary to what some people thought, it took virtually all his time and energy. There was far too much personal recrimination and abuse in politics, and he apologized to anybody he might have insulted.

Meanwhile, Moores tried to put a "going out on top" spin on his resignation: the PC Party announced the results of a so-called political poll that showed them way ahead of the Liberal Party. The media soon revealed that the poll had been conducted out of the premier's office by some of the premier's own staff and that they had targeted for their phone calls the wives and families of PC cabinet ministers and caucus members to ask them what party they would support.

Many in the public seemed to believe that it was pitiful for the Tory Party to trump up a favourable political poll to attempt to let Moores resign with some tatters of honour remaining and that, sadly, all it did was cheapen his resignation. But as I was finding, there was still some bite left in the wounded wolf. With his usual adroit and crafty timing, Frank used the opportunity I had given him—my stupid blunder in my handling the police reports—to pass over the leadership to his successor, and with an immense advantage.

THE CONTENDERS TO replace Moores as PC leader, who would automatically become premier, started to line up. John Crosbie in Ottawa would have been the most formidable candidate, but as a prominent front bench Opposition MP, and obviously feeling that his PC Party under Joe Clark had Trudeau on the ropes, and seeing himself, rightly, as an important federal cabinet minister after the next election, he announced he wouldn't be a candidate for the leadership. That left the field to the three top contenders—Brian Peckford, Bill Doody, and Leo Barry.

Moores pledged that he would remain neutral in the leadership race, but, instead, he reneged on that promise behind the scenes, and it soon became an open secret that he was supporting Bill Doody.

But Brian Peckford, with the support of others in his caucus who, like him, were disgusted with and alienated against their former boss, won the leadership, and he got sworn in as premier in late March of 1979. Peckford would have been a daunting, probably unbeatable, opponent in a provincial election under the best of circumstances. But on top of that, the Liberal Party was rent with dissension over my controversial action.

In the spring of 1979, there was serious disagreement in our Liberal caucus over the police reports and the outcome of the Farrell case. I believed that those who were criticizing my actions had a strong point. But I was being contacted by many in the party who told me that what I had done in the bizarre circumstances was understandable and defensible. To clear the air, I called a leadership convention for early July 1979, announced my intention of running, and with the approval of caucus continued on as leader of the party and of the Opposition until the outcome of our convention.

But a few weeks later, in May, federal PC leader Joe Clark led his party to victory over Trudeau and his Liberals and formed a minority government in Ottawa. The fact that Peckford's earlier choice for national PC leadership was now prime minister, on top of his own profile from recently winning the leadership, plus the dissension in the Liberal Party, made conditions ideal for Peckford to call an immediate provincial election. Some Liberals tried to make Peckford look bad for calling an election in the middle of our Liberal leadership race, but, frankly, I never met any ordinary Newfoundlander who gave a damn about that.

To try to salvage the Liberal Party from its disarray and, I thought, to improve its chances in the upcoming provincial election, I asked Don Jamieson, now in Opposition federally, to take over as leader. Some prominent Liberals, including Joan Cook, later to be a senator, told me I shouldn't do it—I should stay on as leader. Meanwhile, Len Stirling was spearheading a campaign with the slogan "Bring Don Jamieson home for good." I saw some people wincing at the arrogance and condescension of that, but by and large everyone I ran into after Jamieson had accepted the leadership, including most of our own caucus, said that Peckford was finished. I recall one of our MHAs saying that Peckford would now dearly love to withdraw that election writ if only he could, because he was headed for one awful clobbering by Jamieson on election day.

Newly anointed leader Jamieson arrived in St. John's from Ottawa to a rollicking welcome. As one flabbergasted Liberal put it to me at the time, "He came back like the Ayatollah." And in fact all his bawling and blaring made poor Don lose his voice at a crucial time during the election campaign, right before the televised debate of the leaders.

During the election, when I took a weekend break home to see the family, I ran into one of Peckford's top organizers down at the Sports Shop on Water Street, where we were both buying something for our kids. I remarked to him that he certainly looked relaxed, facing certain defeat. He responded that their polls showed that Peckford was going to beat Jamieson easily, and then he added that the numbers showed that I would have done better in the election as leader. I thanked him for being so kind but told him I didn't believe his poll or his comparison.

A few days later, on June 18, 1979, Peckford pummelled Jamieson at the polls. The PCs gained three more seats than they'd won in the previous election, when Ed Roberts had led the Liberals and Smallwood had played the role of spoiler. A personal aside: I was gratified by the generosity of the good people of Twillingate district who, despite Peckford's overall gains, re-elected me by a bigger margin than they had in the previous by-election.

THE FIRST THING Peckford did after becoming premier was put distance between himself and Frank Moores. PC insiders told me that the price of the support of Bill Marshall and others in the Tory caucus for his leadership bid was for Peckford to make a clean break from

Moores's methods as premier, and to indicate as much publicly when he became premier himself. Peckford had no problem with that. He had a well-developed sense of grievance against anyone who went back on their word to him, and reportedly had few qualms about separating himself widely from the man who'd promised he wouldn't support anyone for leader and then pushed behind the scenes for rival Bill Doody. Besides, Peckford was said to be only demonstrating an obvious truth: his own character and Frank's were as different as chalk and cheese, or, as one Tory bigwig put it—"like steak and shit."

Hence, Peckford declared a review of deals made during Moores's latter days as premier and didn't hesitate to compare his former boss and mentor to Joey Smallwood in allowing himself to get sucked in, against the province's best interests, by outside dealmakers. In return, Moores lashed out that Brian had been a great cabinet minister under him but had turned into a ranting and raving maniac when he became premier, "just like that bloody Joey."

Moores and his friends thought that Peckford and his government were deliberately going overboard to embarrass him. Frank found himself charged for unlawfully building a fishing lodge in Labrador, but got off on technical legal grounds. The Public Accounts Committee of the House—on which Peckford's Tories had a majority of members, including former ministers in Moores's own government—hauled Frank before it to answer their allegations that he'd used public money for political surveys commissioned by his party.

Frank defended himself successfully against those "McCarthy-like" tactics, as he called them. Then Peckford wondered out loud about Frank's poor judgment when he had moved into Mount Scio House as the premier's official residence after Lord Taylor had left as president of Memorial University. Before long, though, Moores and his friends were maligning Brian himself for having renovated, refurbished, and refurnished the same château at considerable public expense and converting it into his own official digs.

Moores and good buddies Bill Doody and John Lundrigan set up a consulting firm in St. John's, but, not surprisingly, considering the atmosphere and economy that prevailed in Newfoundland and Labrador at the time, they failed to make a go of their enterprise. It was embarrassing, not to say heartbreaking, that, after leading the government here for seven years, former premier Moores had to skulk out of his own province himself, joining thousands of Newfoundlanders on the mainland, in order to survive financially.

CHAPTER SIXTEEN

Joey in "Retirement"

AFTER BRIAN PECKFORD had won that 1979 election, Joey Smallwood called me up at home. I was surprised, since we'd had almost nothing to do with each other for years. "Don't be disheartened, Bill," he said. "You are only a young man. You can easily be back as leader of the party and premier within five to ten years." It was an interesting gesture from a man of seventy-eight who'd been nursing a grievance against me for seven years. I thanked him for his thoughtfulness and almost asked him why he'd called Tom Farrell that fateful night and set in motion, even though inadvertently, the resulting train of catastrophes. But I didn't have the stomach. Steve Neary had already surmised to me by now that the old guy was so well-acquainted with political setbacks himself that he had done it simply because he had a soft spot for politicians who found themselves on the ropes. Perhaps he was doing the same thing to me, now.

Four or five years went by before Smallwood and I spoke to each other again. By now I was practising law, hosting *Open Line* on VOCM Radio, and writing columns and books. Joey was working on his monumental *Encyclopedia of Newfoundland and Labrador*, and sometimes I thought it might be pleasant for old times' sake to have a chat with him about it. But there never seemed to be enough time—or, to be frank, enough inclination—to act on the thought. I saw him once in the supermarket, pushing his cart along by himself, and I moved toward him, but someone else got to him ahead of me and stayed talking. I turned away and checked my groceries out.

Then, in the late summer of 1984, he called in to my radio show. He mentioned that he'd put out the first volume of his encyclopedia three years before and that the second volume had just recently been published. He was calling *Open Line* now, he said, to inform the public that he was about to go on the road in a motorhome to sell his books directly to customers.

In true Joey fashion, his biggest sales pitch on the air was not how informative or interesting or entertaining the books might be, but how heavy they weighed. The encyclopedia might seem to be a little expensive per volume, he said, but we had to remember that one of the books weighed five pounds and the other was actually six pounds in weight: eleven solid pounds of knowledge about Newfoundland and Labrador.

His intention was to publish five volumes in all, he said, and lest that seemed a trifle ambitious for a man in his eighties, he reminded listeners that he was "sinfully healthy." I had already read the first volume, and had just bought the second, and we had a great chat about the whole colossal project. It would be the last time I heard his voice because, within weeks, he would suffer the most catastrophic event of his life.

Before that, though, he did go on the road flogging his hefty tomes. From what I could gather from his son, Bill, who called my show later, sales were not brisk. An old friend of mine told me that he was eating dinner at a hotel in a town in Newfoundland and Labrador during this time and saw Joey there eating at a table alone. My friend knew him well from political days long past and went over to ask him how he was doing with selling his books. Not as well as expected, replied Joey. He still had eleven sets left that he'd now have to tote back to St. John's when he departed in the morning.

On the far side of the dining room, a long table was filling up with the members of the board of directors of the large corporation that was the area's economic mainstay. My friend knew some of them, excused himself from Smallwood's table, and went over to say hello. One of the directors, having confirmed that the man sitting over there was indeed Joey Smallwood, wondered if my friend would ask him to come to their table so that the directors could meet him. My friend went back and asked, and Joey said, yes, he would go over, if they'd buy a set of his books. My friend walked back to the directors' table—shuttle diplomacy at its highest, he laughed to me. The chairman of the board agreed with Smallwood's condition and he got up and went over. The chairman invited Mr. Smallwood and my friend to sit down and asked Joey what he would like to drink. There was little hesitation: Harvey's Bristol Cream sherry. A bottle of that was ordered, and the chairman of the board excused himself for a few minutes. He came back waving a piece of paper. "I have here," he said, "a requisition for your books for the board of directors."

"One set?" asked Joey.

"No, all eleven sets," replied the chairman. "We would like you to come to the company suite later, if you're free, and autograph them for us." After dinner and a good few Bristol Creams later, the twenty-two books, all 121 pounds of them, were lugged to the corporate suite, where Joey then sat behind a table and personalized each set, while denting another bottle of Harvey's Bristol Cream sherry. He would ask each director his name—John Smith, say, or James Jones—and then he'd write on the flyleaf, "To my good friend John Smith, with great esteem," et cetera, or, "To my good friend James Jones, with boundless admiration," and so on, ending each dedication with the great flourish of his signature: Joseph R. Smallwood.

That went on for a couple of hours, interspersed with a soliloquy from Joey, at the end of which there were protestations of undying love from all sides, and Joey asked my friend to help him up to his room. Once there Joey said, "You're going to have to help me undress. I've had far too much to drink." My friend struggled to get his jacket off, and his vest, and his shirt, and his shoes, and his trousers. Underneath all that clothes, on this warm summer evening following a scorching day, Joey was wearing a set of woolly winter long johns.

When my friend told me that, I had a nostalgia trip: my memory flashed back to Joey's anecdote years ago to us in his dining room when he'd described the agonizing discomfort of his Confederate colleague, Gordon Bradley. Joey had told us he had possessed something approaching disdain for Bradley's lack of energy, particularly his listless inertness during those long summer weeks in Ottawa as part of the delegation in the late 1940s discussing possible terms of union. Then they discovered, said Joey, that, underneath his heavy dark suit, during all that Ottawa summer heat, Bradley had on his woolly winter long johns. My old friend, who'd helped Joey, and I agreed—there was nothing new under the sun.

IN LATE SEPTEMBER of 1984, Joey suffered the cerebral hemorrhage that would partly paralyze him and deprive him of his greatest faculty, his power of speech. In typical Newfoundland fashion, the black joke going around, though not unkindly spoken, was that it took Joey's equal, God Almighty Himself, to finally shut him up. Work on the encyclopedia continued, spearheaded by his granddaughter, the estimable Dale Russell Fitzpatrick. But there was grave doubt that it could now be completed because of Joey's condition, especially when, before long, a sheriff's officer visited his home at Roaches Line carrying a writ claiming almost $200,000 in printing debts.

The spectacle of the speechless, paralyzed octogenarian, "the last father of Confederation," being harassed by a legal process was too much for many to bear, either in this province or across Canada, and there was a great outpouring of support for him and the encyclopedia, the final magnificent monument of his life. Singer Tommy Hunter called me on *Open Line* to say he was planning benefit concerts, and the media reported that a group named the Chocolate Bunnies from Hell were inspired to follow suit. Bill Smallwood met with Premier Brian Peckford to discuss the establishment of a foundation to finish the job.

The Joseph R. Smallwood Heritage Foundation was set up with a mandate to complete the five-volume encyclopedia envisaged by Joey. Leading citizens like Paul Johnson, Campbell Eaton, and Mose Morgan lent their names and efforts to it. Mose Morgan, whom I didn't recall as a great admirer of Joey when I'd studied political science under him at Memorial some thirty years before, and who had no reason later to support the man who as premier had passed him over as president of the university, was forever on the phone and at public functions badgering and wheedling out of us MUN alumni donations to the project. Finally, the task would be fully accomplished after Joey's death.

MEANWHILE, IN 1986, Joey was belatedly made a Companion of the Order of Canada in St. John's at Government House. His frail condition prevented him from travelling to Government House in Ottawa. A few people who'd been close to him over the years told me that, as the person who had brought Newfoundland into Canada, Joey thought that he deserved a British knighthood, which should have been awarded before Confederation had occurred and activated the Canadian ban on the honour. Perhaps he did want that, but I personally never once heard him even hint at it. Quite the contrary. He had told me that in our history, every self-serving, money-grubbing politician-merchant or politician-lawyer contrived to have himself knighted and called "Sir," or, more to the point, to have his wife called "Lady" this or "Lady" that for life. One of our political stalwarts, he said, managed to get himself elevated to the British peerage for his "contribution" to the First World

War effort—the lives and limbs of teenaged Newfoundlanders in the trenches and quagmires of France and Turkey.

Some commentators said that Joey called himself "the last Father of Confederation." Perhaps they had heard him say that, but, in all the time I spent with him, I never heard him use that term for himself once. He was also reported to have been shocked by the ingratitude of British governments for another reason. They would not make him, the person most responsible for bringing its oldest colony into union with its greatest dominion, Canada, a member of the Imperial Privy Council and entitled to the designation "The Right Honourable Joseph R. Smallwood."

If so, I didn't get the impression from him that he had lobbied very hard for the honour, because I was sure that between them all—Lord Beaverbrook, Eddie de Rothschild, and their buddy, Prime Minister Winston Churchill—Joey could have had the title easily in the 1950s if his little heart had been really set on it. He did get an offbeat consolation prize later. In 1989, Joey, who had never evinced great love of the ocean or of going to sea, had a new Marine Atlantic ferry, the MV *Joseph and Clara Smallwood*, named after himself and his wife.

IN THE SAME year, around the fortieth anniversary of Confederation, new PC premier, Tom Rideout, called a spring election. Luckily, I was invited to speak at a celebration of Newfoundlanders in Toronto and had a good excuse to pass up the wicked temptation of an offer to run. At the Toronto event I passed out some Smallwood medallions someone had struck for the anniversary. I was amazed at how popular they were among the young as well as the old.

Meanwhile, in that election, eighty-eight-year-old Joey voted to help put in the first Liberal Government since he'd been ousted from office over seventeen years before. Observers said he didn't seem to mind that he was voting to elect a government of his old bitter adversary, Clyde Wells. In fact, he sent the message that he was happy Clyde had won and become premier. But those around Joey on election night,

Steve Neary told me, saw his face light up even more when he heard the irony of what happened to Wells personally. Way back in the 1966 election, he'd been dragged to victory, just barely, in Humber East under Joey's leadership. Now, in this 1989 election, Wells was defeated under his own leadership in his same home district by lawyer Lynn Verge. She had been an articled student in Wells's law firm earlier, and had been advised by him that there was no place for her in his firm as a lawyer because, being a woman, she might have babies.

Joey was also pleased that Wells had come around to his thinking in another way: whereas back in 1972, Wells was reported to be shocked that Smallwood would hang onto power with a smaller percentage of the popular vote than Moores in an election where the number of seats was tied, Wells himself was quite content now to take power, even though his party had a smaller percentage of the popular vote than Rideout's. (The Liberals had half of a percentage point less than the PCs.)

WHEN HE'D BEEN premier, Joey had made a deal, he told everyone, to turn his house on Roaches Line over to the provincial government for one dollar after he and his wife died, in order to satisfy Revenue Canada. In other words he and Clara retained only a life interest in the property. He'd never hidden the fact that their mansion on his ranchlands had been built and paid for by his business friends and supporters, the Ashleys, the Crosbies, the Goodyears, the Lundrigans, and others after Prime Minister Diefenbaker, out of spite, had evicted him from the former Canada House on Circular Road. When Joey got out of politics, however, he had a change of heart and wanted full title to the house returned to him again. Reportedly, an approach made to Brian Peckford was turned down. But evidently, Liberal premiers Clyde Wells or Brian Tobin did agree, and the heirs of Joseph and Clara Smallwood duly inherited the house when both were dead.

I don't know what else the family inherited from Joey's glory days, but Andrew Crosbie told me that, during the erection of that house or some other work that his construction company did on the ranch, one of his company's huge bulldozers, worth hundreds of thousands of dollars, disappeared off the face of the earth. He told me that Bill or Ramsay Smallwood had explained to him that they'd borrowed it to do some work off site and that, in the process of travelling to its destination, the massive bulldozer had fallen into a bog and vanished. Andrew said that the bog was plumbed and fathomed extensively, but to absolutely no avail. No trace of the mammoth bulldozer was spotted or heard of by anyone ever again. Joey himself was uncharacteristically silent about the miraculous disappearance of the monster machine.

CHAPTER SEVENTEEN

The Last Days of Frank and Joey

IN 1983, A few years after Moores had moved away to Ontario to conduct more lucrative consulting and lobbying activities, Brian Mulroney phoned me to say he was in St. John's and asked me to come to see him at the Holiday Inn. I was then becoming more and more involved in the media, and I divined when I got there that he wanted to show me the pages from national newspapers that he'd spread out on the furniture of the sitting room in his suite. The papers were all opened to articles and editorials that touted him as the best hope for the future of the PC Party of Canada.

I gleaned between the lines of our conversation that Frank Moores had been busily working on his behalf to undermine Joe Clark as the current leader of the party and of the Opposition, and had succeeded in keeping Joe from obtaining the percentage of support he deemed adequate in the review of his leadership in Winnipeg in 1983. Over two-thirds of the vote, 66.9 per cent, was not enough of an endorsement for Joe, apparently, and he resigned as leader to run in a leadership convention he called for later in the year. These events and his support of

Mulroney's leadership bid, according to politicos and reporters I talked to, made Moores much sought after socially and for lobbying activities, and built his financial fortune. But it was very much a bittersweet success.

After Mulroney became leader and then prime minister, substantially as a result of Moores's organizing, fixing, and payoff talents, Frank became a top "adviser" to the PM. I followed his career somewhat—or, I should say, friends and contacts in Ottawa and Toronto regaled me with stories of Frank's shenanigans. He cajoled Mulroney into appointing him to the board of Air Canada, a crown corporation at the time. This was considered by knowledgeable observers to be one of the world's great patronage appointments and meant he could fly free, first class, nearly anywhere around the globe at any moment. It didn't seem to bother him that his lobbying firm represented other airlines and that therefore he was in a complete conflict of interest. He did resign as an Air Canada director, though, when his lobbying firm took on Airbus, the European aerospace manufacturer, as a client. He might have been better off, as it turned out, if he'd stayed in Air Canada and dropped Airbus.

One top Canadian journalist told me—swore up and down—that Frank Moores had made, all in all, according to reliable calculations, over $30 million as a result of his lobbying activities. Others pooh-poohed the figure as too high or too low. Moores himself denied being anything near a wealthy man from his lobbying and public relations. "Well," commented my cynical or realistic journalist friend, "he would deny it, wouldn't he?" He also told me to ask myself why Moores had had a falling-out with Mulroney, the man he'd made prime minister, and why Mulroney refused to speak to him for years: "You don't suppose they had a vicious big scrap over divvying up the gargantuan spoils, do you?"

In the mid-1990s, the Royal Canadian Mounted Police sent a letter to the Swiss government alleging that, when Mulroney was prime minister, he and Frank Moores took kickbacks on the purchase of Airbus planes by the Crown corporation Air Canada. The accused intermediary in the exchange of money was the sleazy international criminal fixer Karlheinz Schreiber. The RCMP wanted to examine their banking records in Switzerland. This sordid Schreiber character and Moores were close acquaintances from way back. More than a decade before, in 1983, they were known to have raised a lot of money together to undermine Joe Clark and to make Mulroney Tory leader. Right up to his death, Moores denied any involvement in or enrichment from the Airbus affair, though evidence then and since has indicated the contrary.

WITHIN TEN YEARS of Joey's removal from power, Andrew Crosbie's business empire collapsed. He'd been forced to sell Eastern Provincial Airlines, lost Atlantic Place, and Crosbie Offshore had gone bankrupt. Then he and his partner were charged with defrauding some German associates of hundreds of thousands of dollars. The partner, a mean squash opponent of mine, was convicted, I was sad to see, and sentenced to prison. Meanwhile, Andrew had contracted brain cancer. The last time I saw him was at a birthday party Penny—my wife—and I held for Penny's mother, Andrew's aunt. He kept on a cap throughout to cover the ravages of chemotherapy, but he was as buoyant and good-humoured as ever.

He died of the brain cancer in January 1991, still in his fifties, the day before he was due to go on trial for thirty-eight charges of fraud and theft. The coincidence had the usual St. John's black humourists out in force, chortling: "Excellent career move, Andrew." Joey was brought to Andrew's funeral service, where he silently wept to himself. Steve Neary had earlier told me that "the Skipper" had a tendency to weep freely at the least provocation these days—a consequence of his stroke. But I believe that, in the case of Andrew's premature death, his grief was profoundly felt.

*

JOEY DIED IN the same year, on December 17, 1991, a week before his ninety-first birthday. He lay in state at the House of Assembly in the Confederation Building that he had built. I went up there and joined the crowd winding around his coffin. The lineup was so long that, although it moved fairly quickly, I had to spend most of the afternoon getting through it. Then there was a funeral service for the "last of the Wesleyan Methodists" in the Roman Catholic Basilica. Notables showed up from all over Canada. I went there to attend, but the press of the crowd was so great I couldn't get in. An usher said they'd find me a place near the front as a former cabinet colleague. But I declined and went home to watch it on television. He was buried at Mount Pleasant Cemetery in St. John's. I pass his physical monument there every time I visit my own parents' gravesite.

During most of my life, I had also passed another, less edifying physical monument to Joey. For years, my father and mother had a country cabin near Upper Gullies. To get there in the old days, we would drive out the Topsail Highway. When we came around the curve in Paradise to approach Octagon Pond, we were always smacked in the kisser by the hideous sight of that machinery plant, one of the components of Joey's great Mao-like leap forward.

The building absolutely obscured and desecrated the view of the famous Octagon Pond. Whenever one of us in the back seat of Dad's car would mention the defilement, he would say nothing, and Mom would simply shake her head. After I joined Joey's government and inquired why he had placed it there, he implied that it was caused by his early admiration of European "socialism" (i.e. communism). The communist governments in Europe did the same thing by placing their factories in conspicuous places so that the population could not miss their presence, thus guaranteeing that everyone knew of their government's big industrialization thrust.

Just after the fall of the Soviet Union, I took a boat along the rivers and canals of Russia from Saint Petersburg to Moscow, and I couldn't help noticing in towns along the way during the ten-day trip exactly the same ugly phenomenon Joey had described and tried to emulate. The only thing Russia had that Joey didn't provide was the greenish-purple sunsets caused by gross atmospheric pollution. If Joey had been alive, I would have chided him jokingly for being such a lousy "socialist" in missing out on those multicoloured chemical sunsets. But perhaps he would have replied that he had done his best. Didn't the Electric Reduction Company of Canada (ERCO) use its sweetheart power deal with the government to pollute Placentia Bay?

Yet, paradoxically, he always decried the loss of Newfoundland heritage and artifacts. We have held ourselves out, he told me, as being the oldest colony, the oldest city in North America, the oldest this and that, but we have taken so little care of our past that if we come across something—a building, a document—we are astonished if it's more than a mere century old.

JOEY WAS A tangled mass of paradoxes and contradictions. All told, he was the most fascinating, for better and for worse, of any man I've ever met. I would have loved the old bastard if it were possible to love someone for whom consideration and loyalty ran only one way—especially if you posed the least threat of rivalry—and to whom admiration for any other human being seemed to have been reserved for modern-day buccaneers and swashbuckling pirates.

Joey often said victory always brought problems with it but that the problems of victory were infinitely to be preferred to the problems of defeat. He certainly would have known. Out of a long life of nearly ninety-one years, perhaps twenty or so years were spent dealing with the problems of victory and success, and seventy years were spent mostly wrestling with the problems of defeat and failure.

CHAPTER EIGHTEEN

Comparing the Great Men

ALEX HICKMAN, LONG-TIME politician and judge, has been reported as saying that Premier Frank Moores was an emotional man. Hickman claimed that Frank's encounter with a person who was having trouble with his unemployment insurance would move the premier to tears, and he would do something about it. Really? Well, here's another man's version of the nature of Frank's emotions.

I was walking up the steps to Confederation Building late one morning in the early 1970s, coming back to my office from a meeting, when a man leaving the building stopped to tell me what had just happened in his encounter with Premier Moores. Frank used to be his MP, he said, and knew him by name and called him his friend. The man said he'd phoned, written, and met with Frank to get his help to straighten out his unemployment insurance problem, but the UI office told the man they still hadn't heard from Mr. Moores. So, this morning he drove in early from Conception Bay North and arrived at the building at eight o'clock to wait for his friend, the premier, to arrive. It was after eleven when Frank's car finally pulled into his parking place. Then, as Frank came through the entrance door, the man went up to him in the lobby and reminded him of his UI problem.

The premier shook his hand warmly, called him by name as usual, and gave him a friendly slap on the back. Then, because there were some people in the lobby, he asked the man to come over to the side with him where it was more private to talk. Frank then led him through a door to the area in front of his private elevator, where they were all alone. There, as the man described it, Frank grabbed him with two hands by the front of his shirt and slammed him up against the wall. "UI is federal, you stupid fucking nuisance," he snarled. "Now you get the fuck out of here, and don't ever come near me again. Because if you do I'll kick the fucking shit out of you."

Two different versions of an encounter by men with UI problems with the emotional Frank Moores. Take your choice.

WHICH OF THESE leaders do I consider the greater of the two? I consider Joey to have been by far the greater man overall, but, strangely enough, I consider Frankie to have been the better premier.

I personally believe Smallwood to be, all in all, the greatest person Newfoundland and Labrador has ever produced. But the irony is that the sources of his true greatness took place before and after he became premier. His top achievement was yoking us, for better or for worse—for better by far, I think—to Canada, one of the most successful countries ever created. But that feat occurred before he took over the government as premier. His next top achievement was creating the *Encyclopedia of Newfoundland and Labrador* series, working assiduously on it, and setting in motion its completion. But that took place after he'd been booted out as premier. The twenty-three years in between when he was premier produced some important accomplishments, many of which have been touched on above, but the balance sheet as a whole, the pluses weighed against the minuses, did not signify greatness. In sum, to my mind, Joey

Smallwood was probably our greatest man, but one of our not-so-great premiers.

AND WHERE DOES Frank Moores rank in our scale of greatness? After he died of liver cancer at seventy-two in July of 2005, I numbered him among our greatest premiers, but only for one very specific reason. Some of our other government leaders since Frank's premiership have achieved great feats themselves: Brian Peckford's creation of the original Atlantic Accord; Clyde Wells dragging the province back from insolvency; Brian Tobin rescuing our education system from denominationalism and making it non-sectarian; Danny Williams's attainments regarding our offshore oil revenues. I hope to write later about those and other elements of the good and the bad and the bizarre concerning our premiers who followed Smallwood and Moores.

But Frank Moores himself was unique in his great accomplishment as premier. Unlike Joey, I don't believe he ranks high in any list of the greatest *persons* in the history of Newfoundland and Labrador. Others have noted that, during much of his premiership and its aftermath, he was up to his neck in scandal and living high on the hog from the gains of conflict of interest and patronage and inside information, and tainted by the unsightliness in a modern public figure of uninhibited boozing and womanizing. And I don't dissent much from that portrayal. Yet, for all that, by becoming premier, Frank Moores created a modern epoch of political thinking and participation in our province, and made a quantum leap from our immature political pubescence to near-adult maturity. He did that by torpedoing the unsinkable Joey Smallwood at the polls, terminating what looked like a "leader for life," and ushering in a brand new era of politics. For that one grand deed, I have considered him a true historic figure and, at the time of his death, perhaps the greatest premier of them all.

*

THE ADVANCE OF time, and the placing of the accomplishments of Moores and later leaders in historical perspective, may change assessments of their rank as premiers. But, to my mind, regardless of how all that falls out in the future, the career of Frank Moores does indeed confirm that the unedifying acts of a person's personal, political, and business life may be redeemed by one outstanding public deed.

Acknowledgements

My sincere thanks to Paul Butler for his substantive editing of this book, to Bruce Lilly for his copy-editing, and to Graham Blair for his graphic design. My heartfelt gratitude to Garry, Margo, and Jerry Cranford, Bob Woodworth, Laura Cameron, Randy Drover, Peter Hanes, Gerard Murphy, and Laura Shandik at Flanker Press for their enthusiastic contributions to publishing, marketing, and distributing it.

Born in Newfoundland, Bill Rowe graduated in English from Memorial University and attended Oxford University as a Rhodes Scholar, obtaining an Honours M.A. in Law.

Elected five times to the House of Assembly, Rowe served as a minister in the Government of Newfoundland and Labrador, and as leader of the Official Opposition. He practised law in St. John's for many years, and has been a long-time public affairs commentator, appearing regularly on national and local television, as well as hosting a daily radio call-in show on VOCM and writing weekly newspaper columns.

Rowe has written seven books: *Clapp's Rock*, a bestselling novel published by McClelland and Stewart and serialized on CBC national radio; *The Temptation of Victor Galanti*, a second novel published by McClelland and Stewart; a volume of essays on politics and public affairs published by Jesperson Press of St. John's; the critically acclaimed political memoir, *Danny Williams: The War with Ottawa*, which appeared on the *Globe and Mail*'s bestsellers list in 2010; *Danny Williams, Please Come Back*, a collection of newspaper articles covering social, political, and economic issues; and *Rosie O'Dell*, a critically acclaimed crime novel published by Pennywell Books, a literary imprint of Flanker Press.

Rowe is a member of the Writers' Union of Canada and has served on the executive of the Writers' Alliance of Newfoundland and Labrador. He is married to Penelope Ayre Rowe CM of St. John's. They have a son, Dorian, a daughter, Toby, and three grandchildren.

Index